Development and Psychopathology

Development and Psychopathology

Studies in Psychoanalytic Psychiatry

Clifford Yorke
Stanley Wiseberg
Thomas Freeman

Yale University Press
New Haven and London

Designed by James J. Johnson
and set in Melior Roman type by Delmas, Ann Arbor, Michigan.
Printed in the United States of America.

Library of Congress Cataloging-in-Publication Data

Yorke, Clifford, 1922–
    Development and psychopathology : studies in psychoanalytic psychiatry / Clifford
Yorke, Stanley Wiseberg, Thomas Freeman.
        p. cm.
    Bibliography: p.
    Includes index.
    ISBN 0–300–04129–2 (alk. paper)
    1. Psychoanalysis. 2. Psychotherapy. 3. Freud, Sigmund, 1856–1939. I. Wiseberg,
Stanley, 1925– . II. Freeman, Thomas. III. Title.
    [DNLM: 1. Mental Disorders. 2. Psychoanalytic Theory. 3. Psychopathology. WM 460
Y64d]
RC506.Y67   1989
616.89′17—dc19
DNLM/DLC
for Library of Congress   88–39160
                                                                                    CIP

The paper in this book meets the guidelines for permanence and durability of the
Committee on Production Guidelines for Book Longevity of the Council on Library
Resources.

10 9 8 7 6 5 4 3 2 1

Contents

Preface

This book has a history that may be worth a summary. In 1977, a few members of the Anna Freud Centre (then the Hampstead Child-Therapy Course and Clinic) felt the need to undertake an expository book on psychoanalytic psychiatry. The idea was prompted by a number of considerations. It was felt that many general psychiatrists did not appreciate the contribution psychoanalytic thinking could make to their work and that, conversely, psychoanalysts often cut themselves off from the more general discipline and thereby contributed to an unnecessary and unfortunate isolation. Furthermore, even where psychiatrists and psychoanalysts perceived their mutual interest, a tendency to specialize in either the adult or the child meant that the developmental point of view, however well it was formally recognized, did not benefit sufficiently from work and study with people of all ages. This is not an argument against specialization. But it does underline the need for the specialists to be better acquainted with each other's work and interests. An attempt to further such understanding was therefore an important part of this enterprise.

For many years, Thomas Freeman had evaluated psychotic patients using Anna Freud's Profile Schema and had brought his extensive material to the center for detailed discussion on a regular basis. These meetings were concerned not only with adult psychosis but with possible childhood antecedents and forerunners of these disorders. In time, Dorothy Burlingham and Anna Freud, together with the authors, thought it necessary to extend this form of inquiry to non-psychotic disorders, and it was in this context that they formed a study group through the activities of which a plan for a book began to take shape.

We soon became aware of the magnitude of the task. What seemed at first sight a matter of comparatively straightforward exposition soon demanded increasing and repeated rethinking of a number of matters too readily taken for granted. Even those disorders whose psychological bases had long seemed understood called for extensive reappraisal. For these reasons, we cannot regard our formulations as having any finality; we hope, however, that they will stimulate the reader to think his or her own ideas out afresh. Likewise, we have made no attempt to be inclusive. Some important psychiatric disorders receive no mention. Others, such as the more serious addictions, are not yet sufficiently clearly formulated to warrant further discussion here (Radford, Wiseberg, and Yorke, 1972; Wiseberg, Yorke, and Radford, 1975).

Our conviction that an informed psychiatry demands a psychoanalytic perspective does not imply that other disciplines—genetics, neuroscience, epidemiology, sociology, to mention some of the more obvious—should not be given due weight. But it is our intention to reaffirm that there is no psychiatry without a coherent and comprehensive psychology, and that the developmental perspective of psychoanalysis is indispensable for the *psychological* understanding of psychiatric states (Glover, 1958; Yorke, 1988).

The book does not, however, seek to explore the contribution to psychiatry of those psychoanalytic schools that have disregarded or found wanting the *basic* Freudian concepts and their augmentation, from the same developmental perspective, by the findings of child analysis. Our reasons for adopting a metapsychological viewpoint, from the standpoint of theory building, are discussed in chapter 12, after the reader has had an opportunity to examine the clinical material on which we have drawn to illustrate the psychoanalytic formulations.

In stressing the value of psychoanalysis for the general psychiatrist, we refer to the model of the mind and not necessarily to psychoanalysis as practiced in the consulting room. We do not take the view that psychoanalysis is the therapeutic treatment of choice for all psychiatric disorders. On the contrary, we believe that clinical psychoanalysis can be effective only if patients are selected according to fairly strict criteria. Psychoanalytically informed treatment is another matter. However, we have chosen not to include a discussion of treatment or management. We hope that, if our formulations are sufficiently lucid and carry some conviction, the logic of appropriate treatment and management of the disabilities we discuss will make itself apparent.

Although Anna Freud died before this book reached its final form, she took the greatest interest in its preparation and saw every chapter in draft form. She herself wrote the opening, theoretical part of chapter 2 especially for this work and asked the authors to supply the clinical illustrations to these new formulations.

Lastly, we want to acknowledge our indebtedness to those many colleagues at the Anna Freud Centre who have suggested or discussed with us material drawn from studies of childhood, both normal and abnormal. They and others are too numerous to mention, but we would like to thank especially Eve Lorenz for her extensive work on the bibliography. Finally, we are deeply grateful to Gina Bon for her tireless retyping of repeatedly changing drafts and to Valerie Thompson (Mrs. Valerie Yorke), whose weekend sacrifices and sustenance are warmly appreciated.

CHAPTER 1 Anxiety, Signal Anxiety, and Panic

In states of anxiety, sensory attention is increased and motor tension rises. These changes accompany a particular affective tonus. In its mildest form this tonus is pleasant and stimulating, but as it increases it becomes progressively unpleasant. When contained, normal anxiety is a more or less continuing mental state that fosters changing perceptions, implies a readiness for action, and gives mental life its alertness and sensitivity to the vividness of experience. It is linked with the pleasure principle and the maintenance of an optimal tension in any current situation. In this sense it is the antithesis of the hypothetical freedom from anxiety that characterizes the state sometimes called nirvana (Freud, 1920; Low, 1920).

People often try quite deliberately to increase their level of anxiety for purposes of pleasure—for example, by riding on a roller coaster, watching horror films, or engaging in physical sport. Here, however, we are principally concerned with unpleasurable states of anxiety and the individual ways taken to deal with them.

Anxiety has a survival value. The affective response to external danger and the necessary physiological changes that in Cannon's terms prepare one for fight or flight illustrate this clearly. Automatic responses of this kind may serve survival well in the face of crude external dangers. Although for a complex organism states of panic have a very limited survival value, it is not difficult to understand the survival value of anxiety that warns of *internal* danger and leads to the institution of ordered measures to reduce it.

Anxiety that alerts us to the presence of danger from within and leads to effective defensive measures is known as *signal anxiety*. To fulfill this function, the anxiety must be contained within a manageable limit. If the limit is exceeded, anxiety loses its signal value and interferes with the individual's functioning. This repeatedly occurs, for example, in young children. It is also characteristic of a variety of pathological conditions.

From the structural point of view the ego can be threatened from three sides. Danger may come from external reality, from instinctual forces of the id, or from the superego. Depending on the source from which the danger springs, the resultant anxiety is termed realistic, instinctual, or superego anxiety. It is the task of the ego to anticipate and respond to these threats. At its most effective, the ego restricts anxiety to the level of a signal that warns of impending danger.

The Concept of Basic Danger Situations

Freud (1926) took the view that the diffuse excitation which overwhelmed the organism in the act of birth was the source and prototype of later states of anxiety. But he distinguished this excitation from the psychic experience of anxiety. Unlike Rank (1952), he did not believe that the stresses of birth had any affective content for the newborn. Later and detailed studies by trained observers have shown that the "trauma" of birth is minimal. Spitz (1947) demonstrated that in normal deliveries the neonate shows "brief respiratory distress and the manifestations of negatively tinged excitation"; later, he wrote, "if the infant is left alone, this subsides literally within seconds and gives way to complete quiescence.... What can be observed is a brief state of excitation, which appears to have the quality of unpleasure" (1965, p. 38). Even the vocalizations of the newborn infant are most often responses to interference by nurse, midwife, or doctor.

For some time, the mother or her substitute must detect danger on the infant's behalf, protect him from discomfort, and assuage his needs. But frustrations inevitably and repeatedly occur, and it is within the context of a functional mother/baby unit that the child's helplessness and painful frustrations first arise. The mother reads or anticipates the baby's signals of distress and initiates appropriate steps to reduce tension and to meet need. Thus imperative drive needs which threaten to overwhelm the child, and which form the basis of later fears of annihilation, are reduced or kept at bay (Winnicott, 1960).

With the subsequent dawning of psychic activity, with the growth of ego and id, with the capacity to differentiate between self and object, and with the beginnings of affective interaction, some indications of psychic anxiety make their appearance. They are readily observed, for example, in young infants who are handed from the mother to the care of someone else. At a later stage, when babies display keen awareness of the presence of strangers, even in a group, mentalized anxiety is vividly exemplified as the child turns fearfully from the intruder and clings tightly to the mother (Freud, 1926; Spitz, 1965).

The absence of the mother soon brings with it the fear of her loss. The child "cannot as yet distinguish between temporary absence and permanent loss. As soon as it loses sight of its mother it behaves as if it were never going to see her again; and repeated consoling experiences to the contrary are necessary before it learns that her disappearance is usually followed by her re-appearance. Its mother encourages this piece of knowledge which is so vital to it by playing the familiar games of hiding her face from it with her hands and then, to its joy, uncovering it again" (Freud, 1926, pp. 169–70). Thus, fear of loss of the mother is a basic danger situation.

We have already referred to prototypical fears of annihilation. The fear of loss of the mother herself (the object) is followed by fear of loss of her love when the infant perceives her as angry or displeased. In time, the turbulence of the oedipal phase brings with it castration anxiety. Introjection and structuralization of the superego give rise to yet another danger—fear of loss of the superego's love.

These danger situations form a developmental sequence. All of them threaten to plunge the child into a state of panic characterized by feelings of utter helplessness. Freud attributed "two modes of origin to anxiety in later life. One was involuntary, automatic and always justified on economic grounds, and arose whenever a danger-situation analogous to birth had established itself. The other was produced by the ego as soon as a situation of this kind merely threatened to occur, in order to call for its avoidance" (1926, p. 162). What is warded off may be called *pervasive anxiety*. It would be entirely in keeping with Freud's formulations to distinguish two kinds of pervasive anxiety. The developmentally earlier one accompanies feelings of helplessness which overwhelm the victim to the point of paralysis. In the later one helplessness is only feared. We suggest that Freud's term *automatic anxiety* be applied to the earlier affective state and that the term *pervasive anxiety* be restricted to the later one. Such a distinction has a threefold justification. First, the two states differ in symptomatic severity. Second, the very young infant's resources are so limited that a state of helpless anxiety *automatically* results from a basic danger situation. Third, in the less severe state, the anxiety can still evoke some sort of containment or defense against the full psychic experience of the automatic state. Later we illustrate this distinction through clinical examples. It in no way affects Freud's hypothesis that feelings of helplessness in the face of anxiety characterize, underlie, and in part define the basic danger situations as these unfold sequentially.

It is the function of signal anxiety to detect the impending danger of such states. Signal anxiety prompts the ego to take appropriate steps wherever possible to limit the threat of a basic danger situation and, with it, those states of anxiety Freud described and that we consider to comprise both automatic and pervasive stages.[1] We sometimes use the term *psychic panic* as a shorthand reference to both automatic and pervasive anxiety when the context appears to justify this simplification.

In signal anxiety, the ego takes an affective sample, a restricted dose, of the affect occasioned by a danger situation. When this sample has the psychic quality of automatic anxiety, the ego recognizes the impending threat and initiates measures to contain it. We have referred to "fight and flight" as measures that may be taken when danger looms from without. But a threat from an internal danger may also be initiated by external situations of one sort or another. For example, an adolescent boy's sexual desire for his girlfriend may suddenly be felt too close to an incestuous wish that brings about an unconscious fear of castration. He may feel massively inhibited in her presence or may leave her altogether. In the first instance the ego has mobilized a fight (or at least a rearguard action) against the drive derivatives; in the second, the boy has taken to psychological flight. These examples of countercathexis and cathectic withdrawal, respectively, may serve

---

1. This slightly extends the conceptual framework used in two earlier but more extensive accounts of the developmental line of anxiety: Yorke, Kennedy, and Wiseberg, 1981; Yorke and Wiseberg, 1976.

for the present as representatives of the host of defenses that may be at the disposal of the ego in coping with basic dangers.

The pathway from the diffuse somatic excitation at the beginning of life to effective signal anxiety is an elaborate one. It is easier to understand if we employ the notion of a *developmental line*.

A Developmental Line: From Diffuse Somatic Excitation to Signal Anxiety

When Anna Freud first developed the concept of developmental lines in 1963, she emphasized that they were concerned not simply with the development of the id or the ego or any single part of the personality considered in isolation; rather, they involved "the basic interactions between id and ego and their various developmental levels, and also age-related sequences of them, which in importance, frequency, and regularity are comparable to the maturational sequence of libidinal stages of the gradual unfolding of ego functions" (A. Freud, 1963b, p. 246). Examples of such lines include those that lead from dependency to emotional self-reliance, from irresponsibility to responsibility in body management, and from wetting and soiling to bladder and bowel control. We are here concerned with a line that leads, via automatic and pervasive anxiety, from diffuse somatic excitation through early psychic concomitants to signal anxiety. The clinical study of anxiety is simplified if we think in terms of progressions, arrests, and reversions along this developmental line. With this as with any other line, developmental distortions and deviations occur.

It is difficult to know at what stage true psychic affects and structured psychic content are experienced. At the beginning of life and for some time afterward, most observers agree that the infant experiences only crude pleasure and unpleasure. This pleasure/pain series can be conceptualized in terms of the rise and fall of instinctual pressures, as an ebb and flow of excitation activating and reactivating whatever primitive memory traces are laid down (Glover, 1950). Disturbances in the pleasure/pain series may have adverse effects on development and may lead, for example, to sleep disturbance or more lasting excessive somatic discharge of excitation.

There is some experimental evidence that shortly after birth some unstructured and fragmented precursors of psychic functioning emerge. These precursors of affect and perception gradually crystallize out of the pleasure/pain series, agglomerate, and become structured. Clear evidence that perception, cognition, and affect have begun to coordinate is seen in the appearance of the "smiling response" (Spitz, 1965). This indicates an unequivocal expression of integrated pleasure experiences and affective communication. The conditional nature of this response ensures the continuing interplay between mother and child and fosters affective and cognitive development to the point at which the child looks, in turn, for the mother's smiling response. When the child is rewarded by this response, his smile broadens. On the other hand, when the response is denied the child, his smile fades and is fleetingly replaced by an expression of unpleasure and perplexity. This precursor of anxiety indicates that the structuralization of unpleasurable experiences is beginning to be developed. In this way the child and mother enter a new phase of psychic reciprocity that brings a new quality into object relations and provides a foundation for the more complex mutuality of object relationships in later years.

The child has made an important move along the pathway that leads from the comparatively undifferentiated mother/baby unit to a clearer distinction between self and object. Moreover, the growth in the mental structuring of experience facilitates the shift from biological excitation to psychical experience of anxiety. The capacity for anxiety and panic also increases while vulnerability to somatic distress lessens. The child has exchanged the extremes of physical distress for a propensity to panic.

Anna Freud (1974) has pointed out that, in the early months of infantile life, pathways between psyche and soma remain open, so that psychic tension may be discharged somatically and vice versa. Somatic discharge pathways are not abandoned when mentalization is established. They remain available, with varying degrees of accessibility, in some children and adults mediating discharges that activate the psychosomatic component of such conditions as asthma and eczema. The early somatic pathways and the later psychic ones retain a variable interchangeability, so that the capacity for reversion along a developmental line can still permit the replacement of psychic panic by *vegetative excitation*. This eventuality will be considered shortly in connection with the traumatic neurosis.

We have discussed the way mentalization makes possible the experience of psychic panic. In considering the way stations along the line leading to signal anxiety, we must turn to those developmental achievements that foster the restriction of anxiety until, ultimately, it can be limited to signal levels. Even in the earlier stages of this process, as the affect undergoes qualitative changes on the road from soma to psyche, the operation of the "compulsion to repeat" (Freud, 1920) plays a significant part in the mastery of unpleasurable feeling-states. The repetition-compulsion is of great importance in both normal and pathological states. The game of peek-a-boo described by Freud and its effect on the child's ability to master the anxiety of separation is a practical application of the working of the repetition-compulsion in which the mother assists the child as if by proxy.

The mastery of overwhelming excitation—the danger from within—increases with the growing sophistication of the mental apparatus and the establishment of progressively effective controls. These involve elaboration of the repression barrier, the concomitant development of secondary-process functioning, and the interrelated acquisition of words and speech. The temper tantrum, for example, can be seen as a manifestation of psychic panic, and it is repeatedly demonstrated during the phase of development in which speech is acquired. This supports the argument that signal anxiety cannot be firmly established at this stage of development.

This is in no way surprising. The development of speech is intimately related to the capacity to think, as it develops from primitive ideation to an increasingly conceptual level. A measure of verbal competence is an important precursor of instinctual mastery. Freud remarked that the man who hurled verbal abuse at his enemy instead of hurling a spear was taking the first step toward civilization. Of course, if the enemy were physically threatening, it might be important to decide between mere words and physical action; but no such choice is available until a fairly elaborate level of conceptual thinking is attained. Such thinking must be "an experimental action carried out with small amounts of energy, in the same way as a general shifts small figures about on a map before setting his large bodies of troops in motion" (Freud, 1933, p. 89). Only then can thought exercise its anticipatory function, its "trial action"; only then can the concomitant affective sampling—what might perhaps be called the use of "trial affect"—be undertaken by the ego. Whether this trial affect can be restricted to a signal level depends not only on the ego's capacity for containment but also on the resources available to the ego to meet the threat of reversion.

Each developmental progression in whatever psychological sphere—structure formation, drive organization, perception, cognition, recognition, recall, intentionality, defensive organization, and so on—will affect movement along the developmental line of anxiety. Some of these acquisitions, such as defense organization, secondary-process functioning, and neutralization, will favor containment. Others, such as a driving upsurge of instinct, serious setbacks in object relations, and a clearer awareness of outside dangers, will counter the foregoing influences and tend to fill the individual with anxiety and feelings of helplessness. It is all a matter of trends, of forces that lead in one direction countered by forces that lead in another; there is an individual need to strike a balance between these opposing trends that, given favorable circumstances, will lead to increasingly adaptive control.

This adaptive control is hard-won. A child who has attained a capacity to exercise signal anxiety has by no means reached the end-point of the developmental line, where some degree of consistency and functional reliability may be expected. Indeed, such a point cannot be reached until the vicissitudes of adolescence have yielded to the comparative stability of adult adjustment.

Signal anxiety begins to operate once speech and secondary-process functioning are established. With the resolution of the Oedipus complex and the relative freedom in latency from the turbulence of earlier childhood, signal function can be expected to operated with some regularity. Even then apparent autonomy, like other seemingly independent latency functions, rests on a supportive background of parents, teachers, and peers as well as social institutions such as schools.

To summarize the developmental line so far, the point of departure is the stage of vegetative excitation, which precedes true affect and occurs within the context of the mother/baby unit. Further progress along the line leads to mentalized anxiety. Its first crude form is psychic panic of a primitive kind, which occurs when the child is plunged into complete helplessness and can be alleviated only by outside intervention. This is the stage of automatic anxiety. Further steps in mentalization and in ego development generally allow the child to restrict the anxiety, although still pervasive, by crude defensive measures. Anxiety now arises as a fear of helplessness when the child is threatened by basic danger situations. We have suggested that the term pervasive anxiety be applied to this way station, to distinguish it from automatic anxiety. Finally, further steps in person-ality development allow the latency-stage child, under favorable cir-cumstances, to use danger signals to prevent the arousal of pervasive anxiety. This is the first sign that the way station of signal anxiety has at last been attained, however tenuously.

As latency proceeds, these capacities become better organized and are more fully integrated into the personality. In normal latency, the process is assisted by the peace that stems from relative instinc-tual quiescence. This peace is disrupted first in prepuberty, when preoedipal trends are reactivated and reinforced, and then by the biological maturation of puberty and the psychological changes of adolescence. A mental economy that, with the help of auxiliary sup-port, formerly restricted latency pressures no longer copes so readily with the intensified urgency of the drives. Old dangers recur with fresh force. For anxiety to continue its operation at signal level, exist-ing defensive measures and ways of coping must be restructured and their effectiveness reinforced. The increase of sexual and aggressive forces involves a remobilization of all pregenital trends; repression barriers are once more threatened; and the defensive organization is subverted at varying and changing points as infantile trends and oedi-pal fears are reawakened. Furthermore, the adolescent is faced with the threat that his rapid physical growth and heightened sexual ca-pacity at last make possible the realization of wishes which, in earlier childhood, remained wishes and wishes alone.

All these changes have important consequences for the develop-mental line of anxiety. Reversions and advances along the line readily occur, as along other lines, with the rise and fall of instinctual pres-sures, since every regressive shift carries with it the wish to reestab-lish progression as the ego struggles to regain its former mastery. Alternations of this kind give adolescence its turbulent character and ultimately lead to the consolidation and stabilization of achievement that culminates in the highest attainment of signal anxiety. The re-gressions of normal adolescence are of a different character from the regressions of neurosis and play an essential part in the ultimate attainment of adult mastery. But this stability can still be threatened at every turn; and it is by no means proof against all the trials and tribulations to come.

In briefly reviewing the developmental line of anxiety, we were obliged to look beyond childhood to adolescence and beyond. Now turning, by way of illustration, to clinical examples and everyday observations, we retrace our footsteps.

There is nothing to be gained by attempting to illustrate vegetative excitation as observed in the course of normative development. Its existence can only be inferred from observation of generalized and wholesale distress as organismic excitation continues to mount, until external succor causes the unpleasurable state to subside and give way to quiescence and satisfaction. But we may justify the notion of reversion to a state of vegetative excitation by considering the phenomenon of *pavor nocturnus*, the night terror experienced by children. Some authors suggest that pavor nocturnus is virtually identical in form and content to the stage IV nightmare as observed in the sleep laboratory (Fisher et al., 1970). The child (or adult) awakens from a nightmare with a terrified expression, sometimes with a bloodcurdling scream, sits up in bed utterly dazed, and is inaccessible to external intervention for some minutes or even longer. The apparent dream trauma that triggers this striking occurrence is in fact a comparatively simple but intensely frightening secondary-process thought—for example, of a house falling on top of the child. In all essentials, pavor nocturnus (and its adult equivalent) is a post-traumatic state in which the ego is knocked out. The child is flooded with excitation and remains inaccessible until that excitation is reduced as mentalization returns with full awakening. The psychic experience of anxiety that supervenes is accessible to parental comfort and ministrations. Vegetative excitation may be reduced via somatic discharge, whether vocalization, trembling, or motor activity.

The suspension of ego functions in pavor nocturnus is confirmed by the child's total lack of memory for the post-traumatic state. It seems possible, however, that in children whose night terrors suggest transient delusions and hallucinations, only some ego functions— such as the ability to contact reality—are in abeyance, and the experience is midway between vegetative excitation and automatic anxiety.

Automatic anxiety is regularly presumed to occur at a stage of development in which the child still cannot express himself adequately or communicate any experience of psychic helplessness in a verbally articulate way. He may scream and display the bewilderment into which he is evidently rocketed by an overwhelming perfusion of affect; but the resistance of automatic anxiety remains an inference. As with vegetative excitation, one must turn to pathology and to shifts

or arrests along the anxiety line in order to find examples that com-
pellingly justify the concept.

Brian

It is generally agreed that so-called borderline children are regularly
plunged into episodes of helpless anxiety.[2]

Brian, aged ten, lived in a world of fantasy and showed neither
interest in nor affection for others. He often threatened to kill his
sister. He had bizarre fantasies about people's bodies: he wanted his
nurse to allow him to turn her head completely round like a wheel,
and he wanted to squeeze "lots of spaghetti" out of her breasts. He
often used neologisms, and his thinking was strikingly concrete. He
was particularly vulnerable to attacks of intense and overwhelming
anxiety apparently characterized by dire and pervasive fears of disintegration and annihilation. At times he rushed about in a blind, panic-
like state: at others he was frozen into apparent immobility. But
whether he exhibited purposeless pell-mell activity or static, trembling terror, he appeared to be flooded with intense psychic and
physical excitation.

On occasion, during comparatively lucid intervals, Brian was
able to describe some of the terrifying mental content that accompanied these episodes of automatic anxiety. Once he described his fear
that everything would drop out of his body, leaving nothing but his
skeleton and a bit of skin; in another instance, he feared he would
literally break into two pieces. Unlike the aftermath of states of vegetative excitation (seen in pavor nocturnus), Brian's supervening states
of relative tranquility allowed him to describe his experiences of
helpless anxiety, bearing witness to the clarity of his memory of these
events.

It has been suggested that at later stages of development, some
states of pervasive anxiety show evidence of signal function and can
with advantage be distinguished from the episodes of automatic anxiety Brian displayed. A boy of three and a half years was in the habit
of accompanying his father whenever the latter went for a haircut.

2. Borderline children are often able to describe in detail states of emotion and
conflict characteristic of the preverbal child. See for example Rosenfelt and Sprince,
1963; Thomas et al., 1966; Yorke and Wiseberg, 1976, 114–121.

The boy enjoyed his outings to the barber's. One day, while his father was awaiting his turn, the boy saw a bald man having his few remaining hairs trimmed. He ran home to his mother in a panic, crying, "The barber is going to cut Daddy's head!" His perception that the barber was using scissors to cut the man's head (since the stranger had very little hair) had brought close to consciousness fantasies aroused by dawning castration anxiety. The fear expressed for his father's safety externalized the boy's own castration fear, together with his unacknowledged hostility toward his father. Signal anxiety had temporarily failed to maintain the degree of repression available to such a young child; although other defense mechanisms against the full ideational content of the fear were called into play, they were insufficient to prevent panic.

Although externalization, symbolization, and displacement could potentially have led to the formation of phobic symptoms and total avoidance of the barber shop, in this case the anxieties were only transiently aroused. Internal measures against debilitating anxiety were reinforced by external reassurance, first from the mother and later from the father and the barber. Repression was temporarily reestablished. Although the child, like others at his stage of development, was vulnerable to pervasive anxiety, he was at no time utterly helpless in the face of this experience, and the reversion stopped short of the automatic anxiety experienced by Brian. The boy, for all his panic, was still able to take (unconsciously) internal and (consciously) external measures against the anxiety.

Healthy adaptation in latency and beyond depends for its effectiveness on reasonably consistent sampling of the affect of anxiety and detection of any potential threat to the ego. The silent operation of signal anxiety ensures that effective defensive mechanisms such as repression are repeatedly called into play to combat danger from within. But this does not render the subject immune to pathology. It may at first appear a paradox that certain pathological solutions to danger may be initiated by signal anxiety.

Harvey

Harvey[3] was ten years of age when his parents sought advice on account of the rapid collapse of his hitherto excellent educational

3. For a fuller account, see Kennedy and Yorke, 1980.

performance. This deterioration followed a change from a coeducational establishment to a boys' school. In spite of a very superior intelligence, Harvey soon found himself at the bottom of the class in almost every subject. Furthermore, he showed apprehension about his new school to the point of apparent reluctance to attend. Soon afterward, he became afraid of the dark, a fear from which he had suffered until the age of five.

Early in his analysis it became clear that Harvey's repression of feminine identifications and homosexual wishes had failed to survive the impact of the wholly masculine environment at his new school. A regressive shift had mobilized oedipal trends with concomitant voyeuristic impulses and primal scene fantasies.[4] The further shift to the negative oedipal phase, with its attendant wish to take the mother's place in intercourse with the father, threatened his ego with overwhelming castration anxiety; and the fantasied observation of, and participation in, dangerous coitus called forth defensive measures through the influence of signal anxiety. A compromise had to ensue. Active curiosity expressed in study and the wish to learn became, by displacement, the vehicle of forbidden voyeuristic wishes; and the retention of academic knowledge was unconsciously equated with inadmissible awareness of sexual secrets. A wholesale repudiation of this knowledge and learning at once resulted through the operation of massive inhibition, and the reluctance to go to school indicated that any failure of these measures might invoke total avoidance.

In circumstances such as these, the measures brought about by the silent operation of signal anxiety often threaten to break down. While the displacement to the taking in of information remained effective during the day, the proximity of his parents in the next bedroom retained for Harvey its danger at night. His old fear of the dark thus returned, though it was controlled by the provision of a nightlight.

In the course of analysis the loss of effective signal anxiety resulted in a panic attack when, at the end of one of Harvey's sessions, his father did not arrive to pick him up. In the course of further work, it became clear that a fear that the father would be killed was reawakened by the involvement of both father and son in a motor accident

4. For a general account of inhibition as well as the process of neurotic symptom formation, see chapter 3.

the day before. The pressure of oedipal death wishes initiated a temporary reversion to traumatic anxiety.

A reasonably autonomous and persistent state of signal anxiety may be fully achieved only with the adult stage of development. In Harvey's case the disturbances described, involving the initial operation of signal anxiety and its eventual loss in a developmental reversion, are not very different from corresponding changes in adult disturbances and neuroses. But Harvey maintained signal anxiety (while it lasted) in the context of family support. When external support is lacking or lost during latency, an untimely move toward independence is sometimes accompanied by frequent, even persistent developmental reversions. Where such a child meets with ostensibly greater success and attains a premature autonomy, his or her achievement may be bought at the cost of distorted personality development. But even the so-called normal adult cannot achieve a permanently stable level of signal anxiety that is proof against *all* the vicissitudes of an "average expectable environment." From time to time internal or external situations result in greater or lesser degrees of panic, although in the normal course of events equilibrium is soon restored and the endpoint of the anxiety line regained. In both normal and pathological states it is all a question of the balance between the quantum of danger on the one hand and the capacity of the personality to cope with that danger, and to resist reversion, on the other. The danger, whether from within or without, may be of such magnitude that the defenses of a mature and effective ego are insufficient to prevent the emergence of pathological anxiety. At the other end of the spectrum, ego functions may be so weak—the personality so immature or inadequate—that any demand may be experienced as a danger and may lead to unmanageable anxiety levels. Of the very wide and multifarious range of anxiety states in adults we have chosen three brief examples.

Elsie

Elsie, a twenty-eight-year-old housewife, whose once doll-like good looks were showing signs of excessive wear and tear, was involved in marriage and motherhood, for which, in terms of maturity and personality resources, she was completely unprepared. She came from a large and poor family that had been held together only by the support of dedicated social work and profuse welfare resources. While her appetite for affection was considerable, her wish to nurture her children was impeded by her own imperative need for dependency. She was a familiar figure at the accident and emergency department of the local hospital, where she presented with various minor physical complaints or, more often, with acute anxiety and the need for a haven. On most occasions, the immediate precipitant was a current domestic or emotional stress. Frequently there had been demands for arrears of rent. On occasion a quarrel with her husband had led to minor violence and estrangement. Elsie responded to all such events, major or minor, with feelings of catastrophe, panic, depression, and insomnia. Only rarely was she able to identify the particular precipitating event among the welter of her everyday worries. Once she had been helped over a particular hurdle, however, she made a rapid recovery.

Because of her poor ego functioning, Elsie experienced even minor stresses as danger situations; but her case illustrates something more. She had not proceeded far enough along the developmental line for signal function to be achieved with reasonable constancy, so that she responded to almost any danger situation with panic and feelings of helplessness.

Eventually she was taken into fairly intensive casework. Once a firm relationship with a social worker had been established, Elsie learned to call for help whenever she felt threatened by a danger. Thus she gradually developed a primitive way of signaling danger, encouraged by a growing confidence that she could rely on the social worker to mother her through her problems. Within this relationship extremes of panic could be contained, and Elsie began to take a part in appropriate problem solving. A further goal for casework was that Elsie would learn to limit her anxiety to a level that would allow her to recognize the current problem and contemplate possible solutions. But the social worker recognized that Elsie, even with further maturation, would not progress to a point where she could take effective action in response to her own independent signal anxiety.

Elsie's history illustrates an arrest on the developmental line. The following case exemplifies reversion along the developmental line following the loss of signal function.

James

James, thirty-five, had experienced an attack of acute anxiety that settled into a chronic anxiety state. The anxiety, though unpleasant and at times disabling, was generally contained within signal limits and did not escalate to major panic. However, when later he was faced with an incontrovertible personal disaster, he had insufficient resources to protect himself against its effects, and he reverted to a disruptive state of panic.

James's father had left the family for no apparent reason when he was five years old. His only recollections of his father were of his physical punishments. While he felt his mother was always fair to him, she seemed cold and unemotional. He had a younger sister of whom he was once very fond, but she had long since emigrated and never answered his letters. James remembered some happy times in his early years but had found it difficult to make friends and recalled periods of loneliness. He lacked confidence and failed to live up to his own expectations. His subsequent life was unsettled and, although he was always employed as a truck driver, he tended to change jobs frequently. His marriage was disturbed by his wife's refusal to accept his excessive need for dependence. His sexual functioning was inadequate.

The first acute attack of anxiety James remembered occurred when his wife went to stay with a friend. He was afraid she would not return. His family doctor prescribed tranquilizers, and the anxiety quickly settled. But anxiety recurred whenever situations arose that appeared to threaten the loss of his wife. Soon the fear was never far from his mind and he remained in a state of chronic anxiety. This state of affairs lasted for about two years, at which point he was referred to a psychiatrist. His feelings of anxiety had persisted and his hitherto satisfactory sleep pattern was disturbed. He was pessimistic. At times he was concerned about his health, especially his palpitations, which he thought might stem from organic disease. He described in detail his fears that his marriage would eventually break down.

Before he could keep his next appointment he was admitted to the psychiatric ward in a state of total panic. His worst fears had been realized: his wife had left him and had written to say she felt much happier without him and was seeking divorce. He was anxious to the point of helplessness, restless and agitated, and his concentration was severely impaired. His pulse was rapid and he was sweating profusely. Despite medication with tranquilizers he remained in this state for two or three days, developing compulsive thoughts of harming himself, though he said he had no real wish to do so.

The detailed history indicated that the patient had been trauma-
tized by the loss of his father at the age of five. This had made him
even more dependent on his mother, who satisfied his material but
not his emotional needs. The trauma was compounded by the effective loss of his sister. His early memories of loneliness were paradig-
matic, and his failure to achieve his academic potential reflected an
associated lack of confidence and impaired self-esteem.

James's marriage threatened him with a repetition of the childhood trauma—he feared the earlier loss would be repeated through
his wife's desertion. He thus lived in a chronic danger situation. At
this stage he suffered from continuing pervasive anxiety. When the
threatened loss eventually came about, he was plunged into what was
a terrifying repetition against which he had no defense. He became
overwhelmed by automatic anxiety, representing a further reversion
along the developmental line.

David

An even more complete reversion, beyond the confines of automatic
anxiety, is illustrated by the case of David, aged forty-two, who had
worked all his life at the coal-face in the mines of County Durham.
He had always lived in a mining village, where he and his family
enjoyed a sense of community and comradeship. He had a zestful
attitude to life and had endured with good spirits the discomforts and
dangers of work in the mines, including his share of minor accidents.
On such occasions, he had always returned to the mine without persisting anxiety. His pit had a good safety record and was without
serious mishaps in recent years.

Six months before David was referred for psychiatric treatment,
he had been caught in a sudden major rockfall and had been trapped
for some hours. He had suffered no physical injury but he described
how a normal working shift had been transformed without warning
by major catastrophe. He thought all his workmates had been killed,
that he was entombed alone and beyond the reach of help. After some
hours he had been rescued; later, he learned that he had been brought
to the surface in a dazed condition, shaking violently and unable to
understand what was happening or what was said to him. This state
subsided over the course of the next twenty-four hours, but he continued to suffer from feelings of anxiety, depression, and dread, which

improved only very slowly. At the same time he began to have repeated and frightening dreams in which he reexperienced, in vivid
detail, the fall of the rockface and the horrifying conditions in which
he had been trapped.

David's condition showed all the features of a traumatic neurosis
described in *Beyond the Pleasure Principle* (Freud, 1920). The essential precondition was his complete unpreparedness for the danger
that befell him, so that signal anxiety had no chance to function. The
result was not psychic panic but massive vegetative excitation. The
reversion along the developmental line proceeded to a stage where
all integrated ego function was temporarily lost. Dreams in which the
trauma was repeated represented the ego's attempt at recovery
through the gradual reduction of accumulated excitation and through
attempts at active mastery of the helplessness of the traumatic situation as it persisted in memory. In treatment, the principal task was
exploration of the trauma in order to facilitate repeated fractional
discharge of excitation.

Although this condition is called a traumatic *neurosis*, it is different from the psychoneuroses proper. The danger situation is not defended against and structured symptoms do not occur. The dreams
do not contain a wish but are oriented toward reexperience of the
trauma in an attempt at mastery. Therapy is directed toward the
abreaction of the traumatic situation—a process that would not by
itself be appropriate or effective in psychoneurosis.

At this point, our illustrations of the developmental line of anxiety have come full circle, for the traumatic neurosis is in many respects analogous to the stage IV nightmare. In both, a traumatic event
initiates the condition; vegetative excitation supervenes, however
briefly; and there is no memory for the period during which ego
functioning is lost. In the case of traumatic anxiety, the trauma comes
from without; in the nightmare, it comes from within. There may, of
course, be other differences, which call for further exploration and
understanding. In the traumatic neurosis, what Freud regarded as a
"protective shield" against external stimuli is breached, which compounds and intensifies the impact of the trauma.[5] Whether a protective shield can operate in a comparable fashion against internal traumata is an important question. Anna Freud (1967) has taken the view

---

5. In some forms of battle exhaustion it is the repeated and continuing assaults of
noise and danger that ultimately penetrate the shield.

that it can, and her opinion is shared by others. It would be important to know, if this is the case, what the shield consists of, how it stands in relation to defense organization in general, how it operates, and how and under what conditions it gives way to internal impact. One must also ask why the effects of the internal trauma are transient while in most instances the traumatic neurosis persists, if untreated, for months or longer. However this may be, both conditions illustrate the operation of vegetative excitation as it occurs in people who otherwise may show no inclination to pathology and whose capacity for signal anxiety is usually unimpaired. The importance of some of these issues for the concept of psychic trauma has been discussed elsewhere (Yorke, 1986).

CHAPTER 2 _Mental Health and Illness in Terms of Internal Harmony and Disharmony_

Developmental Disharmonies

The study of the neuroses and psychoses of adult life tells us that pathology arises if a person's urge for drive satisfaction reverts from an age-appropriate mode of gratification to a formerly outgrown, infantile one.[1] Whenever this happens, and for whatever reason, the revived infantile urges clash with those parts of the personality that have maintained a mature level, and internal conflict arises. This, in turn, is followed by symptom formation—that is, by one of the ego's manifold attempts to restore inner peace by forging compromises between the unacceptable drive representative and the opposing ego and superego agencies.

Or it may be the ego organization that regresses owing to psychological or organic causes. The ego may even be threatened by complete dissolution. Many or all of the vital ego functions may be affected, which then reassume modes characteristic of early childhood, before secondary-process thinking and impulse control were established. Here also, symptom formation can be shown to follow the disturbance of internal balance between drive and egoactivity.

Seen from this point of view, mental health in an internally structured personality can be understood as the harmonious interaction between inner agencies that have reached and are maintaining the

1. The theoretical section of this chapter is by Anna Freud, whereas the authors provided the clinical illustrations.

same level. Symptoms of mental illness can be seen as the result of the ego's striving to reconcile what are in essence mutually contradictory impulses and aims.

Mental Equilibrium in Childhood

To achieve the degree of inner equilibrium compatible with normality is very difficult in early years, when the forces determining the child's development are external as well as internal. What needs to be integrated at this time are the potentialities inherent in the inherited constitution, the vicissitudes connected with the gradual structuralization of the personality, and the influences emanating from the parental environment that is responsible for the atmosphere in which development proceeds. While the task of attuning these influences to each other is difficult under any circumstances, it remains manageable provided that the momentum and quality of all or most of the responsible factors are within a normal range and their onset and rate of advance do not differ too much. However, with inborn dispositions, individual patterns of growth, and family backgrounds as divergent as they are, this is by no means always the case.

Disturbances of Equilibrium Due to Deviations from the Norm

So far as quantity and quality are concerned, each of the factors named can depart considerably from what is normative. When this happens, the consequences for healthy personality development are always adverse and, at times, disastrous.

CONSTITUTIONALLY DETERMINED DEVIATIONS. The innate givens that underlie an individual's instinctual development can distort that development in more than one direction. Most frequently they do so by lending undue weight to one of the early pregenital stages, usually either the oral or the anal stage. As a consequence, the drive representatives of this particular phase dominate the child's sex life and prevent him or her from reaching primacy on either the phallic-oedipal or, later, the genital level. Such developmental distortion also creates a point of almost irresistible attraction (a fixation point) to which the individual's wishes for drive satisfaction return whenever frustration is met in later life; that is, the distortion encourages the very drive regression that psychoanalysis has found responsible for initiating neurotic symptom formation.

Apart from these interferences with the normal course of developmental progress, sexual or aggressive endowment may be deficient in quantity, which may mar the individual's efficiency in adult love or work life. Or sexual or aggressive drives may be excessive and exceedingly difficult to accommodate within the framework of an otherwise normally equipped personality.

DEVIANT MODES OF STRUCTURALIZATION. Individuals differ no less in the structuralization of their personalities (that is, its division into separate id, ego, and superego agencies). The ego may only incompletely emerge out of the undifferentiated id/ego matrix; the resulting structure is unstable. Id and ego retain a tendency to merge readily again, and the child is apt to respond according to the primary process, which favors drive satisfaction, at an age when his ego should already have developed its independent status and should be capable of thinking and acting according to the secondary process, to maintain drive control. The division between the two agencies may also be too final and immovable. The ego is thus deprived of the normal possibility of acting in accordance with, and as a helpmate to, the drives, and it establishes within itself a basic hostility toward the drives. Likewise, the later emergence of the superego out of the ego can be either too complete or too incomplete, too stable or too unstable, for normal functioning. When ego and superego are never in full agreement with each other and can never act as one, unjustified guilt feelings prevail at the slightest opportunity and interfere with the child's enjoyment of developmental achievements and advances. When, in contrast, the monitoring and critical function of the superego hardly rises above the level of the ego or is easily corrupted to fall in with the latter's wishes, character development is in danger of taking a turn toward the egocentric and dissocial.

Within the personality structure the quantitative factor is decisive for the maintenance of peaceful growth. The three inner agencies need to be matched in strength to avoid either compulsive or impulsive excesses of development. Alterations of intensity in any of them, during the transition from one pregenital stage to the next or, inevitably, with the onset of adolescence, cause internal upheaval and are responsible for much of the diffuse pathology of the formative years.

DEVIANT ENVIRONMENTAL FACTORS. Parental involvement with a child's developmental progress can err on the side of too much or too little. Where care, comfort, stimulation, support and guidance are deficient, the developmental advances of the emotions, the intellect, moral functions, social adaptation, and so on all suffer. When, in contrast, a child is overprotected, overstimulated, or too tightly restrained, the prospects for building a sense of identity and becoming an independent personality are stunted from the start.

Disturbances of Development Due to Breakdown of Synchronization

A young child's normal development involves seemingly preordained synchronization in the unfolding of the drives, the ego functions, the superego, and environmental interventions. This picture is disturbed when timing goes wrong on any of the four sides.

The cannibalistic impulses and fantasies that are the legitimate mental representatives of the infant's oral stage normally appear before any organized ego activity exists with which they might conflict. Normally, therefore, they are unopposed and do not form a source of disturbance. But there is trouble when such impulses persist beyond their time, or when critical ego activity sets in too early, or when, as in later life, regression revives cannibalistic impulses that then come into conflict with all the moral and aesthetic principles of a mature superego.

The archaic fears of darkness, of being alone, of loud noises, and so on are normally at their height when the infant can count on support, comfort, and reassurance from the adults who take care of him and act as an auxiliary ego, or when his own ego's awakening reality sense can help to dispel panic. They become a serious threat to peaceful development only if parental support is withdrawn too early, as happens to neglected children, or if the ego matures too late, as is the rule with the mentally deficient.

The separation-individuation phase of the second year of life is negotiated successfully when there is adequate synchronization between three factors: motor development, which provides the means for the child's physical departure from and rejoining of the mother; the ego's awakening wish for exploration and adventure; and the mother's readiness to grant the child a measure of independence. If any of these influences comes in too early or lags behind the others, development is interfered with and the infant, instead of advancing, misses out on an important step.

The fate of the anal-sadistic impulses is even more crucially connected with timing. Normally, there should be at least a short period in which the infant can indulge these drive representatives without meeting either external or internal opposition. All too frequently, however, environmental pressure toward toilet training and condemnation of aggression sets in at the peak of the anal-sadistic phase. The child may concur or identify with both of these attitudes, which puts to an end any possible enjoyment of dirty matter or the urge to attack and hurt people who are at the same time important love objects. The child's efforts to come to terms with the offending parts of himself lead to the precocious employment of such defenses as repression, reaction formation, and the turning of aggression against the self. Later come such manifestations as disgust with dirty hands, excessive tendencies toward orderliness, and repetitive behavior. These are similar to the later obsessional symptoms, although they are diffuse and lack the coherence and organization of a full-blown obsessional neurosis. And while the obsessional neurosis and character are fixed structures, difficult to dissolve even in psychoanalytic therapy, this early, developmentally caused symptomatic picture is transient. It disappears again when drive development advances beyond the anal stage—that is, when its representatives lose their intensity and, in their weakened form, pose no further threat to either external or internal authority.

During the oedipal stage, it is essential that the ego's defense organization be in tune with the advance in drive activity. Children who meet castration fears or penis envy, rivalrous jealousies and death wishes against the parent of the same sex, equipped only with primitive defense mechanisms, develop pathology more far-reaching than that of the common infantile neuroses.

Development versus Neurotic and Psychotic Pathology

Although important as a background for adult psychopathology, the irregularities of infantile development easily escape notice. Once they are overlaid by the later neuroses and psychoses, the symptoms produced intermingle and become more or less indistinguishable from each other. The confrontations between drive and ego activity—which in the immature being are due primarily to the quantitative, qualitative, or temporal developmental deviations described above—are matched in the structured personality by the internal conflicts due to secondary drive regression.

However, for purposes of therapy the two types of pathology need to be distinguished. The pathogenic sequence of frustration, regression, internal incompatibility, anxiety, defense by repression, return of the repressed, and compromise formation that is characteristic of the neuroses is relieved by analytic work that lifts all partners in the process to the same level of consciousness and thereby enables the patient to find different, healthier, and more adaptive solutions to his conflicts. Developmental pathology, on the other hand, may not answer to defense analysis. Even if confronted with the details of their aberrant development and the reasons for it, child or adult patients may remain unable to alter what has happened and what is, after all, the very basis for their personality structure. If anything, treatment directed toward developmental assistance may, in the earliest years, help to correct some of the most glaring developmental discrepancies.

Anna Freud has discussed mental health in terms of a harmonious interaction between the inner agencies themselves and between these agencies and outside influences. Such harmony can be achieved only if the inner agencies have reached and can maintain comparable levels of development and if the external influences with which they interact reflect an "average expectable environment" (Hartmann, 1939). But it is axiomatic that such development can be harmonious only in a maturational sense—that is, in terms of both quantitative and qualitative progress. The agencies are always in latent dispute once adequate structuralization has occurred.

For the child, and often for the parents, even the most normal of developmental shifts may not feel harmonious. Every move forward from an existing developmental phase that is familiar, safe, and gratifying toward one that feels uncertain and even dangerous is a threat to the child's well-being. And every step that was formerly satisfactory may become untenable in the face of fresh maturational processes and new external influences and expectations. Comfort gives way to frustration and exacerbation of conflict. But lasting remedy is not to be found in a return to the past, to old ways of adaptation that have been outlived. The resulting discomforts and dissatisfactions encourage change in search of relief. Even though the past never loses its powerful pull on the present, in terms of adaptation the old has to give way to the new.

Take, for example, the move from passive to active anality. The anal indulgence, on the one hand, and passive acceptance of maternal ministrations, on the other, give way to an active striving for control of both body and objects. The wish for drive expression is opposed by maternal expectations, and growth comes about from the ego's attempts to conciliate and resolve the conflict.

Minor degrees of developmental disharmony are ubiquitous, but the disharmony may be sufficiently severe to constitute pathology. It may also form a nidus for further pathological development. In many instances of neurosis in childhood, the influences of these disharmonies may be observed or at least inferred.

Clare

Clare was a wanted baby born to warm and affectionate parents. Her two brothers were two and four years older than she. She had a close and pleasurable relationship with her mother throughout her early infancy, and both parents shared in her handling and care. By the age of ten months her warm relationship with her mother was matched by an unusual degree of closeness with her father. Shortly before Clare's second birthday her mother became pregnant again, and as the pregnancy progressed the closeness between Clare and her father intensified. By the age of three, her fondness for her father bordered on the excessive and he responded with irritation and withdrawal. He began a new job, in another town, that took up more of his interest and time and spent some months away from home arranging to move the household.

From this time on Clare refused to wear dresses or any kind of girls' clothes. Her absolute refusal continued for the next four years. Though widely regarded as graceful, beautiful, and intelligent, her popularity and social accomplishments did little to offset her obvious unhappiness; and her dissatisfaction was typified when, at the age of seven and a half, she said to her mother, "There is something spoiling my life: I want to be a daddy when I grow up."

The way Clare's unhappiness was brought about can be described sequentially. A predisposing factor may perhaps be found in the narcissistic wounds occasioned by her mother's pregnancy. Clare responded by taking a premature step toward an even closer relationship to her father, thus fostering an unusually early and strong oedipal tie. Frightened by the incestuousness of this bond, the father appeared to withdraw and so added to the child's conviction of parental disaffection in favor of the new baby (a girl). The changed family circumstances occasioned by the move may have reinforced Clare's view of these experiences. Her response was to abandon her developing femininity; and there followed an intensification of her penis envy.

To put the matter another way, the child made a premature entry into an oedipal phase colored and intensified by what had gone before. The oedipal conflicts defied successful mastery, and Clare's sexual organization reverted to the earlier phallic phase. Conflicts were reactivated at this earlier level. Clare's wish to be a boy found forceful expression; she abandoned her femininity and with it, ostensibly, the wish to possess her father. But although she displaced her father and regained, in fantasy, her mother, she maintained her tie to him through identification ("I want to be a daddy"). The result was therefore a compromise.

Although this solution by compromise formation lacked both the structure and the symbolic quality of an adult neurotic symptom, it serves as a childhood prototype of neurosis. But it illustrates more than this. *Clare's difficulties in coping with her oedipal conflicts were increased by the fact that she met them prematurely.* Maturation had not yet proceeded sufficiently to allow her to make a more adaptive resolution of her difficulties. The process of symptom formation was partly fostered by a disturbed developmental chronology, although in Clare's case this disharmony was no more than a predisposing factor, and the clinical form was that of an infantile neurosis.

Progression in development within the normative range demands that the contributions from the various mental agencies as these emerge and mature and the external influences that further this developmental process must be in harmony. Where there is temporal, qualitative, or quantitative disparity—the disharmonies described by Anna Freud—the resulting interaction means that development goes awry, and a primary source of pathology results. This pathology is a consequence of the imbalance itself, which is perpetuated by the synthetic function. The lines of development suffer interference, and the disturbance is carried forward from one phase to the next.

Certain disorders of character betray the effects of imbalance between the psychological agencies. This is evident in children who are at the mercy of imperative drive discharge. The discrepancy in these cases between the force of the drives and the restraint of ego controls may result from excessively powerful impulses or from weakness within the defensive organization; it may arise from inborn constitutional endowment; or it may be brought about by such environmental influences as the reinforcement of drives through parental failure to set appropriate limits. Any one of these influences may result in a compromise that is settled too decisively on the side of drive discharge. Unless the balance can be redressed the inequality will be carried forward through successive stages in personality formation and will have fateful consequences for adult life.

Keith

Keith, the fourth of six children in his family, was four years old when he entered nursery school. The family home, in a poverty-stricken area, was overcrowded. Keith's mother appeared to have cared well for each child during early infancy, but thereafter she failed to provide sufficient verbal stimulation. Neither parent and none of the older children was articulate. Language served the function less of communication than of holding the stage in a competitively noisy household. Standards of cleanliness and social behavior were poor, and expectations for Keith's achievements were set by his elder siblings, all of whom attended remedial schools.

Keith was described as follows:

> an outgoing friendly urchin, likeable but almost unmanageable. He threw himself into activities with gusto, but without control, getting immense enjoyment but upsetting everyone in the process. He was easily discouraged in activities which proved at all difficult; his vocabulary was limited and his indistinct speech was used mainly for bellowing his wishes at maximum volume; he could not wait his turn or share toys; he bashed every child who got in his way or had something he wanted; and he usually reacted to frustration with major tantrums. His bowel and bladder control were precarious; he had a runny nose; and he was often grubby and smelly. (Edgcumbe, 1975, p. 141)

When he entered nursery school Keith gave no sign that he was troubled by his inability to control his impulses or to limit the gratification of his wishes in their various modalities. But he *was* concerned when his behavior incurred reproof, and he became despondent when he earned the disapproval of the nursery staff, to whom he had become very attached. During his relatively short stay at the nursery, the conflict between his wishes for immediate gratification and his wish for love and approval began to be internalized, and he made great efforts, at times successful, to control his impulses and moderate his wild activities. He also began to take some pride in improving his appearance and in cleanliness.

In summary, it can be said that the poor conditions of Keith's home and the low expectations set for him, together with the primitive verbalization employed by the whole family, interfered with his development of secondary-process thinking. As a result, his development was backward in almost all respects. Faced in the nursery school with greater expectations from those he admired, Keith's aberrant behavior led to conflict that was previously lacking, conflict that in time became internalized.

Up to this time, Keith had been set on a deviant course of development that would have led to even greater disturbance in later life. Timely intervention at the nursery school, at a point when the disharmony was nascent and not yet fully fixed by the operation of the synthetic function, helped him achieve a more normal line of development. But it is unlikely that his achievements would help him to escape altogether the consequences of an unfavorable early start.

Alice

Alice, the second daughter of young and immature parents, was first seen at the age of three. Her mother had been hospitalized with severe depression when Alice was two and a half, and the children had been looked after by various relatives. After her return, Alice's mother sometimes lay in bed all day, neglecting the family and the house. Alice's father, cold and detached, refused to help and spurned any affectionate approaches Alice made to him. In short, these adults were parents only in name.

Unlike her elder sister, who met domestic chaos and lack of parental care with passivity and withdrawal, Alice dealt with these circumstances in a strikingly active way. She made herself responsible for the regulation of family activities, calling the parents in the morning and encouraging them to get meals. Her determination and persistence sometimes succeeded in spurring them to action. In providing for herself she hid her needs from her mother and shielded her from the demands of maternal care. Alice felt that she would lose her mother altogether if she made demands on her or showed in any way that she minded her neglect. The mother was impressed by the child's "realism and good sense," an illustration of which was provided during therapy. Alice was ashamed of her worn clothes and dirty shoes.

She confided her shame to her therapist, who mentioned it to the mother. She responded, in the child's presence, "Why didn't she tell me? Of course she can have her shoes cleaned!" Alice looked happy but said, "If you open the polish tin I can clean my own shoes."

From the beginning the therapist was struck by the child's sense of reality and excellent orientation. She nonetheless seemed a solitary child whose negativism was "a stubborn assertion of her self-sufficiency." Although she was sturdy and stomped about like a tough little urchin, she often looked like a waif.

Alice paid a price for her precocious independence and self-reliance. At times she withdrew into fantasy to an unusual degree. Her reversal of affect, by which she kept sadness and anger at bay, replacing them by apparent happiness, allowed her to cope. But her blocking of affect through fear of total loss of the mother added to the picture of an apparently inhibited child whose capacity to form relationships was impaired. She was aware of her needs in spite of her fear of showing them, and it was only after she had been in treatment for some time that she tentatively asked her therapist, "Could a person ever sit on your lap?"

Two unfavorable factors had a decisive bearing on Alice's developing pathology. She received too little caring and emotional nurture, so that she could not reveal her needs and have them met or show her feelings and have them assuaged. This environmental deficiency was compounded by her propensity for premature ego development. There was therefore a discrepancy between the instinctual needs of a three-year-old, on the one hand, and the ego development of a much older child, on the other. Alice developed ways of coping that, however helpful in dealing with the circumstances of the time, led to pathology. Her style of relating to herself and others, her affective suppression, and her excessive self-reliance were brought together by the ego's synthetic function and were well on the way to forming inbuilt components of a distorted personality.

It is not difficult to see the influences of developmental disharmony on the pathologies of such children, particularly if they come under analytic observation at a comparatively early age. But once development has proceeded to the point where structure is not only established but firmly set, the disharmonies may not reveal themselves so readily. Indeed, it can be extremely difficult to reconstruct from pathology in an adult patient the developmental steps that may have led to disharmony among the structures and contributed to later pathological processes. The ego's synthetic function may have done its work all too well. In later chapters we take the view that disharmonies may lay some of the groundwork for later neurosis of symptoms or of character, for non-neurotic developmental disturbance, and for psychosis. It remains a matter of considerable clinical difficulty to elucidate the contributions made by disharmonies to the ultimate clinical picture—with the clear exception of the adult obsessional neuroses (chapter 4).

CHAPTER 3 *The Neuroses: A General Introduction*

Activity and passivity, femininity and masculinity, love and hate are opposing trends in the organism from early life. Where opposition between them is pronounced, these internal conflicts may predispose to later disorder and become incorporated in, and augmented by, external or internalized battles.

External conflicts need no elaboration. They mark the progression of the child's early object relations. Internalized conflicts, on the other hand, can occur only when certain preconditions are met: when, for example, true superego precursors and identifications emerge in the form of internal checks and controls that take on a moral or interdictory quality formerly attributed to the parents. The child can now be truly divided against himself.

Without internalized conflict there is no neurosis, but neither is there normal progress or development. Such conflicts may or may not be reexternalized, but active, dynamic, internalized conflict is characteristic of every postoedipal child and adult. In normal circumstances, internalized conflicts are both expectable and tolerated. Whenever the customary bounds are exceeded, anxiety, guilt, or other forms of mental pain become more threatening. Countermeasures, whether pathological or otherwise, are called into being. But in general, stabilization of conflict comes about as repression increases in effectiveness; the firmer structure of the repression barrier guarantees the amnesia for infancy so characteristic of later phases. But such defense mechanisms as projection, externalization, and reaction formation are also frequently used by children and adults, in response to signal anxiety, to prevent the emergence into consciousness of the contents of conflict or painful affect.

The Simpler Solutions of Conflict

The mechanisms of defense cannot always be effective in this way. Conflict may become intensified, may be thrown out of balance, or may threaten to intrude into consciousness. Even in these instances, neurosis is not an inevitable outcome: economically simpler solutions may suffice. Sometimes the ego allies itself with either the superego or the id so that one side in the battle emerges victorious. The outcome is either the stricter control of a wish or its gratification. In such circumstances there may be no conscious manifestation of conflict.

Sometimes the ego may be temporarily or permanently weak. Its controlling functions may be impaired and unable to respond to superego pressures, even when severe. Such an individual may, for example, complain of uncontrollable rages—afterward he may feel extremely guilty about his outbursts but be powerless to prevent their recurrence. In other circumstances, a weak superego may grant the ego too easy an acquiescence in permitting discharge of drive. In these disharmonies conflict is not so much resolved as short-circuited.

Conflict may sometimes be contained if those situations which threaten to increase its intensity are avoided. A man of twenty-three was in the habit of meeting his girlfriend after work; they visited the local pub together with male colleagues from his office. One evening his girlfriend could not join him. For reasons not at all clear to him, he felt unable to join his friends for their usual drink. He felt vaguely uneasy about his refusal. Analytic work revealed that powerful, latent homosexual wishes were aroused when normal restraints were weakened by alcohol. His girlfriend's presence protected him against homosexual temptation.

Inhibition is one of the simpler means of keeping potentially painful conflicts within bounds, but the outcome can be crippling. At an extreme, some people avoid any kind of human contact that might stimulate drives and their associated affects. A less drastic form of inhibition is seen in some cases of frigidity and impotence, where courtship and wooing may be unimpeded, at least up to the point of repeated failure in sexual intercourse. Whether this failure is simply the result of a physiological inhibition under the pressure of psychological interference is a matter we leave open. What is exemplified in these conditions is not the inhibition of a drive per se but the inhibition of its culminating expression.

Though courtship may at first be unrestricted in such cases, repeated impotence may lead to its abandonment—through fear not of the drive itself but of the pain and humiliation of repeated failure. Measures directed against painful feeling-states must thus be distinguished from inhibitions arising directly out of conflict.

Painful feeling-states can be avoided in a number of ways. Anna Freud dealt with this subject at length in her book *The Ego and the Mechanisms of Defence* (1936). On the basis of her work with children, she illustrated, characterized, and defined a number of ego restrictions. She pointed out that when the active exercise of an ego function becomes psychically painful rather than pleasurable, the activity may be abandoned. She cited the case of a young boy who, during a certain phase in his analysis, had developed into a gifted football player. He became fearful that the bigger boys would envy his ability and behave aggressively toward him, and this led him to withdraw his interest from football. But the energy originally invested in this activity was redeployed. His former enjoyment of writing now became devotion, and he developed an increasing contempt for sporting activities.

An ego restriction of this kind arises from a need to avoid psychic pain, not from a need to block drive derivatives. Unlike inhibition, it involves no damning up of instinctual drive energy or the sublimations that derive from it. The energy invested in those interests is merely diverted to others and the ego is enriched in another direction. This process is normal for an infantile ego coping with painful affects. It is significant from the developmental point of view since it may be repeated and extended and may result in ego impoverishment or distortion.

Inhibitions must also be considered in relation to sublimations. In sublimation, an ego interest or activity that derived originally from a component instinct loses its sexual or aggressive meaning. A child with anal preoccupations may develop into a very good plumber; one whose voyeuristic tendencies were striking may become a good photographer; and many a skilled surgeon may, through his or her craft, use sublimated instincts that initially derived from sadistic impulses.

But it is not uncommon for sublimations to be undone. In prepuberty, for example, sublimations acquired in latency may break down, and a child may be threatened with conflicts aroused by unmodified drives. Take, for example, a girl with a keen interest in piano playing. With the increase in instinctual strivings, her touch, on which she had often been complimented, became reinstinctualized, and a conflict over masturbatory touching was thereby reactivated. The simplest way of dealing with this conflict was to give up piano playing altogether. She was not aware of the unconscious inhibition but, like her family and friends, simply experienced the loss of this interest as a natural consequence of newly developing ones.

Such a loss in a case like this one might be a matter for regret but it would hardly be thought of as a disaster. If, however, a skilled concert pianist were to lose a similar sublimation, an inhibition would indeed be disastrous. Someone whose reputation, self-esteem, deep commitment, and livelihood depends on a skill cannot easily relinquish or divert it. A more complex psychological solution for his predicament, one that meets adaptive requirements, would be called for. Symptom formation of one kind or another would almost invariably ensue.

A common way of dealing with a potentially distressing conflict is through inhibition of affect. Fear of anger may stem from the fear of rage, and the fear of rage from the fear of a murderous drive. Such people may consciously fear their violent propensities but may never experience the affect of anger. For them, anger and murder are unconsciously equated through the operation of the primary process.

In some people, fear of affect in general is so great that their experience of emotion is highly restricted. They may appear cold and aloof and their experience of life may be seriously impoverished. In some people the inhibition is less generalized: they are terrified mostly of positive affects and inhibit all expressions of tenderness, warmth, and concern. Such men and women may give the impression of being inhibited in the colloquial sense and are often so described by others. Some individuals avoid personal contacts because they are afraid of arousing strong feelings in themselves they cannot control. This disability lies in social restriction of the affects themselves. But while these people remain socially isolated they may find other fields of affective expression—toward pets or toward the arts, for example. All these limitations form important components of character.

The Symptom Neuroses

The symptom neuroses have always occupied an important place in psychoanalytic thinking. The exposition of the process of dream-formation, arising out of Freud's self-analysis, not only paved the way for the firm foundation of the new science but also provided the key to understanding such hitherto baffling conditions as conversion hysterias, phobias, and obsessional neuroses. In all these cases the basic psychic ingredients are transformed into their manifest products by processes so strikingly similar that an indissoluble link between the psychopathology of everyday life and the psychic phenomena encountered in the consulting room became established. Both dreams and symptom neuroses are regressive phenomena; both show admixtures of primary and secondary process; both show compromise formations between derivatives of the id and defensive aspects of ego functioning that are normally unconscious; and both represent striking, if irrational, dramatizations of psychic conflict. It is therefore not surprising, since the id has so forceful a say in the outcome of both dream formation and symptom formation, that wish fulfillment should be such a fateful constituent in the protogenesis of each.

What generally conceals both the fact and the nature of the wish from dreamer and sufferer alike is the disguise the ego imposes in order to make the expression of that wish more acceptable. But to the psychoanalytically informed observer, these disguising functions of the ego disclose the very instinctual origins they seek to distort and unwittingly reveal the nature and quality of their sources. The two major contributants to the compromise formation may be revealed through psychoanalytic techniques.

A major difficulty always stands in the way of such a discrimination: namely, the regressive process, which plays such a significant part in the formation of dream or symptom, causing the archaic to rub shoulders with the contemporary; the novel and unexpected to be tinged with déjà vu, and psychological crudities to acquire a modern veneer.

Even an apparently simple dream may illustrate some of these points. A young woman in analysis vividly recalled a fragment of a dream in which an unidentified voice was heard to say, "There must have been a little space." The preceding day the analyst had canceled her session at short notice. During the time when she would normally have been attending her analytic hour, she was standing in her living room, which she was planning to refurnish. Noting the disposition of the existing furniture, she looked toward a corner of the room and found herself thinking, "That's too big a space."

She recalled this fact when she reported the dream to the analyst. She also remembered a previous time when she had been thinking of buying furniture. She had arranged to meet her fiancé to shop together and was bitterly disappointed when he failed to show up. This recollection and the thoughts that followed as the session progressed made it clear that she was far more upset by the missed session than she had hitherto realized. In part, the dream had made good the disappointment by capitalizing on a passing daytime thought about the "space" and, in its wish-fulfilling way, turned it into a "little" one.

So much for the contemporary contributant to the dream. What about the archaic one? At this point in the analysis the patient was reexperiencing, in the transference, the struggle against infantile incestuous wishes. There was a genital "space" for her father. It was only a "little" one, to be sure, because it was only a little girl's. Thus the archaic wish too found expression. The dream thought also contained a frustrated contemporary complaint about the analyst: surely he could have found, during the day, a "little space" just for her?

The unconscious wish from the id, then, found expression, but only in disguise. The longing for the analyst in the present and the revival of sexual wishes for the father from the past were turned, through the defensive operations of the ego, into a coherent but apparently meaningless and detached phrase: "There must have been a little space." The day-residue (a preconscious thought remembered by the ego) was chosen for reasons of representability. Through the primary-process work of condensation and displacement, space in the room became both analytic space and infantile genital space. Its use was thereby overdetermined, and a repetition-compulsion had played its part.

Before we turn our attention from the compromise formations of dreams to those of neurosis, let us bear in mind the fact that, in young children, wishes may be expressed simply and very directly. A child may dream, for example, of eating mountains of ice cream without any distortion except the impossibility of doing so in real life—which is, after all, hardly a distortion of the wish. But in young children wishes are not a matter of war between conflicting agencies of the mind, for these agencies have barely begun to exist. The child may sometimes be at loggerheads with the external world, but that is a different matter.

In turning from the dream to the symptom, we are not only turning from the "normal" to the "pathological"; we are turning from phenomena that occur only under the specialized physiological conditions of rapid eye movement (REM) sleep to phenomena that occur in, or persist into, waking life. While this is a matter of considerable interest and has received a good deal of attention from many quarters, it does not affect the arguments set out here. It serves only to make the similarities between the two sets of phenomena seem all the more remarkable.

Dennis

Let us now examine, briefly, a symptom neurosis in a child. Dennis was twelve when his schoolteachers began to complain about his behavior. He was provocative to the masters but complained bitterly if they responded in a critical, angry, or punitive way. More strikingly, whenever another boy brushed against him, Dennis screamed as if he had been half-killed and rolled on the floor, clutching his belly in apparent agony. The schoolteachers had been unable to modify this bizarre behavior.

Certain other changes were also described at the time of assessment. Dennis was increasingly "difficult" at home. Nothing suited him; he was increasingly unfriendly to the point of offensiveness; and although he had hitherto mixed fairly readily with the rest of the family, he was now comparatively isolated and spent hours alone in his room. Another significant change had passed almost unremarked at the time of the referral and emerged only during a careful anamnesis. Dennis was not provocative to his French teacher. She had always taken a special interest in him, and he had responded well to her encouragement and produced excellent work and examination results. Recently, however, his work in French had fallen off; he showed much less interest in the teacher; and he no longer seemed capable of responding to her concern.

One or two further facts were noted from the history. As a small boy Dennis had been rather close to his father, enjoying the comradeship of their long walks together. There was something of a conspiratorial relationship between them. His father bought him special

sweets and tidbits in spite of his mother's disapproval of eating between meals. At such times Dennis was warned not to tell his mother.
He was also rather intrigued by his father's behavior in the toilet,
where he would spend hours conversing through the open door with
the rest of his family. Father's constipation was almost a family topic.

His mother was always warm to Dennis but less demonstrative
than his father. She was often ill, suffering from severe attacks of
colic. When Dennis was about four and a half his mother became
pregnant. At about this time it was noticed that Dennis became upset
when his father and mother dressed to go out together and that he
failed to settle down with the babysitter—whom he had always
liked—and had difficulty going to sleep. He took a great interest in
the pregnancy, and when his sister was born he looked after her in a
most proprietary fashion.

These points of history were among those which allowed the
diagnostician to make a tentative formulation. The disturbance had
been precipitated by the reinforcement of instinctual drives at the
start of puberty. Dennis withdrew from his primary objects as oedipal
attachments were threateningly reactivated. He withdrew too from
the woman teacher who had become an uncomfortable focus of displacement from the mother. Both mother and father were kept at a
defensive distance by offensive behavior and rudeness whenever
their presence could not be avoided.

But oedipal reactivation prompts instinctual regression to the
negative oedipal phase and the earlier tie to the father is reinforced.
Dennis gets himself attacked by the schoolfellow-fathers and becomes
their victim as he rolls on the floor in the agony of bodily mutilation.
Physical contact with the other boys is tantamount to homosexual
assault while, at the same time, he is turned into a woman through a
wished-for castration. The histrionic enactment embodies something
of the father's exhibitionism; but the bodily enactment itself incorpo-
rates elements of identification with both the mother's illness (colic)
and her pregnancy. The boys' physical contact represents contamination that includes anal elements revived through the exacerbation of
anal-stage interests and pregnancy theories.

It is easy to trace the regressive transformations of instinctual life
that follow the flight from positive attachments to negative oedipal
and anal fixation points. It should be underlined, however, that the
neurotic symptoms of the enactment not only express homosexual
wishes toward the father in disguised form, including displacements

and identifications, but also reveal with some clarity the child's struggle against his instinctual wishes. His behavior displays a fear of men, a horror at the thought of their contact, and thereby expresses, simultaneously, his forbidden sexual strivings and the repugnance they occasion.

Before we turn, by way of contrast, to an adult case, a brief summary of the steps in the formation of the boy's illness may illustrate the similarities as well as the differences between the childhood and adult disorder. The disturbance was precipitated by instinctual frustration in prepuberty. The regressive shift of instinct reactivates earlier fixation points. The ego retains its repugnance to the threatened encroachment of infantile instinct that ensues, and a loose compromise formation results. But the resulting neurosis observed in Dennis lacks the integration, structure, and stability of the established adult neurosis to be found in Jean.

Jean

Jean, a thirty-year-old schoolteacher, suddenly developed a combined paralysis and postural distortion in her right hand. Her fingers were rigidly flexed on her palm and her thumb thrust straight outward in an unnatural manner. The onset of the symptoms was preceded by a few days of excessive anxiety and guilt following a painful incident. Uncharacteristically, she had lost her temper and hit a boy pupil in a physical display of anger that both shocked and surprised her.

For some time Jean had felt vaguely dissatisfied with herself and her life; she had suffered from irritability; and her mind was focused on her discontent and on an unsuccessful and unhappy sexual encounter. She felt she had been forced by the man but could not afterward altogether unburden herself of a brooding sense of guilt and responsibility. The anamnesis suggested a strong identification with a tyrannical father as well as with a passive and suffering mother. Her general character gave indications of undue masculine traits.

Analytic exploration revealed two additional factors. Ostensibly, she was an unwilling and violent aggressor in the episode with the child and an unfortunate, if passive victim in the sexual encounter. At this point we should relate Jean's personal history to the process by which her symptoms were formed.

In 1912 Freud discussed the "types of onset of neurosis" in some detail, distinguishing a number of ostensibly different types while

emphasizing their tendency to overlap. In summary, what is significant for the onset of neurosis is the frustration of an instinctual drive
resulting, in one way or another, in a disturbance of the mental economy. The threat may be posed by the access of instinctual pressure
that accompanies the biological reinforcements of puberty or the
menopause; it may stem from the frustration of instinct occasioned
by internal or external barriers; or it may derive more or less directly
from developmental holdups. To these may be added developmental
disharmonies that have never been properly mastered. In all cases an
economic crisis has transformed a predisposing factor into a precipitant.

The frustration of impelling sexual wishes was clearly the point
of departure for the formation of Jean's neurosis. There was an urgent
need for drive satisfaction—sexually through the man, destructively
through the boy. These gratifications were unacceptable to the rest of
her personality. She could no longer accept sexual intercourse corrupted by the wish for aggressive penetration or the tyrannical eruption of that same aggression in the humiliation of her pupil.

Instinctual withdrawal will not in itself solve conflicts of this
kind. Withdrawal from real objects means that fantasy life is overinvested. Into this fantasy life childhood components begin to intrude:
blocked from discharge in the present, Jean must fall back on the
illusory satisfactions of the past. The process of regression is reinforced by the pull of her fixations. The instinctual organization, like
that of the dreamer, embarks on a retreat to childhood.

But regression serves only to intensify earlier infantile conflict.
Instinctually, Jean reverts to the oedipal phase; but this retreat does
not fulfill the hope of satisfaction. The wish to castrate and possess
the penis—the return of the repressed—poses an intolerable threat to
the ego, which still functions more or less at an adult level and remains in touch with the demands of external reality. Moreover, the
infantile wishes are reinforced by strong adult drive energies. Jean's
ego is required to meet both the demands of instinctual pressures and
the demands of adult standards and precepts, including those im-
posed by the superego.

The ego must strike a balance. The childhood sexual wishes
arouse a reaction that shows itself only as conscious repugnance. The
wishes can reach awareness only if they are disguised. For Jean, the
wish to acquire the father's penis is realized and encoded in the
stiffened hand, while its uselessness and paralysis represents the re-

pudiation of the wish. Thus both sides of the battle, the id and the ego, are represented (in combinative disguise) in the symptom itself. This new formation unifies both the wish and the reaction against it in a split-off part of the personality that, acting like a foreign body, imposes as punishment irritation and suffering which serves to placate the superego.

Neurotic symptoms bear the stamp of regression and compromise formation. Freud's recognition of these self-same factors in dreams underlined the link between normality and pathology. As in the dream, the processes of condensation, displacement, and overdetermination play the same part in Jean's paralysis as they do in the formation of phobias and obsessional neuroses.

CHAPTER 4 The Symptom Neuroses

Conversion Hysteria

The account of the formation of Jean's symptoms (see chapter 3) is confined to the key processes of regression and compromise. Jean's symptoms are those of conversion hysteria, but in all the symptom neuroses the processes by which these come into being are strictly comparable.

The symptoms cannot be considered in isolation. They must be understood in terms of the psychological and developmental matrix in which they are embedded. The nature and quality of the end result—the symptoms within their enclave—depend on the type of fixation, arrests or deviations, mechanisms and modes of defense, and the personality development, including the stages reached on the developmental lines and the genetic and constitutional factors. Symptom neuroses are a paradigm of the personality.

The personality of the conversion hysteric accommodates itself readily to somatic expression. Such individuals possess a generalized bodily erogeneity. As in the young child, the body remains in the forefront of the self-representation. This is not only a matter of physicality and proprietorial pleasure in the body: the pleasure also retains much of its original instinctual quality. The mental representation of the body is invested with insufficiently neutralized instinctual drive energies. It is widely held that genetic and other constitutional factors make their contribution to this physical diathesis. This prevailing erogeneity partly accounts for the bodily exhibitionism so commonly encountered in hysterical manifestations of all kinds.

Such considerations help us to understand the striking fact of somatic compliance in the formation of conversion symptoms. Within the eroticized body image specific parts of the body unconsciously take on the significance of the genitals. These areas, with their particular cathexes, provide the somatic stage for any dramatized solution to conflict.

The developmental factors that, together with constitutional ones, contribute to this state of affairs include the quality of the mother's mental investment and physical caring as well as that of other important people in the child's life. The mother's attitudes and her behavior toward the child's body may themselves lead to its over-evaluation. Within this somatic matrix specific influences may map out areas of particular and excessive instinctualization. Both real and fantasied aspects of relationships contribute. (The interrelation between the two is an important theme in the development of Freud's theory of hysteria.) For example, the interaction with the object world may foster fantasies of seduction appropriate to the child's maturational phase. The child's oral, anal, or other interpretations of coitus help to determine the nature of his fantasied relationships with the mother and father during the oedipal phase.

The child's particular physical endowments can become a source of pride and pleasure to child and parent alike. Physical illness, the concern it arouses, or the treatment it calls for may likewise instinctualize certain areas of the body. The ingestion of "nice" or "nasty" medicines, for example, may emphasize somatic orality. Particular areas of the body end up carrying a special instinctual investment. In the course of time, it displays, somatically, specific aspects of former relationships. The early object is retained and unconsciously represented within the relevant somatic memories.[1]

The fixation points in hysteria are predominantly orophallic. Instinctualized areas of the body come to represent, through a process

1. The persistence of an object relationship within the framework of the somatic symptom is a key distinction between conversion hysteria and hypochondriasis (Schilder, 1935). In the latter, the somatic investment is predominantly narcissistic and object cathexis is represented poorly in the symptom, if at all. For an account of the role of "physicality" in neurosis see Wiseberg and Yorke, 1986, and on psychiatric disorders in general, Yorke, 1985.

of displacement, the mouth or the genital—one's own, or the object's, or both. These fixations maintain a regressive pull that is ready to take effect if the individual withdraws from a disappointing object in the real world. They form vulnerable points in the personality. Moreover, they constitute the repressed instinctual elements that threaten to return to consciousness whenever the repression barrier is breached.

How do these considerations apply in Jean's case? Why, for example, was her hand the locus for physical disturbance? And what overdetermination does it illustrate?

Jean's hands were always of special significance for her. She regarded them as clumsy and ungainly, felt self-conscious about them in company, and never knew what to do with them. After her recent sexual encounter she had experienced vague and repugnant masturbatory urges, which she strongly resisted: they disappeared with the onset of the physical symptom. Also at this time her hand-writing, which had never been good, deteriorated drastically; even her corrections of pupils' essays were barely legible. Her mother had sometimes written bad checks and had cheated Jean's father of money by forging his signature. Jean remembered her father's physical punishment—smacks—with some resentment. And, of course, the hand was the offending instrument in her aggression against her pupil.

Behind the masturbatory impulses, reinforced by the sexual encounter, was a childhood primal-scene fantasy, including identification with both father and mother, aggressor and passive victim, rapist and violated. The hand was not only the instrument of illicit masturbatory deeds and a weapon of aggression in its own right; it was also Jean's symbolic penis, which the psychic man within her longed so much to possess. In addition, Jean underwent, in psychological terms, a reversion along the developmental sequence that leads from bodily discharge of excitation to increasing capacity for mental discharge. Because of this regression, the hand became the physical agent for the expression of the symptom, for the somatic dramatization of unconscious mental conflict (cf. Glover, 1948). From the side of the id, the posture of the hand, the position of the thumb and its protrusion, the martial readiness of the fist were a collective indication of the instinctual contributants to the symptom. But in the very same symptom the ego's defenses also found representation: the first, the penis, the vehicle of assault was paralyzed and useless, effectively preventing any current expression of past and illicit wishes. The symptom thereby transmogrified the parties to the conflict. This selfsame symptom also served the interests of self-punishment, partially gratifying masochistic tendencies.

The contemporary precipitants of Jean's state of mind prior to the paralysis have been described; brief scrutiny of the hysterical symptom itself has pointed to some of its infantile forerunners. Key questions remain. What was the nature of the psychic events that intervened between the precipitants and the onset of the paralysis? And what fostered the regressive shift involved in symptom formation?

During the prodromal phase of the illness, Jean had tried, unconsciously, to contain her continuing conflict in contemporary terms. In effect, she made a last-ditch attempt to stem the rising tide of instinct. All that she was aware of consciously was anxiety, which she attributed to two recent, painful events in her life; and she tried to continue much as before: to be a good teacher, to mark the children's essays to the best of her ability, to contain her irritability and aggressive inclinations, and to avoid manifest sexuality.

In the end, these efforts were unavailing. Unconsciously her fantasy life was overinvested, and this paved the way for the retreat of the drives. Instinctual forces no longer pressed for gratification in the world of real objects, where outlets were blocked; instead, they were deflected to modes of satisfaction once sought out in childhood but subsequently bypassed or left behind. Jean's fixation points were primarily in the phallic-oedipal phase—it is characteristic of conversion hysteria that preoedipal fixation points, particularly those of an oral character, exert a powerful effect. During Jean's treatment, fantasies of biting off and incorporating parts of the object's body were reconstructed, and much material originally expressed in the phallic mode reappeared in terms of oral ambivalence. Jean unconsciously equated the penis and the breast. Contributions from the earlier phase lent to the later one its unusually ambivalent and sadistic quality, and in the emergence of subsequent fantasy made Jean at one and the same time the attacker and the victim, the active and passive child-participant in a mutually destructive adult sexual act.

In Jean, the processes of symptom formation were crystallized around the hand. We have noted some of the reasons the hand was particularly significant for her and so eminently suited to symbolize and unify the various elements of her internalized conflicts in a single representation. The hand, like a dream element, was selected for its qualities of representability; it condensed disparate, warring contributants into a single part of the body. Of all the symptom neuroses, conversion hysteria alone gives mental conflict a direct physical expression. Ostensibly, the mind relinquishes its interest and ceases to be the focus of its own distress. The uneasy terms on which the battle is settled are apparently concluded on a bodily and not a mental field; although, despite the *belle indifférence*, there may be consequential grounds for the patient's mental concern. To the patient, however, this is a secondary, not a primary, matter.

Representability is an important determinant for the choice of body area; but the readiness with which a particular part of the body lends itself to symptom formation is decided beforehand by two interrelated processes: the first, is excessive drive investment; and second, the somatic residue of object relations that the body part contains. In the analysis of an adult it can sometimes be difficult to reconstruct with precision the preparatory developmental steps that led to somatic compliance in the face of mental conflict. But there is no doubt that the excessive instinctualization of Jean's hand lent itself to her manual deformity. Nor is it difficult to see how past and current object relations took part in the formation of this symptom. In treatment, the clinical material suggested that in relation to her primary objects, the deformity symbolized the mother's "grasping" attitude. Later, Jean came to see the delinquent propensity of this side of her mother's character (i.e., her forgery of checks). The symptom also made concrete a fantasy of tearing off and retaining the father's penis.

If Jean had been treated in childhood the analyst could have discerned the contemporaneous significance of the hand in her early relationships. It is precisely in this respect that the psychoanalytic observation and treatment of children can teach us so much about developmental processes—for in children these processes can be directly observed rather than merely and crudely reconstructed.

Our discussion of this case has emphasized the instinctual manifestations of childhood. To what extent are childhood neuroses similar to those of adulthood, and in what respects do they differ? There are striking similarities in terms of precipitation, regression, and compromise. But it is important to recognize the different circumstances in which childhood neurosis occurs. First, the structures involved— the various parts of the child's personality and their interactions—are incompletely formed or consolidated; a ready backward movement by any one of them underlines the frailty and vulnerability of the parties in dispute. The external world has an even greater impact on

children than on adults. External influences not only play a more
conspicuous and observable part in the initiation of childhood illness
but in some cases they help to maintain it (in others, however, they
reduce it). In its formation the childhood neurosis superficially re-
sembles that of the adult but otherwise it is far less structured and
integrated. As in the adult, regression may be inexorably at work, but
developmental progress is on the side of the child.

In very young children, the processes that lead to symptoms take
quite elementary forms. A fleeting hysterical identification was observed in a boy of two and a half who was watching a television film
about the assassination of President Kennedy. He suddenly complained of pain in the head and promptly fell into a deep sleep.
Carried to bed without awakening, he slept through the night. The
following morning he was entirely well and had no recollection of the
incident.

In its simplicity, the symptom closely reproduced the event that
precipitated it: there is no distortion through symbolization, only a
displacement from father to president. The fantasied injury to the
father is transferred to the child himself, thus protecting the father
against a death wish.

Childhood Fears and Anxiety Hysteria in the Adult

Conversion hysteria is singularly effective at dealing with mental
conflict in such a way that psychic functioning is preserved relatively
intact. Conscious anxiety is generally minimized and appears only
as secondary concern about a bodily symptom.

This is not the case in the anxiety hysterias, which involve recurrent and acute anxiety. But since the source of distress is located in
the outside world, the true internal cause of the anxiety is avoided.
This presents a paradox. Unconscious attempts to reduce the pervasive anxiety of a danger situation (see chapter 1) ultimately lead back
to situations in which panic seems unavoidable. The subject withdraws from this intolerable internal anxiety only to live in constant
fear of encountering it from without. An uneasy peace can only be
bought, to a degree that varies from case to case, at the cost of restricted activity.

As in conversion hysteria, precipitating factors are followed by
regression, and the instinctual life of early childhood threatens to
break through. A compromise results: an internal danger is trans-

formed through symbolization, condensation, externalization, and displacement into an external threat.

Most children lack the capacity to develop well-structured neurotic or psychotic symptoms. The young child is closer than the adult to his family (i.e., primary objects) and to his internalized conflicts; disguise of unconscious mental content, though often significant and sometimes powerful, is less elaborate; the repression barrier is less stable; and the inexorable progression of development makes it more difficult to maintain symptoms in a structured form—a difficulty reinforced by the child's less well developed integrative ego capacities. For these and other reasons, true phobic neuroses do not occur in children.[2]

However, defensive displacements and symbolizations are ubiquitous in young children. For example, a fear of anal loss may be exacerbated when a child hears the toilet flushed at night. The child might associate the sound with the disappearance of his body products or even with potential bodily annihilation. Consciously the child may only be afraid of the noise, but the noise represents the way the body is disposed of.

Many childhood fears can be assuaged by simple reassurance. A child of four or five, for example, may get a splinter in his finger, show considerable alarm, and tearfully behave as if his finger were about to fall off. An empathetic parent will quickly lay these fears to rest.

Let us take a rather more complicated childhood fear. A group of children in nursery school were horrified to find a dead bird in the garden. The teacher, in an attempt to deal with their distress, conducted a funeral and burial for the bird. For all but one of the children these measures were successful and any fears aroused were allayed. But one little boy remained fearful even though the bird had been taken away. He became afraid of the garden and subsequently avoided it altogether.

The contrast with the other children is striking. This child's fear borders on a phobia that already seems to have developed a degree of autonomy. A quantitative factor is clearly important. The degree of fear initially experienced by the boy must have greatly exceeded

---

2. The case of Little Hans (Freud, 1909) appears to be an exception to this assertion. It seems possible that in this celebrated case the fact that the child was treated through the father had a bearing on the reconstructions.

that of his playmates, approaching the anxiety level aroused by a basic danger situation. Two measures were employed to reduce anxiety, displacing his fear from the bird to the garden and attempting to bind the fear to the displacement. The new representative of the feared situation acquired a certain autonomy, and, characteristic of a phobia proper, the fear could be dealt with only by avoiding the frightening object.

In such childhood "phobias," the symptom constitutes only a relatively small and perhaps transient part of the clinical picture.[3] By and large, "neurotic" disorders in children are accompanied by learning disorders, behavior disturbances, impairment of bodily functions, general fearfulness and timidity, dissocial behavior and withdrawal, depressive affect, sexual anxieties, and the like. Symptom neuroses in childhood assume a diminished perspective when compared with the major place occupied by the symptom in the adult's mental economy. Some clinical illustrations of symptom neurosis in adults follow.

John

A skilled car mechanic of twenty-four who worked in a large garage sought help with anxiety and a number of phobias. The symptoms had been present for eighteen months, beginning with certain organizational changes at his place of employment. John's boss, the service manager, now occupied an office overlooking the area where John worked. John had always regarded the manager as rather severe and had begun to anticipate criticism and reprimands if he was seen to be unoccupied during brief natural pauses. He was particularly fearful that his chief would be angry if he was seen talking to the female typists around the tea trolley. Whenever John needed spare parts, he had to walk through an office where female clerks prepared invoices; he was puzzled to find himself self-conscious there, believing that people were scrutinizing his walk. His gait became stilted and gauche; he felt increasingly awkward in his movements and became afraid of falling. He shook, felt dizzy, and broke into a sweat. In time, his anxiety spread to include fear of crowded shops, fear of walking

---

3. A number of so-called phobias in both children and adults are not really phobias at all. "School phobias," for example, are often based not on a fear of school but on a fear of losing the mother. In adults, certain obsessional features are similarly misnamed.

into the local pub, and, to a lesser extent, fear of traveling. During his interview with the therapist, he said he recognized that his anxieties were quite disproportionate to any real threat.

Although John's self-esteem had always been precarious, he had made a reasonable adjustment, had a number of male friends, and enjoyed spending evenings with them. He had never been really confident in the company of women, however, and his sexual experiences had been few and superficial. In this respect he felt inadequate. In contrast, he was reasonably successful at his work and was considered a good mechanic. As a child, John had experienced his father as distant and somewhat forbidding. His relationship with his mother had been more gratifying, though he felt there had been distance between them.

When John's oedipal conflicts reappeared in adolescence, he failed to enter the genital phase with any degree of security. This was reflected in his inability to enter into a genital sexual relationship with a woman. Although intercourse was sometimes successful, his friendships with women lacked stability, concern, and real consideration. He had failed to overcome the common adolescent problem of uniting in one relationship both affective and sexual satisfaction.

John suffered from generalized phobias of public places and anticipatory anxiety. The way these unfolded suggested the underlying pathology. His inability to negotiate the oedipal phase successfully and to enter the genital phase left him uncomfortable in the company of women and vulnerable to neurosis. Under the new office arrangements he was for the first time working with both sexes and under the eye of his boss. This situation stirred up his oedipal conflicts, which fostered a regressive shift to the negative oedipal position. His failure to master his rivalry with fantasied condensation of father and boss exacerbated his castration anxiety and led to a castration wish. His wish for his father's love revealed itself in an unacceptable (to him) feminine exhibitionism. He externalized his own disapproval of this exhibitionism onto his boss and, by extension, onto people in public places. The negative (passive) oedipal position was also symbolized in his fear of (and wish for) the loss of erect posture (fear of falling).

Symptom formation in anxiety hysteria does not differ sequentially from that of conversion hysteria. The same pathways are followed: from precipitant to regression, from regression to exacerbation of oedipal anxieties, from oedipal anxieties to reinforcement of drive pressures at a fixation point (in John's case, the phallic stage), from drive reinforcement to an imbalance between the id and the ego, from this imbalance to the threatened return of the repressed, and thence to the resolution of this threat in a compromise formation. The similarity of the fixation points links the two types of hysteria, which are orophallic (although in John's case the oral elements were to begin with conspicuous only in a fear of drinking in public).

Diana

A married women of thirty, Diana was articulate, intelligent, and attractive. She complained of anxiety when faced with social occasions, particularly if they involved eating.

Diana described her mother as a beautiful and imaginative woman who told extravagant tales of having married beneath her. Diana's father was said to be a drunken, vulgar, neglectful ne'er-do-well, unpredictable in temper, chronically in debt, and totally indifferent to the welfare of his family.

When she was twelve Diana became sexually involved with a neighbor, for whom she danced in the nude while he exhibited his penis. This secret affair lasted for some two years, but at fourteen Diana became frightened of her sexuality, partly on account of conscious fantasies that she had damaged her genitals by the masturbatory excitement these activities aroused. She was overwhelmed by feelings of shame and inferiority, her life became dominated by them, and she increasingly withdrew from other people. But with late physical maturation at eighteen, she once more became outgoing and started to live a colorful and sexually promiscuous life in which she repeatedly found herself in situations of excitement and danger.

Diana distinguished two types of heterosexual objects: men whom she regarded as despicable but with whom she experienced great sexual excitement, and men she respected but to whom she remained sexually indifferent. While abroad in the armed services, she met and married a senior officer and gave up her promiscuity. But as with all men she respected, she was unable to achieve sexual gratification with him.

Before her marriage Diana attended a party at which she was introduced to her fiancé's Commanding Officer. There was a tradition in the Service that the future wife of a subordinate had to be "approved." When she was presented, Diana suddenly felt panicky, was afraid of falling down, and began to shake. These symptoms began to recur in similar social conditions, and she had to force herself to attend parties involving officers and their wives. When, some time later, her husband became involved with another woman, all Diana's feelings of shame and inferiority returned. Her symptoms were exacerbated, and she could deal with them only by taking alcohol and/or tranquilizers in secret. She daydreamed of men who would provide her with a uniquely satisfying sexual experience that would once and for all dispel her feelings of genital inferiority and prove conclusively that her frigidity was her husband's fault.

Diana had hitherto dealt with her oedipal anxieties in two ways. Following the sexual affair with her neighbor, any affective interest in boys was inhibited; but when at eighteen, her heterosexual interests were rearoused, she developed a second set of coping mechanisms. She had brief, casual relationships with a series of men. In these encounters she regarded herself as seduced, if not raped; and so she disowned any responsibility for them. In her marriage to a man she consciously admired and loved, these coping mechanisms were useless and were replaced by a loss of sexual pleasure. Her wish to please her husband was expressed in simulated orgasm, which served also to hide her shame at her inability to reach a climax.

It might be expected in a case of this kind that the patient's conflicts would be contained within the frigidity—contained, that is, within a sexual inhibition, in which case a structured compromise formation might have been avoided. This proved impossible for Diana. Indeed, elements of compromise are to be seen even in her coping mechanisms. In her association with men she despised, her enjoyment was counterbalanced by a reaction formation of repugnance. This repugnance, however, retained a link with the consciously despised father, while any guilt so aroused was dealt with by denial of responsibility.

In Diana's case matters could not stand still. Her introduction to her husband's Commanding Officer marked the onset of her neurosis. It represented a public acknowledgment of her engagement, with its clear sexual implications. The engagement was no longer for her a declaration of adult love: its oedipal coloring was too strong for that. Diana had already withdrawn from current reality, and the declaration of her engagement became a confession, in front of the assembled adults, of incestuous intentions. Unconsciously she felt she had aroused the bitter antagonism and envy of the officers' wives. Regression consequent on withdrawal from adult object relations ensured that these women were experienced as the avenging mother. Other conflicts were simultaneously rearoused or exacerbated. The conflict over her exhibitionism in public situations; the projection of her envy of the phallic woman; the fear of falling down (fear of loss of erect posture); primitive retaliatory fears; fears of orality (connected with fears of parties involving eating)—all these could be discerned from the anamnesis and presenting picture without the fuller knowledge of Diana's childhood development that was revealed during treatment. Following is a condensed account of that development.

INFANTILE NEUROSIS AND ADULT NEUROSIS. From Diana's analysis the following details of her infantile neurosis could be broadly reconstructed. She was her father's favorite child and enjoyed an exciting relationship with him. They played rough-and-tumble games together: she loved to be tossed in the air and caught in her father's strong and safe grip. She always wanted her mother and older brother to watch these acrobatic displays. Her father enjoyed feeding her and indulging her oral longings. But as the oedipal phase intensified, Diana's delight in her father as a playmate became fraught with danger. The mobilization of sexual wishes for her father brought, first, a fear of being overwhelmed; second, an access of guilt; and third, a fear of punishment from the maternal rival. This fear was intensified by the externalization of her own wish to displace and eliminate her mother; unconsciously, she believed that her mother's destructive wishes toward her matched her own destructive inclinations. Perhaps because of her father's undue emphasis on feeding her, earlier oral conflicts were exacerbated; a delight in food was followed by a lack of pleasure in eating amounting to anorexia; a more general fear of pleasure ensued, and she became so averse to attending children's parties that her mother soon abandoned all attempts to persuade her to do so. For a time she was plagued with a fear that other little girls would bite her and she avoided their company; but this fear was rapidly overcome in latency. Diana turned against her father, much to his evident disappointment and dismay: her attachment to her mother became intensified and she repeatedly sought out her company, but this relationship was characterized by frequent quarrels. Her mother was not successful in her attempts to persuade Diana to eat more. The child became tomboyish and repeatedly sought to emulate her brother's physical achievements. This was the source of her abiding but secret wish to be able to urinate while standing.

Once established in latency, Diana regained her social interests and once more became gregarious. The main residua from her earlier difficulties were conscious shame about her ne'er-do-well father and persistent, high-spirited, and competitive assertiveness with her peers, which, nevertheless, cost her nothing in popularity. However, the intense and pervasive curiosity that had characterized much of her childhood was followed in latency by a need to plead ignorance of the most everyday matters. Although Diana never developed a learning inhibition as such, she tended to hide her growing store of knowledge, enjoying it secretly but never displaying it to full advantage in school examinations.

It may appear that the infantile neurosis just reconstructed parallels surprisingly closely the anxiety hysteria Diana displayed as an adult. Reconstruction points to the contribution of acrobatic displays with the father to Diana's exhibitionism and to her excitement in falling and being caught, before these pleasurable activities became conflictual.[4] It also points to the considerable oral elements that entered into her relationships with her father, to the fears of parties and the fear of being bitten, to her childhood anorexia, and to the contribution made to her penis envy and phallic identification by her failure to emulate her brother's athletic attainments.

It is important to remember, however, that this account is based on analytic reconstruction and not on direct observation of childhood, let alone on a child analysis. It is characteristic of the analytic treatment of adult neurotics that what reappears from childhood is distorted by subsequent development and experience. Periods of prolonged struggle, for example, may reappear in memory as isolated traumata or single dramatic events; conflicts are condensed and frequently oversimplified; and all those areas in which the child's development proceeded smoothly and unhindered do not, by their very lack of disturbance, reappear within the context of a transference neurosis built around the person of the analyst. The picture of childhood disturbance remains inevitably one-sided, unmitigated by the many elements of progress that must, to some extent, have helped to redress the balance at the time when the child's difficulties made their first appearance. For these reasons among others, we are not justified in supposing that an adult neurosis simply reproduces at a

4. See, in this connection, Dorothy Burlingham's paper on the role of the preoedipal father (1973).

more structured and sophisticated level an infantile neurosis of closely analogous character.

We have followed in detail the formation of an adult anxiety hysteria and have tried to indicate some of its similarities with and differences from the fears and phobias of children. Not all phobias are symptoms of anxiety hysteria: phobic elements may appear as part of the clinical picture in depressions, psychoses, obsessional disorders, and even organic psychoses. This emphasizes the enormous gap between surface presentation and underlying pathology.

The Obsessional Neuroses

The study of obsessional neuroses and obsessional phenomena is one of the most fascinating if baffling pursuits in psychology and psychiatry. In classifying obsessional phenomena in terms of their presenting clinical picture, we cannot improve on the following account by Glover (1948):

> The name given to this group of neuroses indicates the leading feature of the symptoms. When, for example, a man of blameless antecedents constantly imagines himself stabbing his wife with a breadknife and is not only unable to free himself from the thought but suffers pangs of guilt on account of it, it is no exaggeration to say that he is *obsessed* in his intellectual field of activity. We may therefore describe this constant preoccupation with a stereotyped thought as an *obsessional thought.* Similarly when a person finds himself compelled to wash his hands literally for hours on end, producing on occasion a soap eczema thereby, or when a housewife is compelled to wash all her carpets every day with carbolic soap, we can characterize this compulsive repetition of a stereotyped form of behavior as an *obsessive or compulsive action.* When a patient complains that he spends hours of valuable time making up his mind whether to wear black or brown socks, thereby risking discharge from his employment for unpunctuality, the condition is well described as *obsessional doubt.* When we find his mind occupied by metaphysical speculations about the "rightness" of some apparently trivial detail of everyday life, e.g., the significance of a certain arrangement of mantelpiece ornaments, we are entitled to speak of *obsessional rumination.* And when his dressing habits involve an elaborate series of dusting observances, dusting the wardrobe, the coat hanger, shaking each article of clothing, putting it on, taking it off, putting it on again, and once fully dressed, proceeding to brush the floor and every part of the bedroom with which his clothes have come or might have come in contact, turning the door handle with a duster in his hand and finally jumping out

of the bedroom door before the real or imaginary dust can settle on him we are justified in describing this series of events as an *obsessional ritual*. (p. 158)

Unfortunately, the word *obsessional* is often used in a variety of ways and applied to very different conditions. It may refer, as in the foregoing descriptions, to the clinical manifestations of obsessional neurosis; or it may point to modes of defense organization. It may misleadingly refer to a wide variety of repetitive acts that have little in common with true obsessions. Some such acts are well within the range of normal behavior and may be illustrated by childhood love of repetition and by the so-called *preconscious automatisms* (Hartmann, 1939) exemplified in adherence to a particular order of dressing or shaving—unlike obsessional phenomena, these habits can be easily changed, without anxiety, merely by forming the conscious intent to do so. These automatisms have an adaptive value in that they free attention for other, less routine affairs.

Pathological conditions to which the word *obsessional* is sometimes wrongly applied include the form of repetition-compulsion (Freud, 1920) that may lead to an impressive pattern of remarkably similar and equally disastrous relationships. It is also mistakenly applied to recidivism, drug addictions, tics, the repetitive actions of mental defectives, and the persistent acts characteristics of organic psychiatric states and some forms of schizophrenia. Some repetitions, though symptomatic, may be adaptive rather than pathological: these may include the blindisms of unsighted children.[5] Although some of these conditions are easy to distinguish from each other, a psychological understanding of true obsessional neurosis is of considerable help in diagnostic assessment.

What characterizes neurotic obsessional symptoms of the kind summarized by Glover? Descriptively, they involve repetitive thoughts or actions that are felt to be as unpleasant as they are unwanted. But they cannot be abolished by an effort of will and can be delayed, if at all, only at the cost of considerable anxiety. Put in psychoanalytic terms, mental content deriving from the id repeatedly appears in consciousness, either directly or in disguise or symbols, issuing in thoughts or actions that not only are unacceptable to the

---

5. Blindisms are repetitive actions such as rocking, eye-rubbing, turning in circles, and so on. The child readily abandons these activities in favor of other interests when someone provides them.

ego but give rise to tensions between ego and superego reflected in the overriding part played in these disorders by guilt.

The obsessional neuroses share with conversion and anxiety hysterias the common feature of neurotic compromise formation, but the two kinds of disorders differ in one important respect. In conversion hysteria the compromise achieves dramatic representation in somatic form, and the compromise in anxiety hysteria, in which the fear is lodged in the outside world, is wholly psychological in its presentation. But *the compromise that results in an obsessional neurosis is located and resides within the thought processes themselves.*

This statement calls for clarification. Let us take a patient plagued by the repeated thought of plunging a knife into her baby. We are at once struck by an apparent paradox: why should this mother, who cares for and is concerned about her baby, have such an undisguised murderous wish? Why does this blatant, repeated breakthrough of a murderous drive occur in this terrifying form? But the paradox is illusory. The baby is in no danger. For the drive itself achieves no direct expression: it is only the *thought* of the drive that presents itself to consciousness. What horrifies the mother is the *thought* that she could even *think* of such a thing. The thought is, at one and the same time, thought and disowned; and therein lies not a paradox but a compromise. Both sides of the conflict coexist in the sphere of thought.

It is true, however, that the *thought* of the drive must stem from the drive itself. The drive remains repressed, but the repression is weak and incomplete, thus the id intrudes on the process of thinking itself. The thought processes that the patient seeks to repudiate are themselves partly instinctualized. But the repudiation is assisted by another circumstance: the affect that would normally be associated with the thought is divorced or isolated from it. Anxiety alone is experienced—anxiety aroused by the nature of the intrusive and unwelcome thought.

In conversion hysteria certain factors predispose both to physicality and to psychic dramatization of conflict (see above, "Conversion Hysteria"). The obsessional individual overvalues the mind rather than the body. But why, in this neurosis, do the compromise formations come to reside in the thought processes?

This question cannot be answered fully, but certain factors appear important. One is a particular developmental disharmony (see chapter 2), arising early in life when the development of the ego and the superego is premature. This disharmony prohibits or interferes with the pleasure of the anal phase at a time when such pleasure is expected to be at its height. It seems likely that maturational factors contribute substantially both to precocious ego development and to instinctual delay where either or both occur. This developmental disparity is carried forward and, under the influence of the ego's synthetic function, imposes a characteristic stamp on the unfolding personality. Other contributants include such environmental influences as obsessional traits, behavior, or frank obsessional neuroses in the parents, especially the primary caretaker.

The mother's attitude toward toilet training may influence the child's rejection of anality. It is unclear whether heredity plays a part, but parental aims, standards, and influences are significant and may form a basis for important identifications. In the case of George (see below) we try to indicate how such influences may come together and serve to promote and maintain developmental disharmony.

Some maintain that the early mother-infant relationship prepares the ground for disharmony in the anal phase. In a 1966 review of the subject, Anna Freud referred to disturbances in the mother-child relationship that adversely affect development. She pointed out, however, that only a few factors in such a disturbance could be regarded as truly specific, citing "damage done to the synthetic function, to the capacity for the fusion of love and hate [and] to the ability to maintain object-love as contrasted with self-love." She continues, "Losing a love object in early life (through rejection, withdrawal, neglect, separation, death) is an experience which can initiate a variety of disturbances. What is significant for the obsessional neurosis is not the event as such but the child's belief that it is the result of his own death wishes and the feelings of guilt attached to this interpretation. . . . We should take into account also that an excellent early relationship to the mother may promote rapid early growth and instead of safeguarding the individual this may be instrumental in creating the very precocity of superego functions which we have met as one of the preconditions of obsessional neurosis" (p. 119).

These early influences enhance the value placed on ego achievement at the expense of bodily pleasure. This imbalance is further encouraged, in most cases, by high ego endowment including, especially, high intelligence. This premature ego development increases the child's receptiveness to other influences through his own intolerance of anal-phase drives. The child misses out on some of the pleasures of this phase, which leaves what may be a permanent gap in his instinctual life.

The nature and quality of the child's superego precursors and the contribution they make to the sadistic character of the superego itself are of central importance. Glover (1948) has emphasized that if melancholia is the "guilt psychosis" par excellence, obsessional neurosis is above all a "guilt neurosis." The superego precursors lay the ground for a preternaturally strong autonomous structure. The influence and strength of these precursors reinforce external influences in prompting the ego's repudiation of anal impulses and drive wishes, whereby they contribute to developmental disharmony. At this stage the foundations are laid for the later self-torture of the obsessional-neurotic person in which the superego draws on anal-sadistic energies in its repeated attacks on the self. Gratification of this bullying superego strengthens the masochistic elements in these disorders.

There are further consequences for the child of the early intrusion of superego precursors. The intolerance of the anal-sadistic phase leads to the premature emergence of such defenses against anal sadism as reaction formation. The child is also pressured to move into later instinctual phases for which he or she is inadequately prepared. In this way, faulty development is carried forward into the phallic and oedipal phases, with all the fateful implications of these premature moves for the emergence of infantile and adult neurosis.

Rapaport (1950) has provided us with the necessary background for the construction of a developmental line of thinking that leads from hallucinatory wish fulfillment through the drive organization of memories, primitive ideation, and conceptual organization of memories, until the capacity for abstract thought is attained. This sequence is in urgent need of further study and clarification, but it seems highly likely that in the obsessional-neurotic individual the development of this line is deviant. Premature ego development, with its early verbal flowering, results in a permanently faulty relationship between "thing-" and "word-presentations." If thought is indeed "trial action" (Freud, 1933), then trial action may, for the obsessional person, be extended at the cost of action itself—as witnessed by obsessional ruminations and thoughts. Or the faulty connection may manifest itself in a tendency for thinking to be short-circuited in enactment, in which case thought has failed in its delaying function and the action is, from an adaptive viewpoint, quite inappropriate.

This failure is a precondition for compulsive actions as opposed to compulsive thoughts. Equally important for the genesis of these disorders is the role of omnipotent wishes, magical thinking, and ritualistic tendencies in childhood. We take first the omnipotence of wishes. Thought and action may be indistinguishable. As Anna Freud noted, we repeatedly encounter clinically the unconscious belief that death wishes kill. In the obsessional individual this is encouraged by the failure of the synthetic function to deal with the force of ambivalence; the ego further compounds this failure through its defective discrimination between word and thing. Either thought replaces action altogether or thought and action become indistinguishable. Vera's is a case in point.

Vera

Vera, a married woman of thirty-five and the mother of two children, presented with an obsessive-compulsive neurosis that had existed, with remissions, for over ten years. Shortly after her first child was born, Vera explained, she had abandoned breastfeeding. Her milk was inadequate, but she felt guilty about changing the baby to a bottle. She would wake in the night afraid that she had not cleaned the bottle properly, and she felt compelled to get up at once to resterilize it.

Three years later, when her second baby was six months old, she thought she noticed something wrong with her husband's testicles. Despite medical reassurance, she could not rid herself of the fear that he had contracted testicular cancer through her vaginal uncleanliness. Vera recalled an incident early in their marriage when, during intercourse, her secretion was inadequate, and she tried to rectify this by micturating a little on her husband's penis. She now started to wash herself excessively, taking innumerable showers and washing her perineum after every micturition or defecation. Characteristically, the fears spread, and she began to take measures to prevent her children from picking up things that might be dirty. She felt obliged to make sure that freshly laundered clothing was in no way recontaminated—if necessary she washed it all over again. On one occasion her husband's penis touched and wet her when they were in bed; she had not only to wash herself but to strip the bed completely. Her husband was so upset by this that he had a nightmare and wet the bed!

Further intensification of Vera's symptoms followed two significant events. First, the death of a distant relative reminded her of her grandmother's death in the hospital some years before; she had feared that she had caused the death by infecting her grandmother during a visit. Second, her brother-in-law left her sister for another woman, and Vera started to question her own right to be happily married. A little later she went to a party and felt jealous of the attentions a male friend paid to other women. She had previously wanted a third child but now feared pregnancy in case this friend had impregnated her—in spite of the knowledge that no physical contact had occurred between them. She could not rid herself of an idea that she knew to be irrational—namely, that she could have suffered a lapse of consciousness during which intercourse had taken place.

The intensification of the compulsive symptoms led to soreness and bleeding of her hands and perineum. The toilet was blocked with masses of used paper. The family's underwear had to be washed *before* it was considered clean enough to go in the washing machine. This behavior drove the family to distraction, and Vera's husband, for whom she had shown so much concern, began to think about leaving her.

Under certain circumstances thought and action may seem almost indistinguishable to the obsessional patient. It was enough for Vera to experience jealousy when her male friend talked to other women in order to feel the irrational conviction that she had had intercourse with him and was pregnant as a result. The thought and the action were treated as identical. She repudiated the omnipotent wish in action, putting herself on the pill and repeatedly counting the tablets in order to be sure she had taken her daily dose.

There is little doubt that precocious ego development carries with it from infancy a tendency to make inappropriate connections between cause and effect. The childlike simplicity of Vera's thinking, which contrasts so vividly with the intellectual sophistication of some obsessional patients, includes a number of magical inclinations. Somewhere within them, "His Majesty the Baby" (Freud, 1914) is permanently enthroned. Infantile omnipotence supports the notion that death wishes are murderous acts. Surely, then, thinking can also prevent such frightening occurrences. During a phase when anality and secondary-process functioning are proceeding apace, thoughts are invested with the same magical quality with which wishes were endowed in earlier infancy.

A patient may behave as if he can prevent his brother's death by counting up to nine. If the faulty connections already adduced for earlier phases of development are now applied, we can understand how a shift from word to deed underlines and underpins the ritualistic measures the obsessional person takes in order to keep disaster at bay. And whenever the connection between the ritualistic practice and the changes it seeks to avoid can be traced in analysis, the link operates not via the secondary process and logic, as might be thought on account of a precocious ego, but via a primitive symbolization akin to magic.

Thought Disturbance in Obsessional Neurosis

Although in the obsessional neurosis the ego binds the anal-sadistic and aggressive drive derivatives in a form of secondary-process thinking, this binding is not accompanied by a comparable degree of *neutralization*. This failure of neutralization results in an instinctualization of the thought processes themselves. Paradoxically, this means that the ego's activities simultaneously contribute libido and aggression and attempt to defend against them.

The degree to which thought processes can be eroticized is quite remarkable; in some of these patients thinking takes on the quality of mental masturbation—analized, to be sure. Words can also be used as aggressive objects, sometimes with remarkably literal concreteness. Unconsciously they are regarded as weapons or lumps of feces disposed of at the expense of the object, although they may also be experienced as phallic and penetrating. Here again we see word-presentations treated, in some degree, as if they were thing-presentations.

In certain instances obsessional thoughts may lose their connection with the secondary process. Freud's patient the Wolf Man passed through a distressing phase when the word *God* was immediately followed in consciousness by the word *shit* (Freud, 1918). This ruminative phenomenon illustrates the defense of undoing and a great deal more. The thought, elaborated via the secondary process, might be expressed, "The father whom I worship is like shit." But the conjunctions and parts of speech permitting this formulation are absent; secondary-process thinking is denied to the ideation so that there is both a formal and topographical regression to the simple antithetical combination *God-shit*. Perhaps the failure of the synthetic function of the ego contributes to this process. The words themselves carry the aggressive and sexual cathexes of the anal phase. The choice of words rests on their suitability to serve as drive representations; like the elements selected for dream imagery, the words that become the foci of this type of obsessional rumination are determined by considerations of representability. In this example the words carry all the condensations, displacements, and contradictions we associate with the primary process; but the primitive character of the ideation (as opposed to secondary-process "thought") means that the contradiction cannot be properly clarified. The intrusive words retain an undue drive coloring. The localized disturbance in thinking suggests a regressive shift to a point in development when ideation is still organized by the drives and has not yet yielded to a form of thinking involving conceptual, temporal, and spatial frames of reference.

It is of interest to recall the extent to which words and things remained closely interchangeable for the Wolf Man. For example, the sight of horse dung was sufficient to compel him to think of the Holy Trinity. The sacred and the profane, love and hate come together in this uneasy association—a routine matter for the id, perhaps, but hardly an acceptable state of affairs for the ego.

The conjunction of two antithetical thoughts is characteristic of this form of intrusive rumination. Reexamining Vera's case, however, it is clear that the conscious thoughts she magically equates with actions are not in themselves contradictory. When Vera thinks that the baby's bottle is contaminated or that her children's clothes are dirtied with feces, her thought is not cancelled out by opposing ideas. She behaves as if she cannot distinguish between the idea of dirt and physical contamination itself; only *physical* action can undo the *imagined* wrong. Only strenuous and persistent washing wipes away the guilt-ridden notion of filth. Vera's washing compulsion may remind the reader of Lady Macbeth's. But, after all, Vera has not murdered anyone. Nevertheless, she behaves as if she were in persistent danger of doing just that.

For any patient with symptoms of this kind one needs to ask, to what extent are defensive measures against dirt, the thought of dirt, or sadistic and aggressive strivings? In Vera's case all three may be equated. This is not the case with many obsessional ruminations: the patient is often only too well aware that it is the *thought* of dirt, of sadistic acts, or of murder that he fears. Freud suggested that thought is "delayed action" and in this respect fulfills an important adaptive function. Ruminations may delay action to the point of paralysis, as in obsessional doubt; in compulsions the contradicting thought brooks no delay and spills over into immediate physical expression.

Symptom Formation in Obsessional Neurosis

What distinguishes the formation of an obsessional neurosis from a conversion hysteria is the degree of instinctual regression and the defensive measures employed by the ego when threatened with the return of the repressed. Whereas in hysteria regression occurs to an orophallic organization, the obsessional neurosis is structured around the instinctual organization of the anal-sadistic phase.

The organization of defenses in obsessional neurosis is responsible for some of its most characteristic features. Some of these have already been considered. Other important defenses include intellectualization and rationalization. Reaction formation can also take place; but in spite of its prominence the anal drive derivatives have a habit of breaking through. A patient's dress and external appearance, for example, may be altogether immaculate while underpants remain dirty; and all the elaborate precautions and rituals taken against aggression may yet allow the aggressive intent to show itself unmistakably. Indeed, the self-torture of the obsessional person may be matched only by his or her torture of others. And while the fact that obsessional behavior is felt by the object as torture does not in itself confirm an intent to torture, there is no doubt that, in the classical form of obsessional neurosis, this intent may be safely inferred. Vera's case bears scrutiny from this viewpoint.

The characteristic defense of undoing ("God-shit"; obsessional doubt) is a biphasic maneuver that may seriously impede constructive thought and action. A male patient of Glover's, for example, repeatedly untied and reknotted his tie. Investigation indicated that he wished to free himself from his wife; the reknotting represented his conflicting wish to remain tied to her (Glover, 1948; p. 162).

Isolation of affect is conspicuous and characteristic of obsessional neurosis. Many years ago Fenichel (1946) pointed out that the obsessional individual was so afraid of his emotions that he feared the things that gave rise to them and fled from the macrocosm of things to the microcosm of words. Hence isolation of affect and the disorder of thinking have common roots. Denial is important. Repression functions unevenly and has a varying importance in different presentations. It is more effective in ruminations than in compulsions. Magical thinking is allied with symbolization in warding off forbidden impulses through ritualization of thinking and behavior.

Some of these features are illustrated by the case of George. This

detailed history typifies many of the features already discussed and
indicates the developmental forces involved, the way they lead to a
pathological outcome, and the processes by which the symptoms are
formed.

George

George, a lawyer, was thirty-five years of age when he sought treatment for severe obsessive-compulsive symptoms. He had married ten
years before and had two daughters aged five and three. Some details
of the history were reconstructed during analysis.

George was brought up in a rather well-to-do farming family with
servants and nannies. He thought of his parents as rather remote. His
brother, two years younger, lost two fingers in some agricultural ma-
chinery when George was four and a half. Shortly afterward George
became afraid of mechanical toys, especially those powered by clock-
work motors. He insisted that his nanny remove such toys from his
cupboard. In time he stopped playing with any toy that could have
been powered, even if it had no motor, explaining that such toys were
"childish." He soon lost interest in toys and games of any kind and
confined his attention to books. He was an avid reader and did extremely well at school, university and law school.

During his adolescence George became somewhat ascetic and
had little to do with girls. He reported a "memory," which he was
unable to confirm, that as a child he had been involved in sex play
with a little girl who had lived with her family in one of the farm
laborers' cottages.

At college and later at law school, George's asceticism prevailed.
In his one or two relationships with women he was controlling and
guarded and eschewed commitment. His sexual performance was
sometimes adequate but he often avoided intercourse because he
feared impotence. His outstanding academic success was founded
not only on his high intelligence but also on a methodical—at times
overmethodical—approach to his studies. He was regarded by his
friends as something of a dry stick, and he socialized mostly with
other members of his intellectual societies.

When he passed the bar he joined a successful law firm and soon
met a young woman to whom he was greatly attracted. She too was
ordered and methodical in her daily life, though she was far less

inhibited than he. At first George was both attracted and frightened by her, but she knew her own mind and taking more or less subtle initiatives, succeeded in getting him to the altar. He had begun to find the relationship exciting, although it evoked some anxiety, and for a year or two the couple lived in reasonable harmony until the birth of their second child—a second girl. Although George had hoped for a boy, he managed to conceal his disappointment even from himself. Following the birth his wife's sexual appetite increased, while his waned. He avoided intercourse by one pretext or another, and his wife became increasingly frustrated, angry, and disillusioned. George went to bed later and later, only when his wife was fast asleep.

Finally, his wife unwillingly accepted his suggestion that they sleep in separate rooms. He was bewildered by her emotional reaction and by her threat to leave him rather than endure an enforced sexual continence: he was quite unable to understand why she should feel so strongly. His obsessional neurosis ensued soon afterwards.

One day George broke a mirror and rather frantically swept up the pieces, covering a wide area in order to be sure that he had left no shard of glass undetected. His first thoughts were that he must be particularly careful lest either his wife or one of the children (he had withdrawn from the second girl) were injured by stepping on glass. These anticipations were quickly replaced when, in searching the carpet, he began to fear that glass might get in his eyes and injure them.

These symptoms rapidly spread until he was fearful in all parts of the house; he needed to lay down newspaper to walk on at every step. His passage from room to room was marked by a trail of paper. Similarly, he could touch or turn a doorknob only if he were protected by paper. The difficulty in protecting himself while at work led to his inability to attend; and he became altogether crippled by his symptoms.

During the course of treatment certain predisposing factors were reconstructed. George had indeed shown early verbal ability and had been the subject of an intellectual and rather undemonstrative interest on the part of his parents. He was expected to be a good and orderly child and he complied promptly with the demands made upon him in bowel training. Although his parents were remote, they made their demands and expectations plain to the nannies who had the boy in their charge. George took tea daily with his mother in the drawing room, for a prescribed period. For this he was expected to be both clean and immaculately dressed.

The history suggests an intensification of George's castration complex that may have stemmed in part from fears aroused by his brother's mutilation. It was manifested in his infantile neurosis, which, as is often the case, took a predominantly phobic form (fear of mechanical toys). Something of the quality of the oedipal phase is revealed in the analysis of George's reaction to the arrival of his second child and the depression that followed it, which was based not only on jealousy of and rivalry toward the baby but on his narcissistic wound at not having produced a son. His inability to sustain a genital relationship led to regression from the oedipal to the anal-sadistic phase, the derivatives of which are epitomized in his fear of the damage he might inflict on his family via broken glass.

These fears also marked the threatened return of repressed anal-sadistic wishes, which were defended against in a structured symptom formation. So far the path leading to such a formation parallels that found, for example, in conversion hysteria; but certain differences are apparent. Somatic dramatization is absent; the disturbance begins in the sphere of thought, though it is soon translated into the actions of the compulsion. Furthermore, the derivatives of the impulse are only partially excluded from awareness, since the thoughts of harming first his family and then himself are only too clear to him. Rather than repressing these thoughts, the ego attributes an alien quality to them. Reaction formation is conspicuous: both impulse and defense remain in evidence in the compromise, a fear accompanied by compulsive action facilitated by faulty ego processes. The symptom itself is overdetermined; primal-scene anxieties, for example, are reflected in George's fear of damage to his eyes. Forbidden looking is punished by the repeated threat of the violent infliction of blindness. Here again, the suffering serves to reduce guilt.

Just as the word *obsession* is used in many ways that as often as not have only the most tenuous connection with each other, so the diagnosis of obsessional neurosis in children, particularly those in late latency or prepuberty, is often made on descriptive grounds alone and may be seriously misleading. Such a diagnosis should be made only with the greatest caution, for many disturbances that seem superficially similar to obsessional disorder are very different from true neurotic illness. Rather than attempt a lengthy addition to this chapter, we refer the reader to accounts of the Anna Freud Centre's experiences with such cases in Putzel and Schacht, 1975, and Yorke and Burgner, 1980.

CHAPTER 5 The Character Neuroses

Character and Character Types

Psychoanalysts have long been interested in the study of character and character types. The study of symptoms led, inevitably, to the wider issues of character, its mode of development, its vicissitudes, its deviations, and the extent to which it is acceptable to its possessor.

Early in the development of psychoanalysis, its practitioners were most deeply concerned with the nature and functioning of the Unconscious. It was inevitable that the role of fixation points in the organization of instinctual life would become a central issue in the study of character. Hence, *character types* were first distinguished on the basis of points of fixation. An important and early step in this regard was Freud's classic paper on "Character and Anal Eroticism" (1908). In this elegant account Freud demonstrated the links between the observable surface phenomena of avarice (or miserliness), pedantry, and obstinacy and some of the underlying derivatives of anal eroticism that help to bring such traits into being. Further contributions to the understanding of the "anal character" were made by Abraham in 1921; in 1924 he described a further constellation of character traits, linking them with derivatives of the oral phase of instinctual development. In 1925 Abraham described the "genital character"—a designation pursued by Reich in 1928 and later years. Reich viewed the genital character as mature or normative, contrasted on clinical grounds with the generic term the "neurotic character."

These writers were certainly not of the opinion that character or character "types" could be wholly or adequately described solely in terms of instinctual fixation points. Even in his early contribution, Freud (1908) drew attention to the role of defenses such as reaction formations and gave weight to the influence of sublimatory processes. In subsequent papers he emphasized the consequences for character formation of certain specific outcomes of castration and oedipal complexes, while his later structural theory allowed him to sketch out the part played by ego and superego identifications. Although he never attempted to formulate a psychoanalytic theory of character, all Freud's contributions have been influential in later psychoanalytic thinking. Baudry (1983) has provided us with a valuable survey of the evolution of the concept of character in Freud's writings and has traced and summarized chronologically those elements that Freud variously considered to be important in character formation.

The current status of the psychoanalytic concept of character is, to say the least, problematic. Two symposia convened by the American Psychoanalytic Association in 1990—one on the theory of character, reported by Abend (1983), and one on the clinical aspects of character, reported by Willick in the same year—indicate the complexities of the issues involved. Baudry (1984) has revised his contribution to the first of these symposia, examining post-Freudian contributions to the field in some detail, pointing to conceptual ambiguities in definition and to problems of classification, and discussing such important issues as character resistance and character analysis as well as character change during the psychoanalytic process. Finding the status of the term *character* uncertain and the literature confusing, Baudry attempts to clarify the clinical usage of such terms as *character trait* and *character disorder*.

The concept of character is so wide and the contributants to it so many and varied that the usefulness of the concept must be seriously questioned. Baudry himself does not altogether reject this point of view. It may seem odd to attempt to discuss character neuroses without discussing character. But despite the problems of definition and the conceptual difficulties involved in formulating it, the term *character neurosis* plays a useful part in the examination of significant clinical phenomena, whereas attempts to define *character* lead one into so many diverse normative and pathological phenomena that the forest cannot be seen for the trees. Perhaps it is to be expected that a matter involving contributants from any and all parts of the personality, must be examined from the point of view of virtually the whole of psychoanalytic psychology.

Although Baudry's discussion is very useful on character, it is not particularly helpful when it comes to character neurosis. Indeed, he refers to the latter simply as "another term related to character disorder" (p. 464), giving it a very brief treatment in which he follows the views of Waelder (1960). Perhaps a little dismissively, Baudry summarizes these views in his own way, claiming, "The term character neurosis is simply a dynamic way of referring to certain types of character disorder which have a particularly close relation to neurosis. A common example would be the integration of an obsessive neurosis into an obsessional character structure" (Baudry, 1984, p. 466). This is not a view to which we subscribe. It is our opinion that psychoanalytic thinking over the years has made it possible to delineate the character neuroses in a way that can more usefully illuminate clinical experience.

The Character Neuroses

Character neurosis is not simply a disorder of character; it is a *neurotic* disorder of character. Internalized conflict leads to compromise formations as in the symptom neurosis but, in contradistinction, these do not form enclaves within the personality retaining an apparently alien or foreign character. Microstructures rather than macrostructures, they tend to accumulate during the course of development, subject to the vicissitudes of maturation, external influence, and the accident of environmental forces.

The oedipal phase plays an important part in both forms of neurosis. But character neurosis differs in one important respect from symptom neurosis: the personality, as represented by its ego and superego agencies, tolerates some transgression stemming from preoedipal drives or the complementary component instincts and evidenced in wishes that are out of keeping with the changing demands of the outside world. This tolerance permits an outcome to conflict without regression and allows the resultant compromise a place within the personality, where it has a significant influence on subsequent development.

The development of character neurosis, then, involves an ongoing accumulation of preoedipal conflicting character traits synthesized in the course of, and assimilated during, the oedipal phase, subject to reworking and further modification in adolescence, and subsequently stabilized in the postadolescent period.

Andrew

Andrew was in his late thirties when he sought analysis. He said that his work was repeatedly and unnecessarily hampered by his difficulty in getting things down on paper, chronic indecision, and procrastination in dealing with messages and answering correspondence. He walked around for weeks with unopened letters in his pockets. He hoped that analysis would free him from some of his inner restrictions, allay his feelings of inadequacy and inferiority, and perhaps dispel the free-floating anxiety by which he was so often troubled.

But Andrew did not consciously seek treatment on his own account. His only child, a boy of nine, was not very happy at school and had difficulty in learning, and Andrew saw something of his own childhood difficulties in his son. Although he could identify with those difficulties, he felt that his own anxieties impaired his capacity to understand the boy. He gave this as the principal reason for seeking help for himself.

Andrew was an athletically built man of average height, with a rather untidy mop of fair hair. He was clean-shaven and neatly but shabbily dressed. With rare exceptions he was punctual and well-mannered to the point of deference. He spoke quietly, in a monotone, apparently without much affect. It turned out that he sometimes experienced strong feelings, but they were not reflected in his voice. He expressed himself with clarity and precision, though he sometimes verged on the pedantic. He tended to overvalue the intellect and sometimes exploited it defensively. He related to friends largely on the basis of shared intellectual interests.

Andrew's mother, an Irish countrywoman, was killed in a car accident when he was three years old. His father, who was driving the car, escaped without significant injury. He was an inspector of weights and measures. Although at first Andrew spoke of him as rather severe and even at times threatening, as the analysis proceeded he emerged as mild and even ineffectual, diffident in the face of the dominance exercised by the women in the family. He seems to have displayed a certain warmth toward his son. Andrew remembered calling out at night for his lost mother; his father would then sit with him and hold his hand until he fell asleep. His mother's family took them into their household, and henceforth the boy was brought up by his aunt and her mother.

Andrew's aunt was the effective mother. At first, Andrew experienced her as cold and rejecting, believing this to be due to his messiness, of which he felt she disapproved. As time went on, they grew closer, and his concern and protectiveness toward her were reexperienced in the analysis. Unfortunately, just as the family situation was becoming stabilized, six-year-old Andrew developed a subacute osteochondritis of the foot (Perthes' disease) and was confined to hospital for nearly six months.

Andrew was bitter and resentful about the hospital and disliked his stay there intensely. Outwardly, however, he was conforming, compliant, and self-effacing. With the approach of prepuberty he became more openly critical of his aunt, claiming that he was seriously neglected. He said meals were never cooked and his clothes went unmended; and although he gave graphic descriptions of this neglect during the analysis he realized in retrospect that his claims were not serious.

In adolescence, too, Andrew's conformity at times gave way to open defiance, and rebellion alternated with sullen resentment and grudging compliance. The learning difficulties that had marred his schooling became more pronounced, and it was some years before they were sufficiently overcome to allow him to undertake the necessary education and training to become a pharmacist. Before he attained his qualification, Andrew's late adolescence and early manhood was a record of unrealized potential, conflict-ridden ambition, restlessness, and brooding dissatisfaction. It is far from clear how he was able to achieve the degree of success that he did.

For many years Andrew felt sexually ignorant. He had a number of relevant childhood memories, such as various harsh cautions against masturbation and the damage it might incur. At the hospital he was severely criticized for inspecting a little girl's body in the lavatory. He recollected another incident in which a small girl came up to him, turned her back on him, pulled down her knickers, and exposed her bottom in an exhibitionistic gesture of contempt.

During his adolescence Andrew was paralyzingly shy of girls; he had no heterosexual relationship until he was twenty-two, when he became involved with a teenager. The relationship lasted for nearly four years, until she met and married someone else. They practiced mutual masturbation, but he was afraid to attempt intercourse and blamed the end of the relationship on his failure to do so. (He was also demoralized by the girl's academic successes compared with his own scholastic failure.) Shortly afterwards Andrew became engaged to another woman, whom he married four years later.

Feelings of guilt and shame always attended expressions of Andrew's sexuality, together with strong feelings of inadequacy. His few attempts at intercourse before his marriage were unsatisfactory. He expressed no conscious homosexual thoughts and recalled only one attempt at a homosexual experience when, during his teens, he tried to seduce a boy and was rebuffed. He was reticent about his sex life in marriage.

Andrew's conflicts over exhibitionism and competitiveness were repeatedly reflected in his analytic material. He viewed with apprehension his wife's impending driving test, and although he told her he was sad when she failed, he could not altogether disguise his relief. From the standpoint of the masculine competitor he barely concealed his triumph over the woman's weakness and failure; but those aspects of his character built on unconscious feminine identification did allow him later to feel a genuine sense of regret and a lowering of his own masculine sense of esteem. His sadness was, in part, the sadness of castration.

On another occasion, a financially successful relative tried to explain to him how he could use his pharmaceutical skills to greater financial effect by joining a drug company. Andrew was furious and bitterly resentful of the advice. He felt disparaged and belittled, just as he felt pushed, bullied, nagged, and rendered ineffective by his wife when she suggested that he ought to be making more money. In the analysis he fiercely denounced his relative and said, almost pitifully, "Why does he want to cut me down?" He lapsed thereafter into a demoralized sadness. When the analyst pointed to the transference implications of what he had said, Andrew at first greeted these remarks with silence. When he finally attempted to comment on his success compared with that of others, he lost his clarity of thought and became confused. Although he appeared to be demonstrating his own inadequacy, he simultaneously rendered the analyst's interpretation ineffective by finding it impossible to understand. In this way the analyst's efforts were defeated: unconsciously, Andrew was trying to make him feel like a fool.

One day Andrew reported reading a book about a wild young man who drove fast cars and smashed them up. He was impressed by a description of a car crash in which a girl was very badly injured and her face reduced to a pulp. From the midst of the wreckage she was crying for help pitifully. Andrew was very disturbed by the story he was telling. He suddenly thought that he was responsible for the accident, but this was followed by a feeling of identification with the girl. He said he had a "horror-struck sympathy." He became particularly upset when the analyst drew a link with the car crash in which his mother was killed. It took time and patience before Andrew could work through his guilty identification with his father, his flight into feminine identification, and the violent sexual fantasies that began to come into his mind and had so colored his oedipal conflicts.

Fixation Points and Defense Mechanisms

Character neuroses share with symptom neuroses compromise formation structured around fixation points. It is not difficult to identify the oral phase fixations in Andrew's personality. Oral derivatives repeatedly found expression in the analytic process. Andrew's complaints of his aunt's neglect hid an underlying fear of starvation, which revealed itself in discreet demandingness that only occasionally flared into anger when his needs were frustrated. Starvation anxiety was generally kept at bay by Andrew's planned overprovision for his oral needs. Andrew did not conspicuously overeat but rather made certain that supplies would never run out. His tendency to hoard had also been augmented by anal retentiveness and did not derive altogether from earlier fixation points.

The case material shows ample evidence of the role of anality and phallic aggression in Andrew's character disturbance. Before examining the nature of the compromises in his neurosis, however, it may be useful to say a little about the nature of his defenses and their important contribution to the clinical picture.

In the course of Andrew's analysis he often resorted to intellectualization whenever ideas threatened to become too charged and strong affect was in danger of finding expression. Under these circumstances his attitude became aloof and dispassionate and he sounded as if he were giving a lecture. But although he also displayed some isolation of affect, he did not always succeed in hiding his feelings from himself. Thus certain of his defensive activities were sometimes tenuous or even ineffective. Sometimes, the conscious concealment of a feeling-state was related to fear or shame. Less consciously, he avoided both shame and guilt by projecting his own self-critical feel-ings. Examples of externalization included the reporting of his wife's dreams when he was anxious about his own, the experience of his own depression as if it were the analyst's, his wife's supposed envy of a successful relative, and a good deal of his concern about his son's failures.

Many of Andrew's defensive maneuvers also betrayed the sources of the drive expressions he sought to keep from awareness. He tended to compartmentalize, to shut off one set of thoughts from another or to treat thoughts as if they were unrelated. This device was traced to fears of phallic and anal touching, while a tendency to withhold in the analysis combined both a defense against and a devia-tive of anal drive expressions.

Andrew made conspicuous use of denial. Current events that might be potential sources of anxiety were simply shut out—some-times from consciousness and frequently from associations. In treat-ment sessions he often dwelled on his professional qualifications, until a chance remark revealed that his wife was shortly taking an important examination of her own. By shutting this out of his thoughts he kept at bay his fears both of competitiveness and defeat at feminine hands. He mobilized reaction formation against anal sa-dism and its derivatives, as well as intrusive phallic aggression.

Compromise Formations

The accumulation of microstructures within the personality of the character neurotic (see above, "The Character Neuroses") is a striking feature of this group of conditions.[1] Each microstructure is the consequence of a compromise formation, which in turn is the outcome of an internalized conflict.

---

1. *Macrostructures* are the main psychic agencies—id, ego, superego. *Microstruc-tures* are aggregates of many psychological components from macrostructures—e.g., elements of drives, affects, cognitive items, and attendant defenses that, for example, make up attitudes and styles of behavior and relationships to others. The aggregates become synthesized and achieve permanence within the personality. Their sources are constitutional and environmental. Character traits are conspicuous among their effects and stem from disharmonies occasioned by these sources.

In Andrew's case the influences leading to microstructures within the personality include, among others, his being selected to be sent away from home. The end result was that he saw himself as unvalued and ineffective—a view that became fixed in his personality.

While the character neurotic tolerates drive derivatives to a greater degree than does the symptom neurotic, this tolerance stops short of polymorphous perversion. Id derivatives are still opposed by the ego and superego, and a compromise has to be found. The compromise is always an uneasy one and involves no true resolution of the conflict between drive and reaction against it. The opposing forces are bound together in such a way that at any one time either the drive or the reaction against it may be in ascendance. The resulting structure is analogous to a rope, whose strands are closely intertwined though individually discernible.

Character neurosis tends to be based on a multiplicity of fixation points and a wide range of defenses and defensive maneuvers. Although the resulting compromise is stable as a microstructure, elements within that structure oscillate in an unstable fashion. The microstructure is carried forward from one developmental phase to the next, but both the personality and the microstructure continue to modify, influence, and mold each other.

These features largely determine the clinical picture. This is certainly true of Andrew. Multiple microstructures clustered around fixation points are repeatedly defended, but defense and drive expression can often be seen side by side. The wide spread of defenses used does not, as might be supposed, make for adaptive flexibility: on the contrary, Andrew's defenses are not particularly effective; but he employs first one and then another, drawing in this way on the width rather than the depth of his defensive organization in order to safeguard an uneasy peace of mind.

Character Neurosis and the Oedipal Phase

Whatever the extent of conflict and pathology in the preoedipal phases, the subjects of neurosis enter the oedipal constellation and continue their development with firmly established internalized conflicts. In normative development the oedipal phase acts as a major organizer of preoedipal trends, bringing them together in an enrichment of instinctual life and endowing developing object relationships with an individual stamp. The oedipal stage and its associated conflicts move forward in the matrix of an individual character; earlier trends that might otherwise have lent an infantile quality to the personality now allow it to develop toward the goals of concern for the object, a greater degree of altruism, and increased freedom from those impulsions of need fulfillment that fail to take account of the needs or requirements of others. In neurosis these forward shifts may indeed be made, but not so decisively. The child enters the oedipal phase, but the oedipal complex itself is unresolved. Furthermore, in neurotic development, the preoedipal contributants do not so much enrich the oedipal phase as color it in a pathological manner. In the symptom neuroses the fixation points are discernible or can be inferred in spite of the opposition of the ego; in the character neuroses the presence of fixation points is also unmistakable, but they are less strongly opposed by the ego: tolerance of the drives is at least sufficient to avoid the wide divergence between the agencies that in the symptom neuroses ultimately leads to crisis, regression, and major compromises in the form of stable symptoms. Unlike the symptom neuroses, the conflicts the oedipal phase sustains in the character neuroses develop step by step, and the compromise formations are microstructures that are elaborated at successive phases.

For the preneurotic child, the move into the oedipal phase and the attainment of the oedipal object tie, with its economic consequences, are fateful. If this developmental goal is not achieved the course is set for a much more devious development. In this respect the oedipal phase may be regarded as a gateway toward a relatively high level of object relations and, indeed, of psychological adaptation, even in the neurotic individual. We enlarge on this point in chapter 6.

In the discussion of symptom neuroses in chapter 4 it was suggested that difficulty in tolerating frustration and recourse to instinctual regression based upon pregenital fixations could be attributed to an asynchronous development of the drives, ego, and superego. The data obtained from the treatment of reactive character neuroses also point to disharmonies in early development, but the synthesis of the interaction is sufficiently strong to transform the pregenital fixations into more or less stable psychic formations. These transformations are assimilated into the ego, which becomes handicapped to a greater or lesser extent in its capacity to maintain satisfying interpersonal relationships. Two examples help to illustrate this thesis.

Karen

Karen was an unmarried woman of twenty-five who complained of intense feelings of inferiority that interfered with her work and prevented her from engaging in social relationships. Conscious of a sense of shame in the company of others, she blamed it for her social inadequacy and failure to advance in her profession. Karen was self-depreciatory and guilt-ridden. Her related depressive mood had led her to take an overdose of the antidepressant drugs prescribed by her general practitioner. At first sight she seemed submissive and acquiescent, but as analysis proceeded it became clear that these traits hid from view quite different personality characteristics. Indeed, her personality had a hard, unyielding quality. She was ungenerous, lacked warmth, and was unresponsive to kindness and consideration shown her. Believing herself deprived emotionally, she tended to justify her considerable vindictiveness on these grounds.

Karen was the oldest of three children: two brothers had been born before she was five years old. She had ruthlessly pursued her mother for the love of which she believed herself deprived. This pursuit, repeated in the transference, was the source of much resistance. Her unconscious hatred of her mother resulted in a dread of separation and a fear of the mother's death. This fear initially showed itself as a school phobia when Karen was five years old.

After stating that she was without sexual feelings, Karen gave way to a series of angry outbursts. She said she used to masturbate but had not done so for many years, and she went on to describe her sadomasochistic masturbatory fantasies. In one she was watching a man with a very large penis repeatedly penetrate a young woman who was bound and tied. During the fantasy she inserted her finger into her anus. In later adolescence she occasionally substituted an object for her finger and the vagina for the anus. Anger preceded Karen's every discussion of masturbation. In this she identified with her critical, prohibiting mother, who, like herself, regarded genitals and genital sexuality as filthy. It was not long before the passive counterpart to the active need to override and domineer appeared in the transference. In fantasy she was held down and overpowered. Derivatives of these masturbatory sadomasochistic fantasies were repeated in the transference.

In childhood Karen was in the habit of retaining urine in order to evoke clitoral sensations. This form of masturbation had its forerunner in constipation. Her mother had treated the constipation by regularly administering enemas; the child gradually came to enjoy the anal sensations. The wish to be held down and immobilized during the administration of the enemas returned as a transference fantasy and was the passive aspect of the sadistic fantasies that were actively repeated in childhood games. She recalled doctor games in which, in identification with the mother, she tried to insert drinking straws into her girlfriend's anus. This game also allowed her to repeat the part of both the father and the mother in coitus. She painted her friend's vulva with water and was able to remember a time in early childhood when her mother painted her vulva, treating an irritation in that area.

The guilt associated with these doctor games led her to avoid the family doctor whenever possible. The pleasure she obtained from retaining urine was offset when she periodically wet herself, for which she was criticized by her mother and sometimes physically punished. The pleasurable clitoral sensations disappeared in later childhood, but Karen tended to become momentarily incontinent of urine whenever she became excited or when playing with other children. She was overcome by embarrassment at these incidents and became reluctant to mix with others in case she wet herself. As the years passed the incontinence disappeared, but the feeling of being different from others and the sense of inferiority remained. The fear of losing control over the wish to masturbate, hence over the bladder itself, which had a prototype in the fear of soiling, was displaced to thought, feeling, and action. Karen feared she was going out of her mind.

Karen's sense of shame was based on a compromise synthesis of her childhood wish to be seen urinating like her brothers and father and the humiliation evoked by her attempts to bring this wish to fruition. Her sense of shame was permeated by an exhibitionistic (urethral-erotic) wish. In adolescence and adult life she experienced shame in the company of others: the wish to hide concealed the need to be seen.

Fixated as she was at the phallic phase, she wished to possess what her father and brothers possessed. No other acquisition or gift could satisfy this longing—hence her ingratitude. Her wish to possess the penis was expressed in derivative forms: she belonged to that category of women who react to their castration complex with a need for revenge (Abraham, 1920). When the analysis was well established she struck up a relationship with a man who disappointed her. For weeks afterward she searched the newspapers hoping to find a report that he had been killed in a car accident. She recalled that she had earlier been seeing a psychiatrist. Whenever she hinted at suicide, he reduced the frequency of her appointments. She fantasized shooting him in the genitals and then making the suicidal attempt.

Karen's vindictiveness was expressed in an attenuated form in the sadistic component of her anality. Her need to belittle (i.e., to castrate) men was repeatedly expressed both in the transference and in her life. Early in development her penis envy and her castration wish had been synthesized. The former led to her sense of inferiority while the latter evoked the sadistic masturbatory fantasy and the subsequent sense of guilt.

The development of Karen's infantile sexuality had been asynchronous. The persistent stimulation of the anus involved in the administration of enemas prolonged the anal-sadistic phase well beyond its time and so established the sadomasochistic component instinct as a major element of her infantile sexuality. As is so often the case (B. Bornstein, 1935), the anal stimulation led to a premature evolution of the phallic phase, which played an important part in the painting of her girlfriend's vulva and in the repeated observation of her father's and young brothers' genitalia. Her clitoral "masturbation" via retention of urine, beginning as it did while the anal phase continued, had a sadistic content and contributed to the castration wishes.

In late adolescence and adult life the excitement caused by the unconscious wish to possess and destroy the penis led Karen to avoid male company because of the compulsion to look at their genitals. The persistence of the anal-sadistic phase also prevented the successful fusion of libido and aggression. Her sadomasochistic sexuality, which persisted into adult life, provoked guilt but was clearly reflected in her behavior. She looked aggressive, and many of her actions had an unconscious aggressive intent. She was unable to transform or soften the aggression, which was strongly reflected in the superego and gave it a harsh and relentless character.

An uneventful childhood development is always punctuated by transient developmental disorders as the instinctual derivatives evolve. These lead to conflict with the mother (external conflicts). In Karen's case, the premature arousal of anal-sadistic and phallic wishes led to a temporal disharmony. Her infantile ego was unable to deal with the pregenital demands by repression, and so conflict with the mother was exacerbated. These conflicts were partially resolved through reaction formations as development and internalization proceeded, and the resulting psychic constructions were gradually assimilated into the developing ego. They became part of a personality that was left rigid, limited, and restricted. For all Karen's guilt, she saw little wrong in the way she behaved toward others.

Isabel

Isabel's pregenital aims and objects were transformed into reactive character traits. She was an unmarried schoolteacher of thirty-two who was depressed in mood and had lost interest in her work and in life generally. Isabel had two younger sisters, both married. She was devoted to the younger of the sisters (three years her junior) and made considerable sacrifices on her behalf. Isabel was kind, sociable, and had no difficulty in making friends. But her severe constipation made it difficult for her to lead a normal life. Each morning she sat on the toilet for at least half an hour—more often than not with no result. For as long as she could remember, she had not had a spontaneous urge to defecate. Because of her morning ritual she could not stay overnight with friends and could go on holiday only if she obtained a hotel room with a bathroom attached.

In Isabel's early childhood her mother administered enemas and suppositories for the constipation. She remembered her acquiescence in these measures. Indeed, conformity was characteristic of her attitude to her mother throughout childhood and adolescence, and this attitude was reflected in her behavior during the first years of analysis. She was never aggressive to the analyst, and she could not remember any envy or jealousy of her sisters. She recalled that when she was five, her younger sister had wanted one of her toys. Isabel did not want to give it up but she was prevailed upon to do so by her mother. From that time on she readily gave her possessions to her sister.

The advent of puberty was not accompanied by genital sensation. Isabel's sexual feelings toward others were diffuse and took the form of daydreams about boys she met in church or at the tennis club. She found her genitals displeasing, but she experienced pleasurable peri-anal sensations and was given to anal masturbation. In her middle twenties she had coitus for the first time, with an older man. She obtained some vaginal sensation when he performed the act *a tergo*. Later she had other affairs but always failed to reach orgasm.

During the course of Isabel's long analysis a number of disadvantageous character traits were identified. In line with her obdurate constipation, she delayed and postponed her work, house cleaning, dish washing, and changing her clothes. She rarely brought an activity to completion. She would feel "weighed down" and stop what she was doing. In her analytic sessions she would start to speak and then stop. She was aware of an "obstruction" preventing her from saying what was in her mind. Even if she disclosed every thought she was sure that others were still left unsaid.

Her description of the act of defecation showed that she equated words and actions with feces and defecation. When she managed to pass a stool she had the feeling that much was left behind. Sometimes she felt feces move toward the anal aperture and then, of their own initiative, pass back up the anal canal. In the same way words came into her throat, as she put it, but she could not get them out. Often when she was about to pass a stool the anal sphincter contracted and made defecation impossible. In all these ways her retentiveness was striking.

After a year or more of treatment Isabel became aware during the day of a slight urge to defecate. She was inclined to ignore this although she continued to sit on the lavatory every morning. She excused her dismissal of the later defecatory urge on the grounds that, even if she went to the lavatory, she would fail to pass a stool. Many months of treatment elapsed before she could respond to the stimulus to defecate. It became clear that the decision to act on or ignore the stimulus depended on the state of the transference. Even when her bowel function had largely reverted to normal, disappointment or anger provoked by negative transference feelings led to constipation.

Isabel could not maintain an interest or pursue an activity to completion, irrespective of her reactions to emotionally significant individuals. For example, she decided to write up some work in which she was interested, mentioned this to the headmaster of the school where she taught, and asked him to read it. He said that he would discuss it with her, but he asked her to contact him again when he was less busy. However, she waited to hear from him for several weeks, and her interest in the work finally disappeared.

A similar reaction occurred in the analysis. Treatment had revived Isabel's interest in golf, a game at which she had once been proficient. After playing for some months she entered a competition and reached the finals. The playoff was to take place a few days after her summer break from analysis began. When treatment resumed Isabel announced that the final had been a fiasco. She had played badly. She revealed that when the analyst had said, at the last session, that he hoped she would enjoy her golf, she took his remarks to mean, "Off you go and play golf, that should keep you happy." She thought he was uninterested in her and was too taken up with his own affairs, and she approached the final of the golf competition with little enthusiasm. Two years passed before she regained her interest in the sport.

When Isabel perceived the facial expressions of her headmaster or senior female colleague as severe, unfriendly, or critical, she became depressed and panic-stricken. When she was disappointed, she feared that she was at fault. For example, the headmaster asked if she would join him in taking a group of pupils on a field trip. She went to some trouble planning the outing and made up a handout for the pupils. Just before the trip was due to begin the headmaster told her that he was unable to go. When she arrived with the pupils at the appointed place she realized that she had forgotten to bring the handout. She felt that the outing was a failure and that she was worthless. Meeting the headmaster the next day, she was convinced that he turned away from her in anger.

Throughout adolescence and adult life Isabel behaved in an altruistic, self-sacrificing way, especially toward her younger sister and her children. As a child she did not compete with her sisters but took great pleasure in their scholastic and athletic successes, even though she herself was an able girl and had shown promise in these activities. When her sisters married, her only reaction was that their husbands were not good enough for them. Her attitude toward her young sister and her sister's children was like that of a self-sacrificing mother. If she thought the children were disturbed or upset she became deeply distressed. When the younger sister divorced her husband, while Isabel was in analysis, these reactions were greatly heightened. She fantasized setting up house with her sister and the children with herself as the breadwinner.

For all her distortions and pathological features, Isabel was able to maintain a level of concern characteristic of the adolescent genital level. But she was never uplifted by her altruism: she always felt that she had not done enough or that what she had done had not been carried out properly. Her altruism also found an outlet in a need to help children she believed to be deprived or neglected. She worked tirelessly with them even when they had disappointed her. Despite her efforts she was always fearful of criticism from parents or headmaster.

The first three years of analysis brought about the restoration of

Isabel's bowel function. She resumed relationships with men but ended them after her sister's divorce. She also recovered her interest in work. However, her character traits persisted, although they were less pronounced. Then, in a new development, Isabel began to neglect herself. She became unwilling to buy food, to cook for herself, or to bathe and change her clothes. She neglected her flat and appeared for treatment in an untidy, uncared-for state. For the first time she began to consult her general practitioner with numerous physical complaints, none of which had an organic basis.

This regression in the transference, with its reexperience of early object relations and reversion to infantile needs, was also revealed in her complaining attitude toward the analyst. While previously she had been pleasant and apparently indifferent to the environment of the house where analysis took place, she was now extremely sensitive to the slightest change. If she saw a strange car by the house she concluded erroneously that the analyst had bought a new car for his wife. She constantly compared her situation with his. He had plenty of money while she had none. He was living off her fees. She was envious of the food cooked for him, of his house and garden, despite the fact that her own home was large. During this period some alterations had to be made to the analyst's house. Isabel reacted with a mixture of rage and despair, believing that the changes were for the purpose of accommodating the analyst's daughter. How could he be so heartless? *She* was the one who needed to be cared for. Such thoughtlessness could break a person, even cause her to die. Until this time she had thought of the analyst as kindly if rather decrepit. Now, she claimed, she saw him for what he was: a ruthless egotist who cared nothing for anyone, especially for her. She was deteriorating by the day while he was prospering. He even looked younger than she. He was passing her by.

Many years previously, Isabel's early yearnings and dissatisfactions had been reawakened by her sisters' marriages. The process of analysis had exposed this envy, jealousy, and hatred, which had been repressed through identification. In order to remove the anxiety and guilt provoked by her greed, envy, and jealousy, Isabel had played the part of the wished-for and all-giving mother and, in identification with her sisters, gave them what she wanted for herself. Identification enabled her to forget the many frustrations and miseries of her childhood. It also led to her character traits of withdrawal and easy loss of interest in line with her father's rather depressed temperament. There was some evidence that he had suffered a bout of depression during her childhood.

Isabel's altruism also had roots in the anal-phallic orientation of her libido and in elements of the Oedipus complex. She recalled, as a little girl, climbing into her younger sister's bed in the morning, touching and smelling her buttocks and anus. She loved the feel of the skin of her sister's cheeks and recalled a wish to thrust herself into her sister's bottom. Throughout her life Isabel had unconsciously wished to play the part of the man with her sister. This wish for masculinity found further expression in her identification with the analyst—a repetition of her childhood identification with her father.

Isabel claimed that when she was ten she had saved her sister from drowning. This event, whether real or imaginary, is not only the prototype of her need to rescue the deprived but also a representation of the wishful fantasy of having given birth to her sister. As derivatives of the Oedipus complex made their appearance during analytic work, this fantasy revealed an element of that complex. On her way to a treatment session Isabel fantasized that a girl in her class had choked while eating and lost consciousness. She tried to breathe life into the moribund child as her headmaster watched admiringly. He then took her and the child in his car to the hospital. This thinly disguised fantasy of giving birth to her father's child (the younger sister) was represented in a dream of the previous night that analysis showed to be a transference dream. Isabel dreamed that a male colleague, a good deal older than she, had presented her with two gifts, but she still expected a third. He gave the third gift (which represented the younger sister) to his wife. Isabel turned away, feeling resentful and unwanted.

In infancy and early childhood Isabel had been subject to a series of environmental interferences that led to a disharmonious development. Anal overstimulation accentuated anal erotism (retention), led to external conflict over toilet training, and prematurely awakened sadistic tendencies. With the birth of the next sister in her second year, she turned toward her father. His responsiveness led to a premature appearance of the oedipal phase. This relationship with the father ended after the birth of the youngest sister. Isabel's anger led to a defensive identification with him that became the basis of character traits which hindered the development of her femininity. Isabel's heterosexuality was weakened by this development, and the younger sister became the object of her phallic drives.

While the symptoms that caused Karen and Isabel to seek treatment were similar in nature—depression and loss of interest in life—their personalities (but not their characters) were quite different. One was demanding, ungenerous, and vindictive; the other altruistic and considerate. In both cases the character traits had their source in the castration complex. Karen's disturbance belonged to Abraham's "revenge type"; Isabel's to his "wish-fulfillment" type (1920). Karen wanted to take revenge on the man because he, not she, possessed a penis. Isabel wanted to act the part of the man through the possession of a penis.

The pathological expressions of the castration complex in these patients can be attributed primarily to disharmonious development with its consequence of severe internalized conflict culminating in disadvantageous character traits. The disharmony was initially created by injudicious acts of omission and commission on the part of the parents. In Karen the pregenital wishes led to external conflict. Her father's lack of responsiveness toward her after the birth of her brothers led to an overvaluation of the penis and hence to urethral-erotic and exhibitionistic wishes. The penis was necessary, the young Karen believed, in order to love and be loved. The hatred provoked by her envy and jealousy of her brothers was heightened by the sadistic component of her anality. Her sense of shame and inferiority grew out of reaction formations set up to contain the pregenital drive derivatives.

In Isabel's case identifications played the major part in creating the abnormal character traits. They achieved this role because she had experienced a satisfying, if temporary, relationship (the father). Object choice gave way to identification, making this the prototype of defense. In contrast with Karen, Isabel's wish for a penis was only an element of the wish to possess (as father) her sister (herself). The aim of the homosexual libido was anal penetration; the object Isabel's sister. The enema tube and anus were equivalent to penis and vagina. Isabel's homosexual wish did not find expression in clitoral masturbation, no doubt because of the absence of genital stimulation in early childhood and because of her fixation to the anal erotogenic zone. Karen had no such real love object, and so her wish fantasy of anal penetration, based on similar experiences (enemas), was acted out out on the self playing active and passive roles. This formed the content of clitoral masturbation with resulting guilt. Isabel was spared this.

Finally, the topic of regression in character neurosis: regression and progression take place from time to time, when one or other of the preoedipal fixations holds temporary sway. One such, occurring in the course of treatment, is reported in the account given of Mabel. These regressions are contained without pronounced conflict and are tolerated by the ego and superego.

In the next chapter a heterogeneous group of clinical states will be studied. Some of these patients presented initially with symptoms not unlike those that brought Karen and Isabel to psychoanalytic treatment. We have called the disturbances described in chapter 6 *non-neurotic developmental disorders* to distinguish them from symptom and character neuroses. This distinction is made on both descriptive and metapsychological grounds. Neurosis-like symptoms often hold center stage in these disturbances, but the symptoms are not a consequence of disadvantageous character traits, nor are they exaggerations of traits that existed prior to the illness, as is the case in the character neuroses.

CHAPTER 6 Non-Neurotic Developmental Disorders

From a developmental viewpoint, symptom neurosis and character neurosis represent the highest forms of psychological pathology. These conditions involve a number of developmental weaknesses or anomalies that predispose the individual to that pathology. Nevertheless, the capacity to resolve internalized conflict through compromise in symptom formation depends on considerable advances in important areas of personality formation—in particular, in the building of the main psychic structures, in progression through sequential drive phases, and in substantial movement along certain developmental lines. Similarly, in character neurosis, although significant instinctual fixations persist, they are accommodated within the personality in such a way that the potentiality for a reasonably adaptive functioning is maintained. Indeed, such potentiality is shared by the symptom neurotic and character neurotic person alike; both have achieved the required developmental advances indicated above. All such people have entered the oedipal phase, with its relatively advanced capacity for attachment to objects, whatever the nature of the difficulties encountered there.

Certain groups of people never achieve the developmental advances required for neurotic symptom formation to occur. Psychopathy, for example, involves significant developmental arrests, and the same can be said of many sexual perversions. Other disorders may involve regression without compromise formation or may follow the processes of psychic dissolution that characterize the psychoses. But there remains a substantial group of disparate conditions that cannot be categorized by any of these types of disorder. These individuals show serious developmental deficiencies, which may include delays, arrests, deviations, or disharmonies; the problems are rooted in early vulnerabilities and weaknesses. For all their similarities, they vary considerably in their form of presentation and in their pathology.

These *non-neurotic developmental disorders*, which may be loosely subdivided according to phenomenology and pathology, sometimes lay a diagnostic trap for the psychoanalyst. Some, for example, closely resemble character neurosis on early examination. Or the patient's level of professional attainment or superficial social relationships may conceal a clearly disordered psychic structure and incapacity for more intimate relationships. The analyst who runs into difficulties with such patients may be compelled to look outside a model of neurosis in order to diagnose and treat them. There is no shortage of formulations extending psychoanalytic thinking on such problem cases. But the analyst obliged to revise his conceptual model of treatment in line with an extended model of illness is sometimes tempted to discard older concepts that have stood him in good stead. In doing so the analyst may undermine the general model of the mind on which all psychoanalytic models of illness are based. These dangers should be borne in mind in any consideration of the relevant literature.

Fairbairn (1956), Winnicott (1965), and Guntrip (1956) recognized that personality deficits and aberrations, on the one hand, and symptoms, on the other, could not be explained satisfactorily on the basis of a compromise between the ego and drive derivatives altered by regression, as in the neuroses. In their opinion the ego in the "disturbed cases" (Rangell, 1982) was itself too seriously disorganized to contribute to this kind of compromise. The defenses discerned by these authors were of a kind appropriate to an ego whose development had been arrested.

Fairbairn, Winnicott, and Guntrip suggested that the conflicts in object relationships observed in these patients are a secondary development. The conditions that lead to these conflicts are, in their opinion, caused by a serious injury to the infantile self. Kohut (1971) came to the same conclusion, although he understood the pathological changes affecting the infantile self in terms of the development of narcissism. Kernberg (1974) and Rosenfeld (1968), on the other hand, have remained faithful to a conflict model, claiming that the ego "weakness" is the consequence of excessive splitting and projective identification.

Studies of developmental pathology (e.g., Anna Freud, 1951, 1962, 1963, 1966, 1974, 1979; H. Hartmann, 1939; H. Kennedy, 1971; E. Kris, 1956; M. S. Mahler, 1968; C. Yorke, 1980, 1983a, 1983b; Yorke and Wiseberg, 1976) offer a means of understanding the genesis and expression of these "disturbed cases" without requiring that psychoanalytic theory be recast as Fairbairn, Guntrip, and Kohut do. The body of theory of which these studies are examples goes some way toward an understanding of how defects in development may arise; at the same time it accounts for the severity of the conflicts that divide the personality.

In order to demonstrate the explanatory value of these concepts as they apply to this large group of heterogeneous clinical states, we describe a number of cases, each of which demonstrates one or more of the striking clinical features to be found in these conditions. Each of these patients underwent psychoanalytic treatment for a number of years. The first case can justifiably be described as a borderline state insofar as ego functioning was less than adequate in tolerance and reality testing. During the treatment, modifications in technique were necessary (Greenson, 1955; Gitelson, 1955) to deal with the difficulties arising from these deficiencies in ego functioning. The second case, involving a severe disorder of self- and object cathexis, would be regarded by Kohut as a *narcissistic disorder* in his particular sense. In the third case, the patient had been clinically healthy prior to the outbreak of her illness.

A Borderline State

The so-called borderline states have received a good deal of attention in the literature. Writers such as Bychowski (1952), Fleischman (1956), Frank (1956), Gitelson (1955), Greenson (1955), Knight (1956), and Rangell (1955) have described the wide range of symptoms that characterize these states.

Patients with borderline features have difficulty tolerating anxiety and frustration. They falsify reality readily, giving way to wishes that they do not regard as unusual or abnormal. Occasionally the falsifications border on the delusional or even attain an intermittently frank delusional quality. Impulsive and potentially self-damaging behavior is frequently found. All these characteristics make these patients difficult to treat with standard analytic techniques. Many (Gitelson, Frank, Rangell, and others) with experience of these conditions believe the analyst must modify the treatment technique to fit the individual case while not giving up an analytic stance. These writers see borderline states as the result of faulty ego development. Important ego functions—reality testing, anxiety tolerance, and stable defenses—are impaired, while others appear to retain their integrity, thus giving the patient the semblance of normality (cf. the "as-if" personalities described by Winnicott, 1955). Disorganization of the ego is often reflected in profound disturbances in early object relationships, whether or not these have been influenced by maturational or constitutional factors.

Billy

A young man of twenty-one was convinced that the hair on his head above his left ear was diseased. He believed that this hair, extending to the crown of his head, had changed in both shape and texture. The hairs, formerly straight, were now crinkly. He was compelled to examine them in the mirror, but fear soon led him to try to avoid this. He was convinced that others knew that his hair was abnormal and therefore remained indoors. If Billy touched his hair by accident or saw it reflected in a mirror or shiny surface he became panic-stricken. He was not reassured when told by a dermatologist that his hair was healthy.

He told the psychiatrist that he had been quite well until eighteen months before, when he had noticed that his scalp was itchy. He consulted a trichologist, who told him he was going bald. Billy was terrified. He found he could not eat, and he avoided company.

About one year before the onset of the illness the patient was introduced to sexual intercourse by a girl he had known at school. He was apprehensive after the act, fearing venereal disease. Nonetheless, his relationship with her continued for some months. Billy then met a girl who belonged to a strict evangelical sect and refused intercourse. She persuaded him to attend religious meetings where he was told that "hell and damnation" was the punishment for sinners. He became confused and conflicted about his sexual needs, and it was against this background that his anxiety about his hair appeared.

Childhood memories indicated that during latency Billy was overanxious and tied to home. Starting school was difficult; he was shy, sensitive, and afraid of teachers and other boys. His achievements fell short of his intellectual capacity. He felt different from his schoolmates. He disliked changing his clothes for games; he found it difficult to urinate when other boys were present; and noticing that other boys were not circumcised made him think of himself as odd. Billy was most comfortable at home sitting in the kitchen while his mother prepared a meal. As a small boy he disliked the idea of giving away a toy because he thought the toy would be lonely. Disillusionment with his parents, particularly his father, was expressed in a family romance fantasy which began when he was about five years of age. At puberty he allowed himself to believe that a friend of his father was his real father, and he told several people about this. He recalled that at about the age of six or seven, when he was at the hairdresser's, he saw his cut hair lying on the floor and felt as if he had lost a part of himself.

Billy was inquisitive and a keen observer. In latency he played games or indulged in fantasies in which he was a spy in enemy country. He established a hideout in a tree and observed everyone who passed by. Even extensive searches failed to find him. In spite of his acute powers of observation and his curiosity, however, Billy consciously learned almost nothing about sexuality until late adolescence. By this time he had withdrawn from and was inwardly critical of his father. He eventually acknowledged that his parents had intercourse and learned how babies were born.

In the course of analytic treatment, pathological features of Billy's development were reconstructed that threw light on the nature of his disorder. Vicissitudes of the transference indicated the extent and quality of his emotional attachment to his parents. Until the successful completion of the treatment, Billy periodically withdrew and experienced bouts of acute anxiety about his hair. He feared the analyst might die or be killed in an air or car accident. These anxieties mirrored similar fears about his father, toward whom Billy expressed resentment only indirectly in silence and avoidance of contact. Only when he lost his fear that the analyst would get fed up with him was he able to reveal his jealousy of other patients and his wish for an exclusive relationship. This wish reflected a similar set of attitudes toward his mother and two younger siblings. He was devoted to his mother yet at the same time he feared and distrusted her.

A series of dreams made it clear that in early childhood Billy had often witnessed the coitus of his parents. He had also been exposed to their violent quarreling throughout his childhood and adolescence. Screen memories indicated that he had seen his parents' sex play. The excitement and anxiety generated by these experiences were augmented by his mother's distress about her psoriasis, which was principally localized in her scalp. Billy watched her spend hours removing the scales from these lesions. Sometimes she put some of her lotion on his hair. She refused to leave the house if she suspected that anyone might spot her blemishes. During the analysis, Billy dreamed that he had lesions indistinguishable from his mother's.

Billy's identification with his mother, strongly reinforced by his observations of sexual activity, predisposed him to passive femininity, which characterized his personality, but did not entirely block the emergence of his masculinity. Billy recalled a childhood fantasy in which he told his mother he would marry her when he grew up. He related a series of dreams in which he was the active sexual partner of a woman who sometimes had some physical characteristic of his mother. Usually he was interrupted in the middle of the lovemaking, or else the analyst appeared in an angry mood. Following a reconstruction of these primal scenes he related the following dream: "I'm driving in a car with my mother. I reverse the car into a gateway. My father's golf clubs are sticking out of the boot, and they are bent by the collision with the gate. I'm upset and hit myself. Then I'm with a girl trying to make love to her."

Billy's wish to interrupt his parents' intercourse was expressed in later memories of trying to intervene between them when they were having a violent quarrel. Through the transference—in which the analyst became a dangerous, treacherous, and frightening person—Billy presented some idea of how he imagined his father in early times. His constant complaints that he was deceived and told lies about the state of his hair pointed to the anger that underlay his frustrated efforts to find out what went on between his parents. Both mother and analyst were deceitful.

The death wishes so easily discerned in the transference, aimed at his father, had never found direct expression in conscious hatred of the father. The following fantasy is illustrative of the guilt resulting from the death wishes: Billy imagined knocking a man down while driving his car. He believed that he had killed him. The man got up, unbeknown to Billy, only to be killed by someone else. Billy would never know that he was innocent. His anger was thus turned against himself, as in the dream quoted above. The anger was also apparent in an incident in which his father struck his mother. Billy picked up a piece of wood and struck himself on his head, cutting his scalp, instead of hitting his father as he had initially intended.

After the onset of his illness Billy dreaded the sight of his own hair while envying and admiring the hair of other young men. Only straight hair was healthy—his own crinkly hair was abnormal; he equated it with women's pubic hair. He recalled a memory from childhood of watching two dogs in intercourse. The dog had straight hair while the bitch—a poodle—had curly hair. He feared they were stuck together. This screen memory contained his fantasy of parental intercourse expressed in terms of hair—father with straight hairs (erect penis) and mother with "crinkly" hair (castrated). In the illness Billy had lost his masculinity (straight hair) and feared becoming a woman (crinkly hair) like his mother.

The identification with his mother and her hair was traced back to very early childhood, prior to the conflict between masculinity ad femininity that began with the emergence of his phallic sexuality. When he was one and a half years old Billy's mother had to be hospitalized because she had miscarried. While she was away he began to pull out his hair during his sleep. This hair-pulling continued, according to his mother, until he was three years of age. She put mittens on his hands when he went to bed to stop him from pulling out his hair. The link, through touching, between hair and penis may well have begun during that period, when he was certainly the witness of parental coitus.

All Billy's sexual anxieties found expression in his thoughts about hair. His wish to touch his hair and his revulsion against doing so repeated his conflict over masturbation. His wish to look at his hair and the dread of what he might see reflected his wish to see female genitals. The compulsive quality of these ideas suggests that they belonged to the phallic stage of his sexual development, which was prematurely aroused through his repeated witnessing of his parents' sexual activity.

The case for a phallic fixation is further strengthened by the way Billy equated his body with the penis. He held himself stiffly and walked with his arms fixed to his trunk. This body/penis equation was traceable to latency-period fantasies in which he identified himself with cartoon figures on television. The first was Mr. Brush, an inverted garden broom with hair made of twigs. The second was Mr. Twizzle, who had extending arms and legs.

The clinical data described suggest the following sequence of mental events leading to the symptoms. Billy's illness was provoked initially by guilt. Genital sexual satisfaction was no longer possible (because of the guilt fostered, inter alia, by religious prohibitions), and other, past forms of pleasure were sought out. Libidinal regression affected both sexual aims and the sexual object. The self replaced the object, while looking and touching provided his gratifications. The childhood wish to look and touch his own and his mother's genitals evoked memories of her pubic hair. This led to anxiety, based on fear of castration, that could not be dealt with by repression.

The hair of Billy's own head replaced his mother's pubic hair and substituted for her genitalia. Billy had formed a connection in childhood between the hair of the head and both male and female genitalia. The traumatic repetition, with his first girlfriend, of the sight of his mother's vulva resulted in a compulsion to look at and to touch that part of his hair equated with his mother's pubic hair.

This symptom did not include a major contribution from the ego or the superego as is the case in hysterical or obsessional neuroses. The symptom was the direct result of a traumatic event, the memory of which appeared in consciousness, due to the failure of repression, but suitably altered through displacement (substitute formation).

Separation from the mother, occurring at a time when profound ambivalence was more appropriate, was carried forward in intensified form through all subsequent developmental stages. Billy had difficulty in coping with the aggressive component that had been turned against the self (hair-pulling) through an identification with the mother (psoriasis). Phallic anxieties and scopophilia were prematurely aroused by exposure to the primal scene and the intensified identification with the mother that resulted. These identifications and anxieties were perpetuated and permanently incorporated into Billy's personality under the influence of the synthetic function of the ego, abnormal chronology, and faulty balance between drive and ego brought together in disharmony.

One result of this development was that any expression of instinct had to be resisted: this is shown by the fact that the patient was happy to remain in ignorance of sexuality until late adolescence. The sensitivity of the emerging ego to any sign of sexual arousal deprived it of access to instinctual sources of energy suitably altered through aim inhibition and sublimation. A form of adjustment was achieved between the ego, the drives, and external circumstances, but it created an impoverished personality. Masculinity was only weakly established, and passive tendencies were uppermost, so that when a precariously based genitality appeared at puberty Billy found his erections a cause for anxiety. When he had coitus for the first time he was essentially the passive partner. His intellectual development was blocked and inhibitions and restrictions characterized his personality.

Conflict played a secondary role in the production of Billy's illness. This is not to say that conflict did not appear at every level of mental functioning, but rather that the prevalence of conflict was a consequence of attempts to reconcile the effects of the disharmonious development of the drives, the ego, and later the superego.

The nature of the symptom shows to what extent the ego was affected and thus prevented compromise formation. *The wish to look revived memories that so dominated Billy's attention that he underwent a circumscribed loss of reality sense.* This loss was not the result of conflict, nor was the compulsive repetition of the traumatic scenes. Billy's loss of reality testing was the consequence of a faulty, disharmonious development that left the ego vulnerable when it had to meet a situation of frustration.

A Narcissistic Disorder

The distinctions Kohut (1971) and Kernberg (1974) draw between borderline states and narcissistic disorders are by no means universally accepted. Rangell (1982) goes so far as to say that the differentiation is in name only. More often than not descriptions of these supposedly different conditions are so similar that clinicians are forced to bring them together under the rubric disturbed cases (Rangell, 1982). Beatrice, the patient whose case is described below, would be regarded by Reich (1960) and Kohut (1971) as suffering from a narcissistic disorder.

Beatrice

A thirty-three-year-old woman complained of a lack of self-esteem combined with a profound sense of inferiority, although treatment later revealed a grandiose, omnipotent fantasy of the self. Beatrice complained bitterly that she could not feel comfortable in the presence of others. She felt ill at ease and inadequate in company, even with people she knew well. Although she made a great effort to impress people and to conceal her weaknesses, she was always convinced that others saw through her pretense and recognized her as the ineffectual and pathetic being she felt herself to be. She thus avoided social contact much of the time.

Beatrice's problems in relationships are most strikingly illustrated by her marriage. She constantly had to be the center of her husband's attention and the sole recipient of his admiration. Her demands for flattery were insatiable and her jealousy inordinate. She fell into a rage if she thought her husband had looked at another woman. She fantasized his watching a beautiful woman only to become furious with him and despairing of her own physical charms. She felt compelled to ask him if he found passing women attractive. His denials did nothing to prevent a row. Beatrice's unreasonable anger with her husband about what were basically fantasies of her own was rarely amenable to reassurance. These externalizations found even more concrete expression in the couple's sexual relationship. Beatrice refused sex for long periods and then accused her husband of lacking interest in her. She also accused him of homosexuality. She called him selfish and domineering and claimed he enjoyed her humiliation and dependence. Despite his accommodation of her wishes, she felt that he forced her to comply with his requirements and that he came and went at his own convenience. It was he who hurt her, in spite of her own mistreatment of him.

After Beatrice's initial idealization of her analyst, his failure to respond to her self-centered wishes for admiration led to the same angry recriminations that she directed against her husband. It became important for her to show the analyst that she could take him or leave him, so she stayed away from sessions whenever the fancy took her. If this behavior pointed to her use of the analyst as a transitional object, her refusal to telephone him underlined the contempt. If, on the other hand, the analyst was helpful or encouraging toward her, she was unable to feel grateful on that account. Her envy of the analyst's skills and good qualities led her to experience his helpfulness as intolerably patronizing; she felt demeaned and humiliated, which fueled her repeated and contemptuous absences.

Later in the analysis Beatrice was able to disclose a source of resistance of which she had long been aware. She was ashamed, she said, of admitting certain wishes and maneuvers. She then allowed herself to describe the background to a fantasy which afforded her great pleasure and satisfaction. For years she had expected her husband to satisfy her every whim and wish. She treated him like a slave. This was but one expression of her sadism. Her masochism was exemplified by the acknowledged wish behind her obsessive fear of humiliation. In her masturbatory fantasy, a number of men (a harem) lay on the floor, immobile but with erect penises. She sat on each in turn and excited him without allowing him to reach ejaculation. The men were not allowed wishes of their own; indeed, they were not people at all. These fantasies not only indicated the impoverishment of Beatrice's real-life object relationships but also pointed to the polymorphous perversity with which they were closely intertwined. In fact, Beatrice had little wish for sexual activity with a partner, much preferring the excitement and masturbation that accompanied her multifarious sexual fantasies. Their derivatives intruded into her everyday relations and threatened to crack her simulated personality, the false ideal through which all but her intimate personal transactions were conducted.

Beatrice shared a number of features with those who manifest a *narcissistic* form of non-neurotic developmental disturbance. She was unable to give love or even to accept it consistently. She responded with contempt to those who offered love and yearned for it from those who ignored or spurned her. This resulted partly from a substitution of envy for gratitude. An infantile omnipotence of thought led Beatrice to expect that others desired gratification of her wishes as much as she did; she responded with resentment to any indication to the contrary. She was threatened by the wishes and needs of others. She made a literal use of primitive defense mechanisms, particularly externalization and projection, that bordered on the concrete and compromised her judgment of reality. For all she received in response to her demands, for all the success the full social operation of her "as if" personality brought, for all the freedom from responsibility her defensive organization granted her, for all her apparent relish of infantile fantasies, and for all the identity of interest she supposed the world around her to share, Beatrice remained a deeply unhappy woman whose isolation and poverty of relationships were nowhere compensated by sustained enjoyment.

To understand the arrests and delays in Beatrice's development, we must look for connections between certain striking features of her early history and later manifestations of her disturbance. Tracing the early development of adult patients always involves the limitations of the reconstructive method: it is impossible to avoid some speculation.

A series of illnesses in the first year of Beatrice's life interfered with the balance of pain and pleasure, weighting it too heavily in favor of the former. Painful excitation was not subject to the usual relief through comparatively ready discharge but was maintained at the cost of adequate experience of pleasure and relaxation. Factors of this kind in the first year of life may affect later modes of excitation, discharge, and tension regulation. Beatrice's pain appears to have been met by her mother's protectiveness and meticulous attention to the child's hygiene. For example, her mother applied ointment to Beatrice's genitals and upper thighs. It is not known how long this practice continued, but one of Beatrice's memories—which may or may not bear the weight of earlier experiences and concealed recollections—is that of her mother's painfully inserting a finger into her vagina. It thus appears that Beatrice was subjected to excessive genital stimulation, some of it painful. This not only affects future sexual organization but interferes with the process of learning to relate and the developing capacity to love. In children such as Beatrice, such genital stimulation tied to trauma or cumulative traumata intensifies narcissism at the expense of object love, provides a foundation for masochistic experience, and fosters sadistic tendencies that interfere at succeeding developmental stages with the growth of the capacity for concern for others.

Beatrice experienced much sexual stimulation from other sources as well. Whenever she was ill she shared her parents' bedroom and had many opportunities to see them unclothed and making love. Dream analysis during treatment repeatedly brought out memories of parental coitus in which Beatrice identified with the active role of the father. This was one reason why fantasies of her husband's intercourse with a series of women made sex exciting for her; it also accounted in part for the strong homosexual component in her libidinal organization.

This historical reconstruction indicates that grounds were laid early for disturbance on certain developmental lines: first, and most important, on the line leading from dependency to emotional self-reliance. Also disturbed were the line from egocentricity to companionship and others according to the nature, admixture, and preponderance of various factors at early and later stages of development.

In analysis, Beatrice vividly recalled that during latency she had wished she were a boy. Her rivalry with her brother was always intense: she wanted to do everything he could do. She recalled her distress at being unable to urinate standing up, as well as envy when she watched her brother competing with a friend to see who could direct his stream of urine farther. Remembering her childhood masturbation, Beatrice recalled her belief that an internal cord connected her genitals with her umbilicus. The cord represented her hidden penis: when she touched her umbilicus she felt pleasure in her genitals. She feared that if she touched herself too much, the string might break.

While such fantasies are not uncommon in neurotic or even normal girls, Beatrice's penis envy was inordinate. When her menses began she was very depressed: they underlined the fact that she could never be a boy and could never possess a penis. (This wish, persisting into adult life, may have been more important than the wish to be a man per se.) Beatrice used the mechanism of denial against all thoughts of menstruation and never knew when her period was due. She masturbated through adolescence and continued to overvaluate and envy the penis (she avoided looking at her husband's penis, particularly if it was erect).

Her mother's attitude toward the adolescent Beatrice is of interest. She excited Beatrice with stories of women who could get their way with men by making the most of their physical charms while frightening her with tales of the horrible consequences of promiscuity. In using her husband to satisfy her inordinate need to be worshiped, Beatrice was once more enjoying the excessive admiration in which her mother indulged. Her husband, like her mother, also protected her against the danger caused by her masturbatory fantasies. Her preoccupations with his supposed interest in other women gave expression simultaneously to her fantasy of possessing the penis and to that of homosexual promiscuity.

Neurosis-like States

A third group of individuals suffer from pseudo-neurotic states, so called because their anxieties, disturbances of mood, or more specific pathological formations superficially resemble neurotic complaints. These individuals are difficult to study in depth, as superficial remissions and sufficient reduction of personal suffering often lead them to abandon treatment; or the therapeutic situation may be undermined through the patient's inability to accept that treatment exists for any purpose other than gratification. Ambivalence surrounding a preoedipal transference may be too intense for the patient to tolerate. But a number of these patients have sufficient insight to recognize the precarious state of their mental health and are therefore prepared to undertake psychoanalytic or psychotherapeutic treatment. They allow the analyst to discover the nature of their vulnerability to mental disorder.

Helga

Helga was an unmarried, childless woman of thirty-five when she was referred by her family doctor for psychiatric treatment. He had become increasingly worried about her continual need for tranquilizers, sedatives, and hypnotics. Her responses to these drugs were also rather idiosyncratic, and the doctor felt a different attempt should be made to deal with her difficulties.

Helga complained of depression of mood, free-floating anxiety, and multiple fears, especially whenever she wanted something for herself. Sometimes she was even frightened to use the telephone if, for example, she wanted to order something from a store. If she went shopping, she invariably took the first thing recommended by the clerk whether she liked it or not; if she found herself dissatisfied she was unable to return the item. In discussions Helga was unable to assert her own point of view if it differed radically from anyone else's. Disagreeing seemed dangerously aggressive for her—but other people's being assertive or disagreeing with each other never struck her as hostile. Rather, she regarded it as the kind of normality to which she aspired but could never attain.

None of these disabilities affected Helga's work as a secretary. She did exactly as she was told, to perfection. In this capacity she had no problem with telephone calls or requests, which were on her boss's behalf; she regarded herself solely as his representative. Her work, indeed, was the one part of her life that afforded her any real satisfaction. She got along well with her colleagues and was quite agreeable with them, but she confined her contacts to the workplace and, in general, neither gave nor accepted invitations. This helped to keep her anxiety at bay.

Helga's personal life outside her work was of a different order. In social circumstances she was afraid of looking conspicuous or of drawing attention to herself: underlying exhibitionism and corresponding scopophilia could be inferred, but its intensity revealed itself only in treatment. Helga had had a number of affairs with men, all of which had come to grief; at the time of assessment, she was desperately afraid that her current involvement was also in jeopardy. Her sexual relationships were fraught: she enjoyed foreplay but felt unable to tolerate penetration, so most attempts at intercourse ended up with mutual masturbation.

Helga's boyfriend was tolerant and helpful not only sexually but in her everyday difficulties. He fulfilled Helga's need for a man in the role of a caring mother: indeed, she chose all her male friends on this basis. Her fear of loss was based more on dread of yet another failure—a blow to her precarious self-esteem—than on the personal loss itself. She was physically attractive with a childlike charm that aroused protectiveness in men. But for Helga, at a certain level, men were interchangeable as long as they fulfilled her needs. Every lost relationship, however, brought with it a sense of hopeless repetition and deep mortification.

Helga was the only daughter of a German industrialist whom she regarded as a neglectful and aggressive ogre who lived only for his work. She could not bear the sight of her mother, whom she had always regarded as intensely critical. Her one brother, two and a half years younger, she had always thought of as the family favorite, and she disliked him on that account. Helga had been born in England, where her father did a lot of business; she returned from Germany in her early twenties to live and work in London—ostensibly to escape from her "impossible family." She remembered little of her childhood, although she thought it very unhappy. She deeply disliked the girls' boarding school to which she was sent at the age of eight. She had made no close friends and had disliked the female teachers, even when they were kind to her. She had accepted the protectiveness of the one male teacher, who taught English. But there was very little of her life on which Helga reflected with pleasure.

In the analysis, an intense transference "neurosis" quickly developed with strong transference resistances against early oral longings. At the beginning of treatment, lying down on the couch mobilized these early wishes so strongly that her very first mental experience in the analysis was a pictorial, wordless breast representation that she found so frightening she had to sit up. As initial work proceeded and the analysis got under way, it became apparent that there was a great deal more to Helga's anxieties than the passive and active components of oral intrusion and incorporation. A certain defiance compounded her wish to sit up; she also felt a strong compulsion to forgo analytic rules and to defy the analyst's supposed injunctions. To follow her thoughts was a submissive compliance to the analyst's tyranny, a submission to his wish to force everything out of her, to demand that she part with her thoughts as if they were feces. She resented his words, which penetrated her ears as if they were verbal suppositories. Helga felt an intense infantile confusion between orifice and orifice, between one body content and another.

Helga experienced phallic-narcissistic preoccupations too (Edgcumbe & Burgner, 1972; Burgner and Edgcumbe, 1972; Edgcumbe and Burgner, 1975). Her wish for and envy of the penis was apparently foreshadowed by the birth of her brother and her envy of him. But her fear of becoming the victim of sadistic penetration, seemingly involving every level of instinctual organization, and the retaliatory wish for a vengeful penetration of the analyst, to reduce him to helplessness in her stead, turned out to have deeper roots. Reconstruction of a hospital visit for the removal of tonsils and adenoids accounted for some of the material when Helga's resistances were sufficiently overcome to allow this work to be done. She had been told by her mother of the operation and indeed, on the occasions when it crossed her mind, had been terrified of the very thought of it; but it did not come into her analytic material until transference developments suggested the need for its reconstruction. It seemed to have taken place sometime not long after the birth of her brother. This destructive experience, as Helga had evidently regarded it, now reappeared time and again in the analytic context, reinforced by the concomitant trauma of being anesthetized.

Under the anesthesia, Helga was at the mercy of the destructive attacker, castrating her and removing parts of her body, overpowering her and reducing her to a terrifying helplessness. This oral violation involved real and not just fantasized damage. The anesthesia reduced her to oblivion under the influence of its oppressive and intolerably analized smell.

The fear of anesthetics and operations had remained with Helga ever since. But further analytic work began to uncover the wishes behind the fears: an uphill task, but Helga slowly began to see that the wish for tranquilizers and hypnotics that had led to her referral was paradoxical, involving more than a wish to be free of mental pain and to sleep peacefully. Did not the wish for such pills include gratification in a chemically induced oblivion? Was there not a masochistic aspect to this desire?

Helga's growing recognition of these important insights was, however, complicated by further considerations, one of which was the quality of the phallic-narcissistic phase to which reference has been made. This phase was not one of phallic primacy: the other preoedipal phases stood alongside it and compounded rather than colored it. Strung together was a kind of loose homosexual organization, drawn from all preoedipal levels of instinctual life, that remained outside Helga's awareness but was betrayed in the analytic sessions through a number of defensive maneuvers. She used her knowledge that the analyst was a man to keep at bay any insistent wish that she experience him as a woman—just as she sought men who would mother her, standing in relation to her as a caring adult to a little girl. She was working, not without difficulty, on these conflicts when an unexpected external event seemed to bring matters to a head.

Helga was admitted to hospital with a severe chest infection. During her recovery, she found herself drawn to the ministrations of the staff nurse, seeking her out increasingly and feeling jealous and resentful when the nurse gave her attention to other patients. Whereas in the analysis she could always deny the existence of other patients, whom she never saw, and maintain the fiction that the physician existed only for her, refusal to accept a disagreeable reality was far more difficult in the hospital, where she was in a semiopen ward.

We have space here only to discuss those findings that appear to justify the diagnosis of a pseudo-neurotic developmental disorder. In doing so we can start with the point just raised; namely, the intense dislike and jealousy aroused in Helga by triangular situations. She sought and fiercely defended against need satisfaction at almost every instinctual level, wishing total control over the object. But on Anna Freud's (1963) developmental line from egocentricity to companionship, Helga had hardly passed the initial stage in which a third person, another child, is seen as an intruder into a one-to-one relationship with the mother. Certainly Helga moved forward in other respects. Her rivalry with boys, for example, was based on a penis envy that had the usual narcissistic basis but that was compounded by a wholesale rivalry with a brother who Helga believed had displaced her and taken over her mother's love. Her penis envy retained the quality of the phallic-narcissistic phase—complicated for Helga by the persistence, with little modification, of the preoedipal phase. But there is no convincing evidence that she reached the phallic-oedipal phase; if she did its attainment must have been tenuous. Helga's thinly disguised heterosexuality defended against a diffuse homosexual constellation of wishes which meant she could sustain a relationship with a man only if he was prepared to adopt a mothering role.

Successful entry into the oedipal phase allows preoedipal trends to be integrated under an oedipal primacy that they serve to enrich. Objects begin to exist in their own right and relationships are characterized by some measure of altruism. But if the phase is not entered in a meaningful way, then the preoedipal components of instinctual life continue to exist alongside each other without appreciable modification, although ego defenses and defensive maneuvers of varying effectiveness continue to be active.

The pseudo-neurotic developmental group of disorders can only be distinguished from the neuroses proper through a careful anamnesis—if sufficient information is available. Unfortunately, the diagnosis usually cannot be made without intensive psychoanalytic scrutiny. Like other conditions, these cases vary in severity, but their diagnosis is frequently obscured by a high level of satisfactory functioning in many areas. Many such patients, for example, are very successful in their work or have high intellectual, scholastic, or artistic attainments. But on the personal level, their object relationships are often profoundly disturbed. Helga, for example, related to people only on a need-satisfying level and could only empathize with others through identification. Other characteristic features of pseudo-neurotic development include a pseudo-oedipal phase in which preceding instinctual phases persist to an unusual degree; a more or less continuing history of disturbance with partial instinctual arrests

rather than regressions; and a pronounced persistence of comparatively unmodified internal conflicts between activity/passivity, mas-
culinity/femininity, and ambivalence at every level, as well as between the component instincts of scopophilia/exhibitionism and sa-
domasochism. Naturally these conflicting trends are variously defended against, but conflict resolution and compromise is looser, less
structured, and far less well sustained than in the neuroses proper.
No two cases are alike, however.

Analytic evidence suggested that Helga's early life was disrupted
by discontinuity of care from a succession of au pairs. The hospital
admission and operation may also have complicated disturbed object
relationships already made worse by the birth of her brother. One
might regard the operation as a kind of last straw, an "organizer"
around which the mental illness became structured (Kennedy, 1986).
Kennedy traces the analysis of a very disturbed boy from the age of
thirteen to nineteen; this detailed study of a severe developmental
disorder is of relevance here, although Kennedy's patient was clearly
borderline. Helga showed some of the features of a patient described
elsewhere as suffering from a post-traumatic neurotic-like state
(Yorke, 1986), although the two cases differ sufficiently to underline
the range and variety of individuals that may be diagnosed as pseudo-
neurotic.

A relatively benign group of cases—in terms of pathology, that
is—can also be considered pseudo-neurotic developmental disorders.
On empirical grounds psychiatrists differentiate many of these states
from the neuroses by describing them as reactive depressions or adjustment reactions. In the vast majority of such cases the patient appears to have enjoyed good mental health before the attack. The symptoms lack coherence; they are labile and sensitive to environmental
influences—external events may lead either to their disappearance
or to their exacerbation. Often the symptoms, for example depression
of mood or anxiety, seem appropriate to the circumstances in which
they arise, except that they are exaggerations of normal affects. Even
when the symptoms are persistent they do not totally incapacitate the
patient as so frequently happens in established neuroses.

These individuals frequently attempt self-injury, generally
through drug overdose. The attempt is almost always preceded by a
disappointment, by the threat of loss of love, or by object loss. The
suicide attempt always substitutes for an earlier aggressive outburst
that failed to establish control over the love object or to satisfy a

particular need. Excessive consumption of alcohol commonly follows closely on the onset of the symptoms. Such patients tend to attribute responsibility for their mishaps to others. They allocate blame for the mental distress caused by the frustration of needs and the threat of loss of love.

The premorbid personality of many of these non-neurotic individuals appears to have been healthy. Before the onset of the illness they cannot easily be distinguished from mentally healthy people. They make permanent relationships and obtain satisfactions from activities of different kinds. A precipitating factor, an obvious external event, triggers every case. Investigation and treatment are often impeded by the fact that the symptoms rapidly disappear: relapse may quickly occur but does not do so invariably. Symptoms often disappear due to a change in circumstances, such as an admission to the hospital. Because of the sudden improvement, the patient often asks to be discharged. A disturbed early childhood is common to all the conditions described. Separation from the mother, seduction, and traumata of different kinds are commonplace. These events play a major role in creating the conditions for the development of a disordered or unstable personality.

Childhood and the Non-neurotic Developmental Disorders

We have referred to a number of cases of non-neurotic developmental disorders that at least superficially present well. The ego has, as it were, pursued a certain autonomy unenriched by appropriate drive maturation. But the presentation often disguises the shaky foundations on which the personality structure rests. How might such a case look if brought to professional attention in childhood? The case of Jeremy may be instructive in this respect.

Jeremy

At the age of ten and a half Jeremy was referred for psychiatric assessment. In light of the history taken at the time, it was surprising that he had not been referred earlier. Jeremy was adopted when only a few days old, when his adopted sister was a little over two. His parents showed little interest in him during his early life. His mother was depressed, his father overworked, and the marriage was faring badly. The parents showed more interest in the older child, who was charming, intelligent, and lively. The children were told early that they were adopted because "Mummy's tummy couldn't grow babies."

At first, Jeremy was an undemanding child, but he practiced head-banging from the age of one year onward. Later he engaged in battles over bedtime. Attempts at toilet training were begun at the age of eighteen months; but occasional soiling persisted until the time of referral. Early temper tantrums gradually became episodes of violence in which Jeremy destroyed his own possessions. These violent outburst were always occasioned by battles with his mother, father, or sister. He had only started to crawl at thirteen months and was slow to talk, though when he did begin he spoke in sentences. Between two and a half and three years old, he refused to eat anything handled by the au pair; very soon afterward he refused to use cutlery on the grounds that it carried the germs of former users. He ate messily and only with his fingers. He repeatedly showed concern over his adoption: on one occasion, for example, he asked if his biological mother hated him. These anxieties were brought to a head when, at the age of five, Jeremy was told that his adoptive mother was pregnant. He was bewildered and dismayed: after all, he argued to his mother, "babies can't grow in your tummy."

By this time, when Jeremy also had started school, all his symptoms were securely established. But for the most part *they remained confined to the home*. The destructive outburst continued but often gave way to periods of dreamy withdrawal. Occasionally his destruction of his own possessions spilled over into school, but the only recorded instances concerned his excellent artwork, which he tore up when it fell short of his expectations. His fussiness over food and "obsessional" symptoms were not in evidence at school. By and large he valued himself very poorly but was intensely competitive in a number of respects.

The persistence of Jeremy's symptoms from almost every level of development was striking—head-banging, soiling, and "obsessional" features. It was significant that these symptoms, including the outbursts of temper, were confined to the home, while at school Jeremy maintained a semblance of normality and some personal popularity, although his achievements fell well short of those to be expected from a boy with an IQ of 147. But Jeremy was a capable musician and a good swimmer and he showed some skill at conjuring. His self-esteem, however, was decidedly low; and his "friends" were boys whose intellects were inferior to his own.

Jeremy's symptoms persisted from almost every developmental phase, with the striking exception of the oedipal. Either he never entered the oedipal phase at all or his entry was tentative and tenuous and failed to provide instinctual dominance.

The organization of Jeremy's defenses was not very effective, though it operated better at school than at home. This suggests an instinctual tie to primary objects from which only superficial displacements have been made. Instinctual arousal in the presence of primary objects could have threatened the defenses in the home setting, leading to the symptoms' confinement within the family. The quality of Jeremy's object relations remained infantile and for all his skills and tentative sublimations, failed to achieve the true stamp of latency.

As for his superego, it was noted at assessment that Jeremy envied children who had no conscience. This seems to suggest an unduly strong superego; but in the absence of recognizable oedipal material it is more likely to reflect the ego's fear of punishment.

Jeremy's obsessional symptoms are of interest in light of these observations. The obsessional neurotic shows evidence of advanced ego and superego functioning. Jeremy's ego may further some adaptation at school, but otherwise ego and superego were not characteristic of the neurotic disorders (chapter 4). His fear of infection, for example, only involved damage to himself from the outside world, particularly his family; thus it was decidedly egocentric. On the other hand, his violence was defensively self-directed. The persistent head-banging directly involved his own body, though in other respects his violent behavior did not extend to his body, stopping short at his inanimate possessions.

It is impossible to say where further development will take Jeremy. But his case seems similar to that of many adults whose superficially good adjustment in the outside world conceals severe and widespread early arrests in maturational levels. Children's capacity for restoring reasonably favorable development, with or without treatment, is often good, and this factor may help to mitigate gloomy prognostications for Jeremy. Deviant development at one stage does not necessarily preclude a later shift toward normality. But an ego autonomy built on such uncertain foundations may lead such a child in the directions taken by the adult cases described above.

A Developmental Psychopathology

The individuals discussed in this section have in common personality defects disguised by a degree of ego autonomy. One patient suffers from transient defects in reality testing; in another primitive defenses are predominant; a third displays a limited capacity for anxiety tolerance, and the last poor superego development. Often more than one of these elements is present.

Fairbairn, Kohut, Guntrip, and Kernberg regard these disturbances in ego functioning not as the primary disorder but as secondary to a distinctive series of psychopathological events. These writers believe it possible, theoretically, to differentiate separate nosological entities within this heterogenous group—borderline personality organization, narcissistic disorders, and schizoid personality disorders (cf. Klein, 1946).

An alternative view is that these abnormal mental states differ from one another only with respect to the kinds of developmental anomalies that can be discerned within the personality of the patient. These anomalies may be explained on the basis of developmental disturbances, deviations, and disharmonies. For example, an inadequate response by the mother to an infant's instinctual needs creates dangers and external conflict. The consequences of such disharmony are most evident when structuralization is not sufficiently advanced to assimilate psychic pressures caused by external and internal stresses.

We may hypothesize, for example, that Helga's traumata occurred before the phase of object constancy was truly established. Such conditions, with their developmental delays, are unfortunate for those aspects of ego functioning that are dependent on adequate internalization of, and identification with, love objects. Ego development is thrown out of step with that of the instincts. Instinctual pressure then heightens external conflicts with intimate objects; and fear of loss of love and object loss becomes a persistent and almost expected danger that repeatedly attacks self-esteem.

By contrast, in Beatrice's development overstimulation became the source of disturbance and disharmony. This sort of anomaly cripples the ego and interferes with the establishment of the superego. An enduring solution to danger situations cannot be attained because the function of repression is impaired. The individuals described here did not resolve conflicts by a firm compromise as in anxiety hysteria.

Failure to achieve such structured compromises produces the labile character of these symptoms and the behavioral problems that are the rule in cases such as these.

The pathological narcissism that is more or less pronounced in all these cases can be explained on the basis of disharmonious development. Autoerotism, intensified by emotional deprivation or over-stimulation in the first months of life (Greenson, 1955), overshadows the process whereby objects reach adequate instinctual investment. The adverse consequences of this lack of concordance are countered by the synthetic tendency, which, as it were, seeks to make good the absence of a satisfying love object without suffering the effects of the loss. The synthetic tendency leads the individual to identify with the frustrating and disappointing object, providing a focus for the libidinal cathexis. This process heightens narcissism. These identifications, as illustrated above, produce symptoms and behavioral difficulties, including sexual deviation (e.g., homosexuality: Freeman, 1963).

A disharmonious or deviant development is not unique to the heterogenous conditions described in this chapter. Disharmony may help create the conditions for the emergence of a neurosis but may not be so pronounced as to lead to an arrest or distortion of ego and superego development. When this does happen it is difficult to sustain the diagnosis of a neurosis. In the psychoses the ego and superego are particularly fragile. Can this fragility be attributed to a disharmonious development? Later we will attempt to show how the concept of disharmony helps us understand why certain individuals become vulnerable to schizophrenic and manic-depressive psychoses, which are in part biologically caused.

Although developmental factors play a predisposing part in all neuroses and psychoses, it seems appropriate to call the disturbances under discussion non-neurotic developmental disorders to emphasize their essential unity. They include cases in which the personality has always been characterized by inadequate ego and superego development, as well as cases in which the personality appears superficially sound before an acute trauma or before the onset of sustained disappointments and frustrations. For all that, it is important to draw a clear distinction, on both descriptive and metaphychological grounds, between these disorders and neuroses and psychoses.

CHAPTER 7 Contemporary Theories of Schizophrenic and Paranoid Psychoses

Freud and Contemporary Theories

Recent writers have drawn attention to passages in Freud's writings on schizophrenic and paranoid psychoses that indicate he far from wholeheartedly espoused a theory implying continuity between psychoses and neuroses (London, 1973; Katan, 1979). According to London, Freud (1911b, 1915b) entertained the possibility that the process of decathexis of objects not only serves a defensive function but is part of what London has called a *psychological deficiency state* involving a disturbance of object representations. London proposed that we can identify within the classical framework a general, unitary theory emphasizing the metapsychological identity existing between the schizophrenias and the neuroses and a specific theory postulating that the psychoses have their own unique source of disturbance.

Most authors have based their own theories of schizophrenia on either the unitary or the specific theory. Some have taken elements of both theories and attempted to make a synthesis of them. London's contribution is twofold. First, he distinguishes between these two theoretical positions, unitary and specific, as taken up by different authors. Second, he points out that the value of a theory lies in its capacity to organize the clinical phenomena and to extend the field of observation. Contemporary theorists have had no difficulty with the first but have failed lamentably with the second. London believes

that this is because the majority of psychoanalytic writers on schizophrenia have overextended their theoretical concepts, forcing their
clinical observations to fit a particular theoretical framework.

Many male patients who are diagnosed as suffering from schizophrenia, schizophreniform psychosis, and paranoid psychosis present initially with the delusion of being persecuted by a person of the
same sex who is or was known to them. In women the persecutor is
usually, though not invariably, of the same sex. The delusion of persecution may continue unaltered over a long period without the development of new content or changes in the cognitive functions. Or it
may recur after remissions, as illustrated by the case of Michael (below). In another, larger group of cases the delusion of persecution is
followed by new delusions and hallucinations, as in the case of Joan
(below). The Schreber case, which Freud (1911b) employed to illustrate his theory of persecutory paranoia or *paranoid psychosis* (Forrest, 1973), belongs to this group.

Schreber's psychosis began with the delusion that he was to be
emasculated and sexually abused as a woman by his former physician, Flesching. This was the stage of persecutory paranoia. Later
Schreber believed that God had entrusted him with a divine mission
and that to accomplish this he must change into a woman. Schreber
believed that he had developed breasts and female genitalia, that
divine rays, sent by God, would impregnate him; and that he would
give birth to a new race of men. He nevertheless endured much suffering from God's treatment of him in the course of this process—the
stage of *dementia paranoides*. Schreber's intellectual powers remained largely intact, enabling him to write the account of his nervous illness.

In a letter to Karl Abraham, Freud (1907) expressed his long-
standing indebtedness to Hughlings Jackson's theory of the evolution
and dissolution of the nervous system (1884). In his discussion of the
Schreber case, Freud described the psychoses as the "expression" of
a loss of advanced mental functions, on the one hand, and an attempt
to "make good" these losses, on the other. These attempts to regain
what had been lost are governed by the nature and form of the mental
functions remaining intact after the impact of the morbid process.
Freud (1911b, 1917) regarded Schreber's delusions of persecution by
Flesching as reflecting this process of restitution. The delusion was
not to be confused with the morbid process itself, whose effect was
to be found in the loss of developmental achievements.

Freud (1911b) identified the morbid process in its psychological expression as a form of repression. The mental representation of a homosexual love object—Flesching in the case of Schreber—lost its libidinal cathexis. The withdrawn libido returned to the self, leading to grandiose wish-fulfilling delusions. Basing his theory of paranoia on that of the neuroses, Freud envisaged the persecutory delusion as caused by a return of the repressed libido to the love object. The repressed homosexual wish reappeared in altered form: hatred had taken the place of love. This unconscious homosexual wish of the paranoiac is entirely different from the sexual wish of the manifest or latent homosexual (Frosch, 1983). One form of homosexuality, in man or woman, enacts the role of the active preoedipal mother with a love object representing the childhood self (Freeman, 1963). The male paranoic unconsciously wishes to act the part of a woman, fulfilling passive sexual aims in a relationship with a man. The paranoic woman follows a reciprocal course in enacting the role of a man. The passive-feminine wishes of the male paranoiac are clearly different from the passive sexual behavior of those male homosexuals whose aim is to acquire the masculinity of their active partners.

Schreber regained relations by means of projection. Hatred that was not perceived within as such found expression as an external perception. Instead of hating, Schreber believed that he was hated by Flesching. Freud (1911b) regarded projection as the principal mechanism in persecutory paranoia (paranoid psychosis) whereby contact with Flesching was restored in the process of restitution. The additional delusional material appearing in such cases and in established cases of schizophrenia has a different aim. A distinction should be drawn between the concepts of restitution (Freud, 1911b, 1917) and reconstruction (remodeling, Freud, 1924). In the former (see the case of Michael), a relationship is restored despite the pathological form it assumes; whereas in the latter (the case of Erica, below), the aim is reconstruction of the self and external reality.

The far-reaching dissolution of mental life occurring in schizophrenia was also attributed by Freud (1911b) to repression, which caused a widespread withdrawal of libido from the mental representations of reality. The movement to repair what had been damaged was less effective in schizophrenia than in persecutory paranoia because of the particularly elementary nature of the mental processes left intact by the morbid process. These less advanced forms of mental function—for example, primitive forms of abstract thought, perception, and motility—determine the mode of expression of the "return of the repressed" and not projection as in persecutory paranoia (Freud, 1911b).

Freud's introduction of his structural concepts in 1923 did not radically alter the existing theory. In psychoses, relations between the ego and reality are disrupted. Though he no longer described the means of this disruption as repression, Freud (1924) adhered to his earlier view that paranoid and schizophrenic types of psychosis are initiated by a withdrawal of cathexis from the object in the face of a danger situation. The course of the illness and its clinical characteristics depend on the balance struck between the forces promoting the decathexis of objects and the dissolution of adult mental life, on the one hand, and the pressure exerted by the libidinal wishes seeking to recathect the object, on the other. The closer the libidinal cathexes come to the rejected piece of reality, the more intense anxiety becomes. The reconstruction is therefore strenuously opposed by the forces that initiated the decathexis and led to repression.

The Prepsychotic versus the Psychotic Phase

Katan (1974, 1975, 1979), though a lifelong advocate of Freud's theory, has suggested that decathexis and restitution are not the processes leading to the symptomatology of schizophrenic and paranoid psychoses. Katan believed that a clear view of symptom formation in schizophrenic and paranoid psychoses has been obscured by a failure to distinguish between the prepsychotic and psychotic phases of the illness. As long as the prepsychotic phase continues, ego functioning is maintained and the content of unacceptable wishes remains repressed. Freud's model of symptom formation—repression and the return of the repressed—fully explains the clinical phenomena that characterize the prepsychotic phase, but it is inappropriate once the break with reality occurs.

Katan has demonstrated that the contents of acute psychotic attacks give expression to the conflicts repressed during the prepsychotic phase. The transformation of these unconscious wish fantasies into the content of delusions and hallucinations follows from regression to what Katan (1979) describes as the undifferentiated state. Here the distinction between self and objects is lost, at least in part; past and present no longer exist. The loss of the ego organization allows the primary process to recast the content of the prepsychotic fantasies and simultaneously alter the form in which the content finds expression. What was formerly part of the patient's mind becomes part of the outside world (primary projection; Katan, 1974).

Freud's theory (1911b, 1924) claims that decathexis (repression) initiates the psychotic attack. This is unacceptable to Katan, who came to believe that the presence of a repressing agency, even if described as "psychotic repression" to distinguish it from "neurotic repression," implies that an ego is operative—even if it is disorganized by the morbid process. The fact that the primary process determines the form and content of delusions and hallucinations from the moment of the break with reality signifies that the ego is no longer an effective psychic structure. This loss of the ego involves the complete breakdown of repression. Like Freud, Katan follows Hughlings Jackson in asserting that advanced mental functions must be lost before elementary mental processes can exert their influence.

Katan (1979) has revived the criticisms of Freud's theory made by Federn (1953) and Schilder (1939). If decathexis is followed by the libido's return to the self, then grandiose delusions should be a feature of all acute psychotic attacks. However, the great majority of psychotic attacks commence with persecutory, not grandiose, delusions. The latter *occasionally* precede or accompany the persecutory manifestations, but it is more common to find grandiose delusions later in the course of schizophrenic psychoses. It was Federn's view that a diminution, rather than an increase, of the libidinal cathexis of the self is the precondition for the onset of a schizophrenic psychosis.

In Freud's theory the persecutor and his activities give expression to the return of the repressed. Although altered in nature, the libidinal wish has found its way back to the love object. Repressed childhood memories and fantasies provide material for the remodeling (reconstruction) of reality (Freud, 1924). This restructuring takes place through projections and hallucinations. Anxiety is a constant feature because of the active pressure of the repressed. Katan takes an opposite view. He believes that the persecutory delusion does not represent the repressed and/or act as a means of restitution; rather, it comes into being in order to prevent the overt expression of libidinal, homosexual wishes that can no longer be countered by the defenses of the prepsychotic phase.

The purpose of the persecutory delusion is to halt the development of genital excitement that would lead to masturbation. This act would signify fulfillment of the woman's wish for masculinity and the man's wish for femininity. The persecutor is so constructed (through primary projection) as to be an object of hate and fear instead of one that evokes sexual excitement. This process occurs as soon as the structural regression to the undifferentiated state takes place. There is no question here of the delusion acting to restore a lost object cathexis (restitution).

The loss of the ego and the return to the undifferentiated state disrupt the continuity between past and present. The prepsychotic phase, like a neurosis, is initiated by a danger situation. The danger arises when a contemporary love object, real or fantasied, assumes the significance of a homosexual object of childhood, with all the accompanying fantasies and affects (Katan, 1979). The defenses operating in the prepsychotic phase attempt to dissipate the danger evoked by the wish to repeat a real or fantasied encounter with the childhood object. Once regression occurs to the undifferentiated state in which there is no longer any distinction between self and object, present and past, the contemporary love object ("a spontaneous transference figure") loses its connection with the love object of childhood. There is no longer any bridge (Katan, 1979) between current experiences and those of childhood. The fact that persecutors have childhood love objects as their prototypes does not invalidate this view. Frosch (1983) is also of this opinion.

In the undifferentiated state, childhood and contemporary object relationships continue to exist, but they are subject to primary process. The contents of the delusional ideas can be used to demonstrate the childhood origin of the persecutor, but the persecutor is no longer a "transference" figure. Referring to Schreber's prepsychotic phase, Katan (1975) says that in this stage, when reality orientation was as yet unimpaired, "Flesching was indeed a transference figure representing the brother ... [but] as soon as the transference relationship led to a genital stimulation the ego dissolved itself. With this dissolution of the reality ego a regression to the undifferentiated state took place" (p. 370). Through the regression the transference situation ceased to exist. ... the chain of events, as I have just described it, beginning with transference feelings for Flesching ended with the formation of a persecutory delusion, Flesching being the persecutor. Through this delusion Schreber tried to prevent an eventual transference situation involving Flesching leading to a genital stimulation. With the regression to the undifferentiated state, the phallic wish-fulfilling fantasies that Katan believes constitute the essence of the danger situation are torn from their childhood roots and through primary projection become aspects of the persecutor.

Owing to circumstances beyond his control, Katan was unable to discover how far his theory would accommodate the different types of schizophrenic psychosis (1979). He therefore made use of the cases Freud employed to illustrate his theory of decathexis and restitution (1911b, 1915b). Two cases were unmarried women (Freud, 1915a, b) who complained of being persecuted by men with whom they had love relationships. Using the delusional and hallucinatory content, Katan (1975, 1979) was able to show that these women, in the prepsychotic phase, had engineered a sexual encounter in order to acquire the means of fulfilling a phallic childhood fantasy. Each woman excited her lover to erection (Katan, 1975, 1979), and by masturbating him satisfied her voyeurism. The fantasized incorporation of this visual symbol of masculinity led to clitoral orgasm. In each case, the woman identified with her lover's "superiority" (Katan, 1979), but the fulfillment of this wish now brought guilt and fear of retribution. Regression to the undifferentiated state followed, and displacement erased recollections of the sexual encounter.

The hatred that Freud's patients (1915a, b) came to feel for their former lovers was sufficient to inhibit further genital, homosexual excitement. The delusional, damaging behavior of the lovers represented the patients' wish to be castrated, altered by the primary process and the primary projection.

The sexual activity these patients engaged in before their psychotic attacks aimed not only at defending against an unconscious homosexuality derived from the preoedipal relationship with the mother, as Freud (1915b) believed, but also at furthering an active homosexual aim. This unconscious intention caused one of Freud's patients to become jealous of her lover's contact with a beloved older female colleague. Their homosexual wishes made these women envy their lovers' masculinity.

Freud's female patients selected by Katan to illustrate his theory suffered from the type of schizophrenic disorder in which the persecutor is of the opposite sex. In these cases the persecutor was a former lover. However, the male persecutor in this type of psychosis is not usually known personally to the patient. At best he is an acquaintance, doctor, dentist, or clergyman. Are such cases amenable to explanation in terms of the concepts of Katan's theory?

Erica

Erica, an unmarried woman of twenty-one, complained that she was being pestered by a young man who had been in her class at university. Although she had only a passing acquaintance with him, she believed he was sending messages to her through the television set. He said that he was in love with her and wanted sexual intercourse in spite of her refusal. In revenge for her rejection, he was telling everyone that they had been sexually intimate. She believed that he had forced her to have sexual intercourse against her will. He had committed an "inhuman act." He stopped her from sleeping and during the day made her dizzy and forgetful. In spite of all this Erica knew that the young man loved her, and and if he did not present himself in person it was because his mother objected to their relationship. She reported that his mother (whom in fact she had never met) had humiliated her. When sitting in a restaurant with her parents, she had heard his mother say, "Take off your pants." She was sure that everyone else in the restaurant had heard this, and she rushed outside in a state of embarrassment.

Erica, a tall, attractive, friendly young woman, was worried by all these experiences. She believed that the young man had loved her when they were in the same class, but she had ignored him. She knew that he had been consumed by sexual desire—for his face had revealed it. She discovered that a female student with whom she was friendly had allowed him to have intercourse with her to relieve his frustration. He was punishing Erica now because of her indifference to him and his needs. During the acute attack she was convinced that whatever was happening to her was also happening to him. She believed that he had made himself mentally ill through masturbating. She also said that they were mentally and physically alike—"He looks like me, tall with fair hair, he has a big round face [like herself] and gives you a long look; I find myself doing that."

Her mother reported that in the months preceding the acute attack Erica had lost her usual cheerfulness and had become irritable. She stopped confiding in her mother as she had formerly done. When the psychosis began she was living away from home. In the previous year she had kept company with a young man, not the persecutor, but had given him up because, she had told her mother, he wanted to have intercourse with her. At no time did the patient tell the psychiatrist about this relationship.

Erica complained that she had been betrayed and oppressed physically and mentally by the man she believed loved her. Later she concluded that his mother had come between them because she was jealous. Katan's theory allows us to draw a connection between the two elements of the delusional content. The operation of primary project in the undifferentiated state means that in the prepsychotic phase (beginning during her real love relationship), it was the patient who was jealous. Erica wanted to betray her real lover, to tell his mother about their lovemaking and cause her to turn against him. It was she who was in a state of sexual excitement, who had committed an "inhuman act." Now, with the onset of the psychosis, both the young man and his mother became objects of fear and hatred and not of sexual attraction.

As the patient scarcely knew the young persecutor and his mother, they must have been substitutes for the real boyfriend and his mother. Katan's theory would suggest that Erica's sexual encounters with her real boyfriend had evoked a clitoral excitability along with a homosexual fantasy with the mother as the object. Instead of the boyfriend's pressing her to engage in coitus, as she alleged, it was she who had wished to play the active part. By doing so, she could excite him and bring him to erection. She now completed her identification with him. Such an active wish could explain her accusation that the young persecutor had forced her to have intercourse. Was it her wish to seize his penis, and was this the "inhuman act" she claimed he had inflicted on her? Throughout, her behavior toward her real boyfriend could be regarded as a design to reach the woman through the man.

This reconstruction of the prepsychotic phase is supported by what is known of Erica's personality prior to her illness. She never wanted to play second fiddle to a man. Throughout her childhood she had wished to be a boy. She played boys' games, and her competitiveness found a satisfactory outlet in games at which she excelled. According to her mother, as a young child she was envious and jealous of her only brother, two years younger than herself. Erica herself had said that she hated her brother: "I never wanted him." Later her attitude changed and she became protective toward him. During a disturbed phase of her illness Erica made some disconnected references to doctor games that she had played with her brother and to seeing an erect penis. It is reasonable to assume that she had pronounced phallic fixations. She harbored a persistent, actively homosexual wish for her mother and she desired to take the brother's place—that is, the father's—with the mother. Was this the childhood prototype of the prepsychotic conflict and the delusional content?

Erica's psychotic ideas continued intermittently over a period of two or three years and then disappeared, only to be followed by new persecutory anxieties. Erica now claimed that a man who owned a trucking business next door to her father's office, where she did a little work, had punished two of his young male employees in a particularly horrible manner. He had stripped them of their clothes, bundled them into an open truck, and driven them around the town for everyone to see. Erica feared that he was going to do this to her. Sometimes she tried to explain these fears. She thought she had always known about such punishment for misdeeds, which parents inflicted on children, usually boys, who were disobedient. Sometimes it was done to a young man the night before his wedding.

Erica was frightened that her parents wanted to get rid of her and said, "They think I should find a man and get married." She was worried because she could not find a man, and she had the impression that people she met in the street thought her odd because she was single. Over the succeeding months she periodically hallucinated a young female neighbor's voice shouting, "Go away,"; "you are not wanted"; "take her away." She knew this woman fairly well and had played badminton with her and her husband.

Some of this later material could be understood to favor the reconstruction described above—the wish for masculinity. Erica's belief that she was odd because she was unmarried and her fear that she would be rejected by her parents for being single suggests that she harbored doubts and fears about her heterosexuality. If her delusional fear of being displayed naked to the populace were the outcome of a projection, then an unconscious wish to humiliate young men because of her rivalry with them could also have been involved. At the same time, as a man, Erica must suffer the punishment inflicted on men because of their misdeeds. The content of the hallucinatory voices indicated that her presence was an offense to everyone. Were these criticisms a result of bad conscience springing from her criminal castration wishes?

Topographic Regression and Its Consequences

Katan (1974, 1979) postulates that the hallucinations occur in schizophrenic and paranoid psychoses when mounting sexual excitement is denied genital expression. This theory rests on Freud's concept of *topographic regression*, according to which a drive that is unable to gain access to motility through the system preconscious regresses to the sensory end of the mental apparatus to cathect the memory traces of percepts and sensations (1900). Katan proposes (although not explicitly) that hallucinatory phenomena depend on topographic regression to the undifferentiated state in which the primary process governs the distribution of drive cathexes. Katan's theory has explanatory value in cases such as the following: Joan, an unmarried woman of forty-five, bitterly complained that the medical superintendent of the hospital in which she was a patient caused her to experience tingling sensations on the inside of her thighs. This happened, she said, when the doctor touched his penis to masturbate. According to Katan's theory, Joan's own wish to masturbate was blocked, topographic regression occurred, activating memory traces of sensations associated with genital arousal. Joan's attention was thus diverted from the genitalia themselves to another representative, part of her body. Her sense of outrage destroyed any possibility that the love object might act as a source of sexual excitement.

For the most part schizophrenic hallucinations appear in the auditory modality. Does Katan's theory accommodate these manifestations? The following case allows us to examine this question.

Maura

Maura, a married woman of thirty-five, said that a colleague at work, a widow of fifty-five with whom she had been friendly, was spreading malicious tales about her. She had trusted this woman and confided in her. She now believed the woman was maligning her, accusing her of promiscuity and readiness to have sexual intercourse with any man. In particular she alleged that Maura had designs on a senior male colleague with whom both women were friendly.

One day, after talking to this man, Maura heard him telling other people that she had "stripped him with her eyes." She thought he must be joking but soon realized that he meant what he said. Clearly, he believed she wanted to touch his penis. After this event Maura's female colleague had become even more outrageous in her accusations. She said, to the men in the office, "You like her because she's like that." Maura concluded that the older woman acted in this way because she was jealous of the attentions the men paid Maura.

Soon afterward Maura thought she heard announcers on the television and radio say, "She is like that." She believed she was being treated like a criminal. Unpleasant sexual and sadistic thoughts forced themselves into her mind: "I didn't want to talk about them," she said; "when I see a man I think he's got an erection." In the psychiatric hospital, Maura reported that while sitting and talking to a woman doctor she suddenly had the fantasy of sticking a knife into her, accompanied by an exciting, vicious feeling. Maura was acutely distressed by these ideas and emotions. One evening when she was at home, she was sure she heard the television announcer mention contraception, referring to girls of sixteen or nineteen. "I did not want my son to hear," she said. "I was pregnant before I married and I was nineteen."

Maura's illness remitted after a year, but three years later she again entered the psychiatric hospital. After her discharge she had obtained work, holding the post for two years. She gave up her job because she felt tired and "out of sorts." After six months of unemployment she found work as a waitress in a restaurant, where she worked until four months before readmission. Shortly after starting to work in the restaurant, she developed the idea that her colleagues were too inquisitive. A little while later she began to hear, when alone or in company, voices belonging to people she used to know. She could not recall what the voices said, but it was sometimes pleasant, sometimes distressing. Sometimes the voice was that of a man; at other times, that of a woman. The voices came from outside her. Maura said she was particularly distressed by the voices of two men who called her a "fucker." They told their names and where they lived. One of the men jeered at her, saying that she had messed up her bed by masturbating. Sometimes the men apologized and claimed that they were forced to speak to her as they did.

In the hospital Maura felt herself the object of criticism. If another patient passed by she heard a critical comment, but she was sure it was not the patient herself but someone else using her voice. At times she had the opinion that others were using her own voice to insult her.

Maura said that she heard the voice of a boyfriend with whom she had kept company at the same time that she was going out with her future husband. She had had sexual intercourse with both men. It was only when she discovered she was pregnant that she decided to accept her husband's offer of marriage. The former boyfriend, a policeman, now appeared to be trying to protect her from a man called Fowler, who knew everything about Maura's life. The boyfriend said that Fowler was foul-mouthed. Then she heard a voice saying, "You know you fuck things, Fowler." From then on she heard other patients calling her Fowler. Fowler's voice became threatening. He said he would rip her genitals open during intercourse; he would tear her to pieces. Maura believed that her former boyfriend had fallen ill because he was similarly oppressed by Fowler's voice. She began to complain of visual hallucinations: her own naked body, her son's penis, her own genitals. Unknown voices commented on her actions, and one of them told her to cut her throat. She tried but could not do so, and her anxiety and distress deepened. These hallucinatory phenomena dominated Maura's attention for many months, and it was impossible to obtain any other material from her. As the hallucinations weakened she wanted to go home and was released from the hospital. When seen subsequently she refused to talk about herself.

On the occasion of Maura's first admission to hospital she had made it clear that her marriage was less than satisfactory. Her husband, several years older than she, was a quiet, retiring man who was content to stay at home after work. She had found domestic work dull, and when her children were old enough to go to nursery school she began full-time work. She found her life boring and would have liked to get out in the evening. However, Maura never expressed this discontent to her husband. A year before her psychosis began she had suffered from frequent micturition and a burning sensation in her genitals. No bacteriological cause was found for these symptoms. Some six months previously she and her husband had given up the use of condoms as a means of contraception and had begun to practice coitus interruptus. Maura found this unsatisfying but did not complain. There is every reason to believe her masturbatory conflict and fears of being unfaithful began at this time.

According to Katan's theory, Maura's auditory hallucinations would have provided a means of discharge for sexual excitation that would otherwise have led to a masturbatory wish with a homosexual content. The wish would involve the desire to seize a man's penis and then to rape a woman. In the first phase of the illness this content was confined to the delusion that Maura's senior male colleague wanted her to touch his penis. To support his theory, Katan would also have referred to the voices surrounding the name *Fowler*. This would support the hypothesis that the persecutor (Fowler) represented Maura's wished-for masculinity. The hallucinatory threat made by Fowler to rip her open in intercourse expressed her wish to play the role of the man in sadistic coitus with herself as woman. By attributing her sadistic fantasies to Fowler she was able to hate him.

Maura's illness first involved a persecutor of the same sex. But this delusion soon vanished, and eventually the clinical picture was characterized by hallucinations. Unlike cases in which the production of a permanent persecutor destroys the perceptual basis for homosexual excitement, hallucinations at best can only temporarily reduce the danger created by sexual wishes arising from within (Katan, 1979). In Maura's case the memory traces of phrases with an unpleasant sexual connotation took the place of clitoral excitement. If Katan is right, it follows that in cases such as this the hallucinatory phenomena continue while the danger of giving way to masturbatory fantasies persists. This hypothesis is supported by the clinical observation that patients whose psychosis is of a predominantly hallucinatory nature do not habitually and persistently complain that they are persecuted by someone they knew before the onset of the psychosis.

Critical or abusive auditory hallucinations are usually attributed to a superego that has been subjected to regression and to externalization. Katan's theory suggests an entirely different origin for hallucinations of this kind: they are derivatives of instinct that have found pathological expression in the auditory modality. Katan holds that the superego disappears once regression to the undifferentiated state has taken place. The opposition to instinct gratification arises not from guilt but from primitive elements in the psychic constitution—from anxiety generated by fears of retribution for the psychic fulfillment of wishes belonging to the phallic phase of sexual development.

Loss of Differentiation between Self and Object

In attributing a decisive role to phallic (homosexual) conflicts in the genesis of schizophrenic and paranoid psychoses, Katan generalizes Freud's homosexual theory of paranoia to the whole range of these conditions. In doing so he ignores Freud's (1911b) doubts about the significance that should be given to instinctual derivatives as initiators of the process of symptom formation. Federn (1953) was the first writer to propose the alternative theory at which Freud hinted: namely, that a defense against instinct may play only a secondary role. It was Federn's opinion that the early symptoms of schizophrenia are caused by diminution in the cathexis of the ego.[1] With the loss of the ego boundary ideas and percepts are no longer distinguishable and reality becomes falsified. The weakening of the ego cathexis rather than a defense against instinct was instrumental in leading to a schizophrenic psychosis. While signs of conflict might be detected, the psychotic symptoms are not the result of a defense. Federn (1953) considered the psychosis itself to be not a defense but a "defeat." It is the defeat of an ego no longer able to defend itself against the impact of instinctual demands, the requirements of external reality, and the conflicts derived from them.

Bak (1971) also defends the view that the instinctual conflicts discernible in the content of delusions and hallucinations are at best contributory and nonspecific. Bak bases his argument on the form the clinical phenomena assume rather than on the content. In this he makes common ground with Katan (1979). While both writers trace the formal aspects of delusional and hallucinatory phenomena to the dissolution of the ego organization, agreement ends there. The homosexual conflict given prominence by Katan, Bak regards as a consequence and not the cause of the disintegration of psychic structures.

In attributing the basic disturbance in schizophrenic psychoses to damage to object representations, Bak has amplified Federn's (1953) theory of a loss of ego cathexis. However, the loss of cathexis, whether aggressive, libidinal, or neutralized, cannot alone initiate the morbid process: object representations must also be rendered defective. Bak therefore postulates a developmental fault to account for the vulnerability of the object representations. This vulnerability has its origins in an exaggeration of the normal tendency during development for individuals to draw on their self-representations as material for the construction of object representations. This exaggeration predisposes one to homosexual object choice—the individual selects someone like him- or herself or as he or she wishes to be. Here Bak merely repeats Freud's explanation of why the homosexual conflict appears in cases of persecutory paranoia—namely, that predisposed individuals choose love objects on a narcissistic basis.

Bak does not take the homosexual content of persecutory delusions as the starting point for his theory of symptom formation. Instead he begins with the prodromal or prepsychotic symptoms. These

----

1. Federn's use of the term *ego* is idiosyncratic. It is given "boundaries" and comes close to the concept of the *self* or *self-representation* but is not identical with it. Federn never defined this term with precision.

phenomena—withdrawal, hypochondriasis, and inappropriate sexual and aggressive behavior—are to be understood as signs of an impending dissolution of object representations and the emergence of an undifferentiated state. Neither the prodromal signs nor those of the established illness—transitivism, delusional perception, and "end-of-the-world" delusions—are caused by the homosexual conflict expressed manifestly or latently in the delusions.

Bak, following Freud (1911b), explains the delusional reality as the outcome of a recathexis of objects, all of which represent aspects of the patient's physical and mental self (see also Frosch, 1983). Bak thus again takes issue with Katan (1979) by asserting that the psychotic reality is the outcome of a reconstruction and is not the result of (primary process) reactions designed to arrest and deflect masturbatory excitement. The anxiety that is such a striking feature of established schizophrenia is not, in Bak's opinion, a response to an instinctual (homosexual) danger but a reaction to the threat posed to the integrity of psychic structure.

Bak contends that the homosexual conflict found in schizophrenic psychoses is an expression of faulty development and a sequel to a disturbance in object representations (loss of object cathexis). He suggests that affective elements other than those associated with sexuality may initiate symptom formation. Such a possibility is not at odds with the view, based on abundant evidence, that prior to the onset of psychosis patients are disturbed by fantasies and conflicts of a phallic nature. However, these wish fantasies and the conflicts they provoke remain repressed until the moment of the break with reality. The case of Michael can be taken as an illustration.

Michael

Michael, a twenty-year-old single man, was admitted to the hospital for acutely disturbed speech and behavior. Shortly after arriving he attacked a male nurse because Michael thought he was making sexual advances. Later Michael claimed that other people were implying he was homosexual. He believed that his brother was forcing him to have homosexual thoughts. It was his brother, said Michael, who was responsible for all the talk about homosexuality.

Michael's brother, whom he very much admired and looked up to, was seven years older than he. In recent months, however, Michael had come to the conclusion that his brother envied him. He noticed that his brother followed him everywhere, had taken to dressing as he did, and copied his gestures and manner. He began to suspect that his brother was homosexual and was trying to undermine Michael's masculinity. Michael also believed that his brother intended to seduce their sister and to get Michael out of the way so that he could inherit the family property after their father's death.

As the persecutory ideas disappeared, Michael became low-spirited and self-critical. Instead of hating and fearing his brother, he worried about him and became concerned for his health. He compared himself adversely with his brother and criticized himself for being envious of him. Michael's psychotic attack had begun shortly after his brother announced his engagement to be married.

Michael's brother was his ideal and he wished to be like him. In health he had gained a vicarious satisfaction from his brother's success at work and with women. The brother's announcement of his engagement threatened this relationship, leading to envy that had been repressed until the onset of the psychosis, when it led to the first symptoms of the illness: the wish delusions. Michael believed that, like his brother, he was extraordinarily handsome and attractive to women, several of whom wanted to have sexual relationships with him. The persecutory ideas soon followed.

In Michael's case, envy, jealousy, and hatred were provoked by a threat to an incestuous object relationship. A dissolution of psychic structures followed, in accordance with Bak's view. The content of Michael's delusions suggests that a repressed wish for femininity was present in the prepsychotic phase. Once the ego had been subject to dissolution, this wish for femininity found expression, with resulting anxiety. Healthy envy leading to the wish to seize his brother's masculinity was kept within bounds until the impending marriage threatened Michael's relationship with the brother—his narcissistic object choice. While this formulation recognizes the presence of phallic conflicts, it relegates them to a secondary position. They found expression in the content of the persecutory delusions only when the former mental representation of the brother suffered from the impact of these events, leaving only jealousy and envy.

Models of Schizophrenia as Neurosis

Implicit in the theories of Federn and Katan is the concept of a psychological deficiency or deficit that manifests itself whenever the vulnerable individual is subject to an affective stress (the specific theory of schizophrenias; London, 1973). In contrast, some conceptualizations take the theory of neurosis, with its concept of instinctual conflict and defense, as their model (the unitary theory of schizophrenia). One such theory is proposed by the followers of Melanie Klein (Rosenfeld, 1954; Bion, 1967). They criticize the libidinal orientation of Freud's theory and assert that a primary role should be given to the derivatives of the death instinct and the measures employed to deal with them. Schizophrenic symptoms are substitutes for pathological infantile (psychotic) conflicts. There is, therefore, no break between past and present in cases of schizophrenia, as the "specific" theorists believe. This temporal continuity makes possible a transference psychosis analogous to the transference neurosis.

Envy, which the Kleinian psychoanalysts believe is the earliest expression of the death instinct, plays a primary role in initiating as well as creating the predisposition to schizophrenic psychoses. In the case described above, Michael complained of his brother's envy. According to the Kleinian theory, the patient would have established his brother as an ideal object prior to his illness. In so doing he would have split off the bad, destructive objects with which part of his ego was identified from the good part of his ego. His latent envy of his brother, inherent in the bad self-object, manifested itself upon the brother's success in winning a bride. The patient greedily wanted his brother's masculinity and procreative powers (the penis) for himself. The first result of incorporating (introjecting) the ideal object was the phase of grandiosity. This was soon ruined by envy, which attacked and spoiled the ideal object. The ruined ideal object could not be kept apart from the bad object with whom the self was identified. A serious danger was created by this failure of splitting, and the resulting terror of internal persecution and destruction of the ego led to externalization of the bad object into the brother (projective identification). Through this process the brother was turned into a dangerous criminal. Simultaneously Michael feared the brother's projections. Hence the brother was trying to turn Michael into a criminal and a woman (that is, to take away his penis, as Michael had castrated his brother out of envy).

According to Kleinian theory, the predisposition to such an illness is formed by an abnormal development of the infantile paranoid-schizoid position that occurs when there is too much envy of the breast-penis and too much hatred. Perception of the ideal object (breast-penis) is unbearable. Instead of projective identification, in conjunction with splitting, differentiating good from bad objects and good from bad aspects of the self, it takes a pathological form. Damaging projections, influenced by the envy and hatred, are directed against the ideal object and the means whereby it is perceived. This process assuages the mental pain provoked by perception of reality. The perceptual ego, as well as the introjected ideal object, is fragmented and projected into an object splintered by the action of projective identification. The infant now perceives reality as filled with destructive and damaging fragments (*bizarre objects*, Bion, 1967) composed of bits of the ego and the object. Ego development is weakened. Sometimes the potential for a degree of healthy ego development is preserved by splitting it off and isolating the bizarre objects. When envy is provoked in later years, as in the case of Michael, the individual regresses to the pathological paranoid-schizoid position of infancy. The psychotic attack follows the revival of this stance with the emergence of the bizarre objects, which are felt as threatening and destructive. Somewhat similar views have been proposed by Grotstein (1977) and Ogden (1980).

The prevalence of destructive and sadistic content in many cases of schizophrenia appears to add weight to the Kleinian claim that libidinal, particularly homosexual, wishes constitute a defensive reaction against pregenital sadistic wish fantasies directed against the parent of the same sex (Klein, 1932). The homosexual conflict therefore is not of primary importance in the formation of persecutory delusions. The example of Maura is representative of cases in which fears of being physically and mentally destroyed dominate the clinical presentation. Did this woman's psychosis begin when envy and jealousy of her male and female colleagues provoked destructive attacks on the combined breast-penis (the combined parental figures in coitus)? Was there a regression to a paranoid-schizoid position, which had a pathological development? Did hate alone turn Maura's woman friend into a persecutor? Can the patient's later complaint that others, men and women, criticized and tortured her verbally in her own voice be attributed to a projection of an ego function suffused with the hatred directed against the combined parent figures? Did elements of the ego, splintered into pieces, enter and fragment objects, thus creating a series of persecuting figures rather than one figure, as at the beginning of the illness? If so, all the persecutors would consist of part of the self and the hated parental objects. With the perceptual system damaged and externalized through the action of projective identification, the reality that caused the mental pain was abolished.

Blum (1980, 1981) and Meissner (1978) have also expressed dissatisfaction with the homosexual theory of persecutory delusions. They believe that insufficient attention has been paid to the role of preoedipal and pregenital influences in predisposition to paranoid states and to persecutory types of psychosis. According to Blum (1980), homosexual love can create a danger situation but it is not the decisive factor in the formation of persecutory delusions. The homosexual conflict so often discernible is, in his opinion, a defense against pregenital (sadistic) tendencies, rage, and rivalry belonging to the preoedipal relationship with the mother. The unconscious homosexuality in persecutory psychosis is derived not from the negative Oedipus complex, therefore, but from an abnormal development of narcissism (Blum, 1981). In this view, the persecutory delusion is the final outcome of narcissistic injuries contributed by sadomasochistic experiences with the mother. Regression revives this early period in which self and object representations are poorly differentiated, facilitating the projection of murderous rage. The persecutor is a narcissistic object endowed with the omnipotence of the preoedipal mother. Although Blum (1980) claims that persecutory types of illness in adulthood are usually preceded by paranoid tendencies in childhood (infantile paranoia), he does not go as far as Klein (1932), who postulates a paranoid position as a normal developmental phase.

Another group of writers (Arlow and Brenner, 1969; Boyer and Giovacchini, 1967; Pao, 1979; Searles, 1963) attributes symptom formation in the schizophrenias to regression, conflict, and compromise between a weakened ego and drive derivatives. Pao's (1979) theory is representative. It is largely based on what is known about psychotic and borderline children. Pao employs Mahler's (1952) concepts and hypotheses to develop his own theory of schizophrenia. According to Mahler, the psychotic child's difficulty in relating to others, his or her destructiveness, perceptual anomalies, anxiety, and symptoms of transitivism and appersonation (Fleiss, 1961) arise because a representation of the mother has not been firmly established, thus interfering with the process of separation-individuation from proceeding normally. This failure, Mahler claims, springs from a lack of "mutual cueing" between infant and mother. Instead of attributing childhood psychotic symptoms to lack of object constancy as a primary deficit

(Rosenfeld and Sprince, 1963; Thomas et al., 1966), Mahler conceives of a core deficiency created by pathological mental events set in train by the absence of mutual cueing.

Pao calls these pathological mental events of infancy *experiential disturbances*. They consist of the painful, unsatisfying, and frustrating experiences of the young child deprived of the beneficial effects of "mutual cueing" (or reciprocity). The "experiential disturbances" do not lose their power as mental development proceeds, nor do they bring about an arrest in development as does childhood psychosis. However, they retain their potential for ill and can manifest themselves at the advent of puberty and adolescence. The experiential disturbances undermine the healthy evolution of the personality by disturbing the capacity for interpersonal relationships, by interfering with the fusion of aggression and libido, by upsetting the developing cognitive functions, and by blocking the transformation of traumatic anxiety into signal anxiety. Experiential disturbances of infancy are not schizophrenic symptoms but rather their precursors.

Basic to Pao's theory is the concept of an evolving personality so unsteady as to require buttressing by means that generally prove restricting and maladaptive. The nature and course of the psychosis are dependent on the extent of this developmental deficiency. It is particularly pronounced in those cases characterized by Pao as schizophrenic type III, otherwise referred to as *process* or *nuclear schizophrenia*. The deficiency is less evident in type II schizophrenia and minimal in type I.

Pao proposes five steps in symptom formation. First, conflict is generated by aggressive or libidinal wishes. This brings about what Pao calls *organismic panic*. In the third stage, the integrative functions of the ego are paralyzed. In this regressed state the ego has to make use of primitive defense mechanisms (denial, projective identification, and so on) because repression is not available. These defenses gain strength in the fourth phase as the ego begins to recover and attempts to find what Pao terms "the best possible solution"—in other words, a compromise. The schizophrenic symptoms are the expression of this best possible solution. For example, the end-of-the-world delusion is the outcome of a compromise between aggressive wish fantasies (oral and anal-sadistic) and an ego so injured that it must have recourse to externalization in order to dissipate the danger of self-annihilation. Whether the conflict that has necessitated the best possible solution can be resolved depends on the magnitude of the developmental deficiency. When the deficiency is limited, as it is in type I schizophrenia, analytic therapy is instrumental in influencing the conflict and relieving the symptoms. Such a favorable outcome does not occur in type III cases.

Form and Content in Unitary Theories

Theories that fall into the unitary category provide an explanation for the content of schizophrenic delusions but fail to explain their form. Frosch (1983) takes up this point in formulating his theory of the paranoid constellation. Although he acknowledges the contribution to this constellation of destructive pregenital instinctual derivatives, its core is in his view formed by an unconscious homosexuality that acts as an organizing principle to resolve oedipal and preoedipal conflicts. The paranoid constellation can only make up the content, not the form in which it is expressed.

The claim that the form results from regression to an infantile mental state in which pathological defenses operate is difficult to sustain if identical mechanisms are held responsible for non-psychotic symptoms. Followers of Klein believe that transitivistic phenomena and appersonations support the idea that the psychosis expresses the death instinct—as represented in bad parts of the self and bad objects—projected into external objects, which then become persecutory. The transposition of aspects of a mental and physical self to others and vice versa, detected in individuals suffering from symptom and character neuroses, is attributed to splitting and projective identification, as in the schizophrenias. In the former these transpositions are unconscious; in the latter they are overt. Does this happen in the schizophrenias because regression leaves the ego only with primitive defenses? Since the same mechanisms are indicated in the non-psychotic disorders, is the ego equally injured in these conditions?

The "specific" theorists have little difficulty with the formal aspects of schizophrenic symptoms because they believe that the ego no longer exists in the part of the mind subject to dissolution. Since ego and id, self and objects, reality and fantasy are no longer differentiated, conditions favor the emergence of delusions and hallucinations. In both acute attacks and chronic states, some ego does remain in the non-psychotic part of the personality (Katan, 1954). However, there is no evidence that it helps form psychotic symptoms. Awareness of these remnants of ego functions may have led such writers as Rosenfeld, Bion, and Pao to infer mistakenly that this is the psychotic ego, striving to expel a destructiveness that will otherwise annihilate the self.

These writers point to the anxiety accompanying delusions, transitivistic phenomena, and hallucinations to support their view that symptoms arise from conflict and defense. They assume that this anxiety led to the schizophrenic psychosis. However, the anxiety observed at the onset and during the course of the psychosis may be a product of the morbid process, not its cause. Bak (1971) and Wexler (1971) suggest that the anxiety accompanying the schizophrenic attack results from the loss of the sense of self brought about by the dissolution of psychic structures (see Frosch's concept of *delusional fixity*, 1983).

It has also been proposed that the anxiety is produced by reconstruction, as the drive derivatives attempt to recathect the abandoned reality (Freud, 1924). According to this view certain affects (envy, jealousy, hatred, anxiety), some the outcome of sexual frustration, initiate the dissolution of the most recently acquired aspects of mental life. The form the psychotic symptoms take and the affect and ideational content of these symptoms result not from regression alone but from a process of reconstruction that makes use of modes of mental functioning appropriate to infancy and childhood.

Theories of the schizophrenias can be differentiated according to whether they regard positive symptoms (delusions, hallucinations and negativism) as the repetition of infantile wish fantasies and defenses or as the outcome of attempts to reconstruct the personality after it has been dissolved. The frequent oedipal content of persecutory delusions is interpreted by advocates of the former theory (Klein, Blum, and Pao) as representing the superficial layer of a psychic structure whose foundations were formed by a severe disturbance in the infantile period. According to the latter theory (Freud, Katan, Bak, Frosch), the oedipal content is thrown up by the dissolution of mental life and employed for the purpose of reconstruction. The concept of transference psychosis (repetition of an infantile psychosis) is tenable only in terms of the former theory.

CHAPTER 8 Nosography and Theory of the Schizophrenias

London (1973) is one of several writers (including Frosch, 1983; Jacobson, 1954) who have pointed out that nosography is of decisive importance when constructing a theory of the schizophrenias. Account must be taken of the wide variation in symptomatology that exists between cases of a given type and between the types themselves, as well as the different courses the various types of illness follow. Theories of schizophrenia frequently fail to explain why some individuals diagnosed as schizophrenic in accordance with the criteria of M. Bleuler (1978) recover while others follow a cyclical course without serious damage to the personality, and a third group proceeds to moderately severe or severe endstates. Theorists frequently fail to tell us why the delusional content remains unchanged in cases that follow a cyclical course but changes considerably in the third group of cases.

Cases illustrative of various types of schizophrenia and the courses they follow are described in our review of contemporary theories of schizophrenic and paranoid psychoses (chapter 7). *Erica* shows a moderately severe endstate, and in her case the delusions of the initial phase disappeared, to be replaced by a new psychotic reality. *Maura* also reached a moderately severe endstate. At the onset of the persecutor was a woman, but auditory hallucinations featuring a male persecutor became the leading clinical feature. *Michael's* illness followed a cyclical course, and the content of subsequent attacks was

137

similar to that of the first. His personality prior to the illness did not change. This case and those that recover without further attacks fall into the category Vaillant (1964) called *remitting schizophrenias* and Langfeldt (1960) designated *schizophreniform psychoses.*

Transitivism (the perception of oneself or parts of oneself in others) and appersonation (the perception of parts of others in oneself) occur in both groups. While these phenomena are observable at the onset of illness in the cases described, they are also found in the chronic condition (Bleuler, 1924). Transitivism and appersonation are the result of identifications (Freud, 1921) characterized by the absence of a boundary separating the representations of self and object. Jacobson (1954) has called them *psychotic identifications;* while Frosch (1983) has named them *primitive identifications* to distinguish them from apparently similar forms of infantile object relations.

The transitivisms and appersonations of the initial phases of remitting cases differ from those that do not remit. In the former the psychotic (primitive) identification is with a real object, while in the latter the identification is with a substitute. Michael and Erica respectively illustrate two types. The identification with a real object at the onset of nonremitting cases soon gives way to identification with a substitute. These differences in content suggest a possible reason for recovery or a cyclical course in the one category, and for chronicity in the other.

Delusional Object Relations in Remitting Schizophrenias

Psychotic identifications observable at the onset of remitting schizophrenias represent mental contents present consciously or unconsciously during the prepsychotic phase of the illness (Katan, 1979). In this phase, the loss of a love object leads to wish-fulfilling fantasies, dangerously acquisitive attitudes toward the loved one, and defenses against unacceptable sexual wishes that find expression through identification. Psychic dissolution allows these unconscious (prepsychotic) identifications to find representation in transitivistic signs and appersonations. Identification can serve various functions.

IDENTIFICATION AS REGRESSION FROM OBJECT CHOICE. When a schizophrenic illness of the remitting kind follows a lost love, the psychotic identification restores the love relationship (Freeman, 1982). It fulfills the wish that the past become the present, the wish for a return to happy times. Appersonations and passivity, further consequences of the identification, are also subject to the hostile component of the ambivalent attitude to the lost love object (Katan, 1979; Tausk, 1919).

IDENTIFICATION AS WISH FULFILLMENT is seen in cases of remitting schizophrenias where wishful, grandiose delusions precede or accompany the persecutory delusions (Freeman, 1981). The patient becomes the person he wishes to be. He now possesses the attributes belonging to the object of his admiration and envy—virility, power, and so on—as in Michael's case.[1] The psychotic patient then fears attack. Persecutory delusions result from a fear of retribution. Persecutory experiences may be seen as arising from within or from without. In the former case, the figure the patient has become is dangerous both to himself and others (Freeman, 1981). In the latter the object is re-externalized and acquires through the fusion of self and object, the hatred and envy attached to the original wish fantasy.

In female patients wish delusions may originate in identification with a sister or other female relative envied and idealized for her feminine charms. In the psychotic attack the patient believes that she is the beautiful and attractive sister. Penny (discussed below), for example, fashioned her hair after her sister's and wore her sister's clothes, however ill-fitting, to emphasize their identity. Again in these cases, persecutory fears arise from a dread of retaliation provoked by envy and acquisitiveness.

In women who present with erotomania before or during a persecutory symptom complex, the delusional content does not suggest a wish for enhancement of femininity. In these cases evidence may point to a prepsychotic real or wished-for heterosexual relationship. The phase of wish delusion, the erotomania, has often passed before the patients are seen. However, they describe themselves exactly as they describe the persecutor. This indicates the existence of an identification with the man, an appersonation, even though the patient now dreads revenge from him for the wish to steal his masculinity.

IDENTIFICATION AS A DEFENSE. In cases of remitting schizophrenia where the initial symptoms are entirely persecutory, the psychotic identification serves as a defense against a homosexual wish. This

1. The same acquisitive wish fantasy is seen in a male homosexual who acts passively toward his sexual partner in order to acquire his admired and envied masculinity (A. Freud, 1952; Nunberg, 1921).

wish is the basis for the delusion of being accused of heterosexual promiscuity by a known person of the same sex. These patients almost invariably refer to their abhorrence of homosexuality. Male patients believe their male persecutors are virile and sought after by women. The heterosexual component of the patient's sexuality leads to envy of the persecutor-to-be, while the homosexual component leads to a homosexual attraction. Through identification the patient achieves his wish to be the sexually active man. While this disposes of the homosexual attraction and confirms the patient in his masculinity, it does not dispense with the prepsychotic envy and hatred of the man who has become the persecutor. The patient is now slandered just as he had wished to malign his persecutor.

In women the sexual maladjustment and its pathological consequences follow a comparable course. When the patient believes she is slandered by a woman, an account of the prepsychotic period often shows that she was jealous of the man or men whom she believed to have an intimate relationship with an admired but envied woman. This woman, who becomes her persecutor, was despised as promiscuous and unfaithful. To counter the homosexual attraction, the patient becomes the promiscuous woman who is reviled by everyone.

These psychotic identifications demonstrate that in the remitting schizophrenias the real object is not entirely lost or abandoned. An object relationship present unconsciously during the prepsychotic phase continues to exist, albeit in a primitive form. This psychotic identification is the centerpiece of a transient delusional reality. Once the danger subsides the psychotic identification is resolved. Self- and object representations of the period prior to the illness are differentiated once more and recovery ensues.

Delusional Object Relations in Nonremitting Schizophrenias

At the onset of most cases of nonremitting schizophrenia, transitivistic signs and appersonations relate to fantasy objects rather than to the real ones of the period prior to the illness (Freeman, 1982). Reconstruction of the prepsychotic phase shows that these delusional objects are substitutes, as in Erica's case. But in some nonremitting schizophrenias, the delusional content at the onset of the illness concerns a real person with whom the patient had a relationship. This figure is shortly replaced by a fantasied one.

Belinda

Belinda, a woman of twenty-three, became seriously depressed after her fiancé left her. She gradually recovered only to fall ill again a year or so later. On this occasion she blamed herself for the breakdown of the relationship. Her self-criticisms, however, left no doubt that they expressed her anger against the former fiancé. A concomitant change in manner further supported the conclusion that she had identified with the lost love object. After some months these depressive manifestations gave way to the delusion that her former fiancé was trying to contact her. He had made a mistake, had not appreciated how much he loved her. Belinda would interrupt her work, go to the door of the bank where she was employed, and claim that she had heard his voice outside. She behaved similarly at home. She also believed that someone was preventing her from meeting her fiancé.

As Belinda became progressively withdrawn she was admitted to the hospital. Her auditory hallucinations continued, and she became negativistic. She accused a female cousin of jealously preventing her fiancé from seeing her. Later she developed an attachment to a male doctor who had spent a short time in the ward where she was a patient. When he left the hospital he took the place of the former fiancé. Belinda now claimed that her jealous cousin had enlisted the support of her former fiancé to stop her beloved doctor from seeing her. Her fiancé hated her because she preferred the doctor, and so he had allied himself with the cousin. This delusion persisted for twenty years despite all forms of treatment.

At the onset of the illness, identification replaced object choice. At this stage nothing distinguishes psychotic identifications from those in remitting illnesses that follow the loss of a real love object. But the replacement of a real object by a fantasy object marks a further pathological development.

During the prepsychotic phase Belinda identified with her lover, which revived phallic homosexual wishes based on a strong libidinal attachment to her young sister, to whom she had been devoted. After her disappointment in love she wished to turn once again to her sister, but she was now married. A danger situation was created by her homosexual wishes and her jealousy of her brother-in-law. Soon after the onset of the psychosis, therefore, a female persecutor—a cousin—appeared on the scene. During the psychosis Belinda could continue to believe in her heterosexuality through the wish fantasy of her lover's attempts to find her. As time passed, she created a new fantasy lover. The homosexual cathexis was transferred from her sister to the substitute cousin. The jealousy, no longer repressed as it had been in the prepsychotic phase, was projected onto this substitute. In order to maintain the "repression" of the homosexuality, Belinda turned love to hate, insisting, "I do not love her; I hate her; she hates me out of jealousy."

It may be remembered that a similar substitution took place in Maura's case. Initially, a homosexual love object became a persecutor. Later a fantasy object, an unknown man, replaced the female persecutor. At the onset of this psychosis identification defended against a homosexual wish, as in nonremitting cases, but later substitution pointed to an extension of the psychopathological process.

Wish-fulfilling identification is also found in non-remitting cases where the acute attack is characterized by grandiose as well as persecutory delusions. The case of Schreber (Freud, 1911b) is illustrative. Niederland (1959) has shown that Schreber's description of some of his actions and his (delusional) ideas can be attributed to the fact that his father's mission in life was to improve the physical and mental health of humankind. God became a substitute for the father, and evidence of the identification with God are to be found in passages of Schreber's memoirs. Identification as a result of wish fulfillment is found too in nonremitting cases where an erotomania precedes persecution by the imagined beloved. In such instances (e.g., Erica's case) the substitution takes place before the persecutory delusions appear.

Over the long term, in cases terminating in states characterized by persecutory delusions and minimal cognitive disorganization (paranoid schizophrenia), the content of delusions remains constant. This suggests that the process of substitution, whether it took place at the onset or somewhat later, has halted. However, in cases that terminate in hebephrenic-catatonic endstates, a complete change of delusional content occurs from that present in the initial attack (Bleuler, 1924).

In hebephrenic-catatonic endstates, the process of substitution extends over a wide field. Real objects are replaced by fantasy objects fused with magical, omnipotent self-representations in primitive (psychotic) forms of identification. This is the basis for the transitivisms and appersonations typical of these chronic conditions (Bleuler, 1924).

Mark

Mark, a young man of nineteen, had an acute psychotic attack a few months after his older brother announced his intention to marry. Mark feared he was dying from a heart attack. He complained that a fellow student at college was watching him and interfering with his affairs. He accused the student of rifling his locker and ruining his chemistry experiments. He also angrily accused his brother of winking at him as if to indicate that he were homosexual. Shortly after being admitted to a mental hospital, he attacked a male nurse, claiming he had winked at him. This acute attack cleared up after some months.

A relapse followed seven months later, in which a wish delusion occupied the center of the clinical picture. The delusional thoughts concerned a girl, an acquaintance of his sister's, whom he had met only once or twice. He invited her to the theater. A few days later he saw her in the company of another young man. He went up to her, told her he loved her, and gave her a poem he had written. The girl told him not to be silly. Mark went home and made some superficial cuts on his throat. In the hospital he said, "I did it to make someone sorry."

As the weeks went by, Mark became increasingly withdrawn and negativistic. He lost interest in his appearance, and his speech became difficult to follow because his thoughts were unconnected and he formed neologisms. In the following years an extensive wish delusion made its appearance. He and the girl were children of God. She was sacred, and she was to marry him. He would receive a pension for restoring the hospital after its supposed destruction. His interest in therapeutic contact terminated whenever it appeared to him that the doctor was unable to fulfill his delusional wishes. While he acknowledged that doctors and nurses had a separate identity, he also related to them and others on the basis of identification (appersonation). Such persecutory fears as he expressed related to his bodily integrity. At no time did he refer to the anxieties present in the acute attack. In this and other cases terminating in hebephrenic-catatonic endstates, a lack of differentiation between magical self- and object-images can be observed (Bychowski, 1952; Freeman, 1968; Jacobson, 1967; Niederland, 1959).

Dynamic, Economic, and Structural Considerations in Schizophrenia

The clinical data described above support the theory (Freud, 1924) that all cases of schizophrenia, irrespective of the course they may follow, pass through a similar initial phase. Following dissolution of psychic structures in the face of a danger situation, a psychotic identification replaces the object relations of the period preceding the illness (see Jacobson, 1954; Nunberg, 1921; Rosenfeld, 1954; and Tausk, 1919). These identifications are not haphazard; they achieve aims of a wish-fulfilling, restorative, and defensive kind. The quality and distribution of the cathexes that subserve the maintenance of self-and object representations are disturbed by the morbid process.

This formulation does not imply an immediate loss of object cathexis. The object representation retains its cathexis but it is no longer differentiated from the self. At this early stage of the illness, therefore, the continuity of mental life is preserved. The object is retained despite a change in the manner of its expression, as revealed in the delusional content. If the psychotic process is not resolved and preillness object relations restored, the second phase follows. Its onset may be rapid or slow. In the second phase, cathexis is displaced from the condensed real self- and object representations to primitive fantasies of self and object undifferentiated from one another (Bychowski, 1952; Jacobson, 1954). This movement of cathexis becomes the economic base of the psychotic, delusional reality and for the reconstruction of what remains of mental life (Bak, 1943, 1971; Freud, 1911b; Frosch, 1983).

In the schizophrenias terminating in hebephrenic-catatonic endstates, reconstruction does not restore the boundary between real and fantasy objects and the self. Relating continues on the basis of psychotic identifications, leading to transitivism and appersonation. It is when this form of relating occurs in a close temporal connection with the remnants of healthy mental life that an aspect of double bookkeeping is to be observed (Bleuler, 1911; Freeman, 1977).

The process of reconstruction is more effective in cases that proceed to a paranoid endstate (Bak, 1971). The identification is immediately transformed into its constituent elements—self and object. Aspects of the fantasy object are retained within the self, and elements of the fantasy self are externalized onto the object. This reconstruction of aspects of the self and object returns the individual to the sense of identity and the boundaries of the self. In the hebephrenic-catatonic type, by contrast, sense of identity and self-boundaries are only faintly represented.

Once the second phase begins the unity of past and present representations of real objects and the reality self is disrupted (Jacobson, 1954). The continuity between past and present is impaired, as is the capacity to distinguish one from the other. Affectively toned preconscious thoughts and memories can reach consciousness only by way of auditory hallucinations. A female patient was asked out by a man. A voice in her head said, "You are not too old to be hit," and she hit herself on the back of the head. It emerged that in her adolescence, her father (now dead) had said these words and had struck her as she had struck herself. These types of hallucination as well as those derived from repressed childhood memories act, as Freud (1924) proposed, to complement and fit in with the psychotic reality (Katan, 1975).

At first Freud (1911b) based his theory of schizophrenia on cases in which the illness had been present for many years. He concluded that the psychotic process was initiated by a loss or withdrawal of object cathexis followed by reconstruction, or "remodeling," as he called it in 1924. The study of schizophrenic individuals who recover or cycle suggests that what appears to be reconstructive—that is, the delusional content—is in fact the product of an identification with a real object. The object is retained, as in cases of psychotic depression, in which the delusions, melancholic or persecutory experiences result from identification with an object that has received the hostile component of ambivalence. Reconstruction plays no part in symptom formation. Remission is the rule in psychotic depressions, as in the remitting schizophrenias. Retention or loss of the object seems to determine the outcome in cases of schizophrenia.

The fact that object choice so easily gives way to primitive types of identification in the schizophrenias suggests a special vulnerability in the personality prior to illness. Jacobson (1954, 1967) suggested that those who succumb to a schizophrenic illness do not adequately differentiate self- and object representations and the ego ideal. The superego lacks stability and cohesion. We attempt below to show how Anna Freud's (1981) concept of developmental disharmony can help to explain such a vulnerability.

We do not attempt to evaluate, clinically or metapsychologically, the persecutory types of illness that originate predominantly in the fifth decade of life and after. These conditions, usually designated paranoid psychoses (Batchelor, 1964; Forrest, 1973; Retterstol, 1966), arise when life is well established, occurring most commonly in women and frequently accompanied by depressive manifestations. They generally proceed to complete remission without injury to the preillness personality. Superego pathology appears to play a major role in the genesis of the symptoms (Freeman, 1965).

CHAPTER 9 A Developmental Approach to Schizophrenic and Schizophreniform Psychoses

The most recent and complete study of the schizophrenias (Bleuler, 1978) has confirmed the long-suspected fact that the personalities of those who succumb to these psychoses are not necessarily grossly abnormal, nor are their childhood experiences characterized by severe emotional upsets. Of the patients in Bleuler's study, 30 percent had, descriptively speaking, normal or nonaberrant personalities, and the parents of 25 percent of them were caring and responsible.

The preillness personalities of the schizophrenic patients described in chapter 7 can also be designated nonaberrant, to use Bleuler's term. Only the appearance of the psychosis aroused suspicions that their prepsychotic personalities had deviant (aberrant) characteristics. But in a great number of individuals who develop a schizophrenic psychosis, the prepsychotic personality is readily recognized as abnormal, characterized by pronounced schizoid and other disadvantageous traits that obstruct the development of warm, consistent, and reliable relationships with others. A history of disturbed parent-child relationships is most often encountered in these individuals.

The discovery of an abnormal prepsychotic personality in conjunction with a history of a disturbed childhood environment originally promoted the belief that environmental factors must play a decisive role in the causation of schizophrenic psychoses. This view has become increasingly difficult to maintain as knowledge has increased

147

of the childhood backgrounds of individuals suffering from so-called personality disorders, neurotic depressions, and alcoholism. These conditions are associated with histories of childhood suffering and deprivation no less frequently than are the schizophrenias.

The fact that schizophrenic psychoses can occur in individuals who underwent apparently unexceptional development requires that other pathogenic factors be postulated to account for the predisposition to the illness. A counter argument claims that the influences rendering an individual vulnerable to schizophrenic illness are so subtle that only the closest examination reveals their presence in what seems to be a reasonably normal parent-child relationship.

The developmental approach to the schizophrenias does not have to concern itself with this heredity-environment controversy. The developmental approach seeks, in the patient suffering from a schizophrenic or schizophreniform psychosis, a faulty mental evolution that has rendered the individual unable to meet the internal or external demands of adolescence and adult life. This failure is most easily demonstrated by patients who develop schizophrenia in adolescence. The nature of their subjective experiences, when compared with those of healthy and neurotic adolescents, shows that they have been unable to take the developmental steps essential for the transition to adulthood.

The adolescent who falls ill with a schizophrenic psychosis is unable to redirect his instinctual wishes from parents to others outside the family. Similarly he lacks the psychic resilience necessary to absorb the effects of the transient affective and cognitive regressions that occur in adolescence. Only by resorting to extreme measures can he control the reawakened preoedipal and phallic-oedipal drives. The adolescent tendency to withdraw from and belittle the parents is excessive, and love is transformed into hate on a scale never encountered in mentally healthy adolescents. This hatred is often displaced or turned against the self. Family romance fantasies disowning the real parents and real family become delusions. The wishful fantasies of adolescence become grandiose delusions, accompanied by an exaggeration of the healthy adolescent's tendency to identify briefly with whomever he currently admires. There are wild swings between instinctual indulgence and self-imposed deprivation. The body is alternately loved as beautiful and as a source of pleasure and hated as horrible and as a source of temptation.

Patients whose schizophrenic psychosis begins in early adolescence at first appear homogenous in as much as their symptoms differ little from case to case. However, detailed examination of individual cases indicates that this is not so. Some individuals have obviously been unable to displace phallic-oedipal and preoedipal wishes from the incestuous objects to extrafamilial love objects. At best, the choice and construction of fantasy love objects may rest on wishful fantasies about the self.

Ivy

Representative of this type of schizophrenia is the case of Ivy, who fell ill at the age of thirteen. The prepsychotic period, which lasted for many months, was characterized by withdrawal from others. Ivy explained her behavior by claiming she was oversensitive about her appearance. At home she kept to her room and particularly avoided her father, of whom she was critical. She confided in her psychiatrist, who saw her regularly during this prepsychotic period, that she was worried by sexual thoughts about one of her schoolteachers, a man about her father's age. The fantasies led to genital excitement and to masturbation. Ivy was afraid God would punish her for this. She hated menstruation, which had started about six months previously. She would have preferred to be a boy, she told the doctor, and her occasional fantasies that she was were accompanied by frightening genital sensations that led her to urinate.

The acute attack began with intense anxiety. Ivy refused to urinate, saying that God was going to kill her because of the genital excitement she experienced when she did so. The older men who had appeared in her previous masturbatory fantasies were now stimulating her sexually against her will. Later Ivy made sexual advances to her father and then assaulted him, saying that he wanted to seduce her. She denied her parentage, claiming a more "exalted" origin. Ivy's condition progressively deteriorated; years later she presented the picture of a severe endstate (Bleuler, 1978).

Penny

In other individuals who succumb to a schizophrenic or schizophreniform psychosis in middle or late adolescence the fixation to incestuous objects is not immediately apparent. Penny was fourteen years of age when she presented with signs of mental disorder. She was one of a family of five children with two older sisters, aged twenty and nineteen, and two younger brothers, aged twelve and ten. Both parents were well and had never suffered from mental upsets. Penny was described as bright, cheerful, and sociable. She had several friends with whom she went to the movies and to the local social center. She had no regular boyfriend. Her menses had begun when she was thirteen years old and had caused no special problem. Penny's behavior at school had been unexceptional, and her academic performance was judged to be above average. She was very close to her oldest sister, who had married two years earlier, but of late she had been rather distant and unfriendly toward her brother-in-law. Her other sister was also engaged to be married.

Toward the end of Penny's fourteenth year her parents discovered that she had been absenting herself from school over a period of three to four months. Both parents worked during the day, and Penny would return home after supposedly setting out for school. When asked why she did not want to go to school, Penny claimed that the other girls were saying she smelled. She had heard girls in her class saying so. This had so embarrassed her that she could not face them. She could not be convinced that there was no truth in her belief or be prevailed upon to return to school or even to leave the house. She said that people in the street and on the bus looked at her strangely, and that this signified she was "smelly."

A few months later Penny was referred for examination by a child psychiatrist. Her parents told him that she had increasingly confined herself to her room and refused to mix with the family: she spoke only to her cat, Tiddles. She kept her bedroom door locked, much to the annoyance of her father, and spent a great deal of time washing herself and changing her clothes. Even her oldest sister said that she could no longer get through to Penny. The parents were particularly upset when they discovered that Penny had cut up some of her clothes. The psychiatrist, fearing psychotic illness, suggested that Penny be admitted to the psychiatric unit of a general hospital for observation.

Penny remained in hospital for about two weeks. She was extremely unhappy and repeatedly demanded that she be allowed to go home. There was no reason for her to be in hospital—her parents must want to get rid of her. She absconded from the hospital and had to be brought back. She made few references to her fear that others believed she smelled, but her parents noted that she was in the habit of smelling her own clothes and those of her brothers and sisters.

At home during the next six months, Penny confined herself to her room, and there was no change in her mental condition. But toward the end of this period a new development took place: Penny cut her hair, fashioning it like that of the younger of her two sisters, who had just married and left home. Penny put on her sister's headscarf and plastered her face grotesquely with her sister's cosmetics. She insisted that a boy in the neighborhood was using a telescope to watch her while she bathed. Other boys were standing outside the house shouting that she was a "good thing" (i.e., sexually available). As she became progressively more difficult to manage Penny was readmitted to hospital.

During Penny's second hospital visit there was no sign of the initial delusional ideas, except for an occasion when she elaborated on the theme of the boy watching her through the telescope. She believed that this boy, with whom she had been friendly for a brief period, was reading and influencing her thoughts. She confided to a nurse her conviction that her parents had arranged for her to be killed while in the hospital. She told the same nurse, after her parents, sister, and brother-in-law had come for a visit, that they were impostors. She refused to speak to them when they next came to visit.

When Penny was discharged after a three-month stay she showed no overt signs of mental disturbance. But as soon as she returned home she reverted to her earlier beliefs and attitudes. Within a few weeks it was noted that she was given to bouts of giggling for no apparent reason. She spent a lot of time looking at her face in the mirror and grimacing. One day she announced that everyone was envious of her good looks.

Penny had now become overactive and was talking to herself and painting her face hideously. She could not be kept in the house—she ran to the neighbors' and the nearby shops, where she helped herself to whatever attracted her attention. She began to make many references to the devil, but it was not clear whether she was the devil or whether she was being influenced by him. When she was incontinent of urine or criticized for masturbating in front of people, she said by way of excuse, "The devil told me to do it." She said to a visiting psychiatrist: "I saw you, I saw you shag that woman."

When her parents or sisters tried to restrain her Penny gave vent to violent rages. She shouted that her mother was a witch and attacked her with a knife. She also attacked her favorite sister, saying that she was trying to steal Penny's feminine charms. "You want to be me because I'm better looking than you: that's why I'm on TV!" Penny shouted at her.

Penny was admitted again to the mental hospital, much against her will. She tried in every way she could to escape the ward. She tore off her nightdress and ran about naked. She exposed her genitalia and in bed, unclothed, she masturbated and was incontinent of urine and feces.

At times Penny admired her body in the mirror, feeling her breasts, buttocks, and abdomen and saying, "I love my body." When a slightly built nurse approached her Penny ran at her in a threatening way, saying, "You hate me because you want to be me. You are sad because you can't have my body and be me. I love being me. I live in the curved world and you live in the straight: you're jealous of my body." She made further accusations against this nurse: "You want my brains so that you'll be as beautiful as I am; you want to make me flat-chested; you're trying to make me like you." These utterances exactly repeated accusations she had made against her oldest sister before admission to hospital. "God will kill you," she told the nurse: "He is young and beautiful."

Penny masturbated in front of the male members of the nursing staff and made advances to them. "Would you like to see my fanny?" she asked, then shouted, "Penis, balls, penis, balls, how are my hairy balls?" With this she tore off her nightdress. At another time she sang out: "There was a crooked man who had a crooked stick and fell on it.... My cat Tiddles has a squint eye and a crooked paw, he licks my fanny and my bum when I'm in the toilet." She exposed her breasts, shouting, "Do you see these marks? They were caused by playing at cats." She then pretended to be a cat and rolled on the floor, mewing, scratching, and making licking movements with her tongue: "We roll on the floor and play at cat games." It was in such a phase of sexual excitement that she suddenly exclaimed, "Jimmy and Davy tore my pants off in the berry field and pushed their willies up my fanny." She illustrated this by seizing a half-used roll of toilet paper and trying to push it into her vagina.

During the following weeks Penny's disturbed state continued. She ran naked through the hospital grounds and smeared her face with urine and the right side of her body with feces. On more than one occasion she ate her feces. From time to time she was violent toward the nursing staff and attempted to destroy any object within her reach.

In the hope that her disturbance might be mitigated if Penny no longer feared permanent confinement or death in the hospital, agreement was reached with the parents that Penny be allowed home on leave. This had a good result: her incontinence and feces-smearing stopped immediately, and she became calm and easily manageable. Her parents noted, however, that she went about touching everyone in the house but could give no reason for doing this. A week after returning home she suddenly attacked her father, biting and scratching him.

Penny was once more admitted to hospital. She claimed she had "gone for" her father because he had had sex with her. She was somewhat more manageable during this admission. She was not incontinent but constantly asked to go home. Instead of tearing at her nightdress and other clothes she just threw them off and walked about admiring her body, taking other patients' belongings whenever she felt like doing so. She was also inclined to make sexual advances toward female nurses and ask them to get into bed with her. Penny remained somewhat manageable, enabling the nurses to take her out for walks in the grounds. She became content to wear her clothes and was willing to sit at the table to eat. Her parents agreed to take her home again on leave. Penny remained calm for some days until her older sister came to visit. She excused herself and went to the toilet, returning with her hands covered with feces. She proceeded to smear her sister, saying, "You have the power now." She had made reference to her "power" in the hospital: it appeared to come from God.

This sister reported that every time Penny came home from the hospital she arrived at her sister's house asking to sleep with her. She seemed determined to exclude her brother-in-law. When her sister refused this request, Penny went to her newly married sister and demanded to sleep with her. This behavior must have been connected with the fact that Penny shared a bed with her older sister from the age of two until she was twelve and then shared a bed with the younger sister until she was married, when Penny was fifteen.

Readmitted to the hospital, Penny was once again determined to return home. The anxiety and urgency that characterized these demands suggested she still believed she was to be murdered in the hospital. "You must take me home, you will give up your job and look after me," she said to her mother. When her mother did not immediately agree, Penny became very angry.

During her quiescent spells at home, which were periodically interrupted by acute disturbance, Penny's personality was found to be changed. She was disagreeable and quarrelsome, she would not help with the housework, and she easily became irritated with her mother. She had little interest in anything but smoking and eating chocolates. If her wish for cigarettes was frustrated she flew into a rage, ran into the street, and asked the first person she met for a cigarette. She neglected herself and had to be pressured each day to wash and keep herself clean. This childlike behavior was also reflected in her insistence on wearing both inside and outside the house an old coat that had belonged to her older sister, even though the coat was far too big for her and the weather was far too warm.

During several acute attacks that occurred over the next six months Penny was violent toward he mother, accusing her of being a witch. Penny said she was not her real mother and that she was not born from her mother or at her birthplace. Penny was a goddess; only she and God were in the world. She had to show her beautiful body and so rushed out into the street. Her father was in the United States; the man who claimed to be her father was an impostor.

The Prepsychotic Phase: An Attempt at Reconstruction

Like so many patients who fall ill with an acute schizophrenic attack, Penny was unable to describe what had happened to her in the months before the appearance of the "smelly" delusion. For this reason her psychotic utterances and behavior were carefully scrutinized, in the hope of gaining some insight into her mental life as it was during the prepsychotic phase, which probably started when she was about thirteen.

Penny's prepsychotic phase was characterized by a self-imposed isolation, a compulsive need for cleanliness, and the cutting of her clothing. The first two manifestations can be explained as a reaction to her fear that her body had an unpleasant smell. This may have been an olfactory hallucination. It is important to recall that prior to her psychosis Penny took pride in her appearance, was particular about the state of her bedroom, and was never careless with her clothes.

Prior to her psychotic attack Penny began to avoid her girlfriend.

She explained that the house was drab and unattractive. Later she said that her friend did not want to visit because the house was poor and her parents badly turned out. This indicates that Penny was ashamed of her parents as are many young adolescents.

Early in the psychosis Penny tried to fashion herself into her sister, who had just married. Later she accused her other sister of being envious of her: "You want to be me because I am better-looking than you." This indicates that Penny had substituted the younger sister for the older one. In the prepsychotic phase she had been unconsciously envious of her sisters' appearance and of their boyfriends. She wished to be as they were and identified with them. Her accusations of envy suggested that these prepsychotic identifications were accompanied by ambivalence, the hostile component of which remained in repression. Her later delusion that a young man was spying on her as she bathed satisfied her wish to be as attractive to men as her sisters were. Her behavior toward her brothers-in-law before the illness showed that she was jealous of their relationships with her sisters. She wanted to displace them, and this wish was made manifest in her desire, during the psychosis, to sleep with them once again.

The prepsychotic wish to have and possess everything the sisters possessed and literally to become them was the source of Penny's envy. The wish to have the sisters as love objects provoked her jealousy. The first wish became reality once the psychosis began and identification replaced object choice. The basis for the second prepsychotic wish lay in the phallic-masculine orientation of Penny's sexuality, which became apparent as the psychosis developed.

It will be recalled that Penny claimed two boys had sexually assaulted her while they were picking strawberries. In then trying to thrust a roll of toilet paper into her vagina, she played the part of the male as well as of the female in sexual intercourse. At first it might seem that by asking the male nurse if he would like to see her fanny she was asking him to repeat what she claimed the boys had done. But another explanation of her behavior is possible, one that has relevance for her prepsychotic period. By exposing her genitals and her breasts she hoped to excite the nurse and cause him to have an erection. That the erect penis excited her was evidenced by her repeated shouts of "penis, balls," and so on. Her cry "how are my hairy balls?" points not only to a wish for masculinity fulfilled but to memories of having observed the penis.

Was Penny's accusation of rape a substitute for a prepsychotic wish to excite and then expose a boy to see his erect penis? By doing so she could identify with his masculinity. During the psychosis these active wishes were projected onto her brothers and father, whom she accused of raping her. Earlier, she had projected her wish to look at the boy she had once known, whom she accused of spying on her through a telescope.

Penny's acute psychosis also drew attention to her masturbation conflict before and during the prepsychotic phase. She confessed indirectly to this conflict in attributing responsibility for both anal and clitoral masturbation to her cat. During the attack she became this "sexually perverse" cat who gained pleasure from licking, smelling, and scratching.

The return of anal erotogeneity at puberty had led Penny to anal masturbation, which shamed and disgusted her. The fear of being thought "smelly" can be regarded as a response to this shame. Her clitoral masturbation was also colored by anal sadism (the smelly, scratching cat), exacerbating the conflict caused by her penis envy and castration wishes.

The prepsychotic phase was initiated by the second sister's impending marriage, which threatened Penny's incestuous attachment to her. In early adolescence, Penny's phallic sexuality was awakened as it had not been when her first sister married two years earlier. She was jealous of her second sister's fiancé. Simultaneously, the dormant envy of her sister awakened. She desired her sister sexually yet hated her—her engagement represented a betrayal. To cope with this danger situation, in the prepsychotic phase Penny regressed from phallic to anal sexuality, from activity to passivity. Her fear of genital masturbation was replaced by the fear of anal masturbation. Her compulsive washing was a direct reaction to the anality, as was the fear of being "smelly." As Penny's phallic homosexual wishes gained strength, however, this defense began to fail. The prepsychotic phase ended with the dissolution of psychic structures and a return to the undifferentiated state (Katan, 1979).

At this point new psychotic object relationships, based on the defusion of libidinal and aggressive instincts and on primary projections, made their appearance. Penny now believed that she was the object of envy, jealousy, and hatred. Her prepsychotic identifications found representation, and she freely expressed sexual wishes of all kinds.

Some individuals who fall ill with schizophrenic psychosis have succeeded in forming temporary or lasting extrafamilial love relationships. Manic-depressive symptoms often accompany their schizophrenic manifestations, and the patients experience remissions during which they appear to have regained mental health, either partially or wholly. Some psychiatrists prefer to call these cases *schizophreniform psychosis*.

Olga

Olga fell ill at the age of eighteen. During the succeeding fourteen years she suffered five psychotic attacks, during which she had auditory hallucinations, persecutory ideas, passivity experiences, manifestations of "double bookkeeping," excitement, elation, and melancholic delusions. Each attack was followed by a remission, the shortest of which lasted one year and the longest four years. Depressive symptoms of moderate severity sometimes accompanied these remissions, but for the most part Olga led a reasonably normal life until she committed suicide at the age of thirty-three.

At the onset of the psychosis the symptoms suggested a manic illness. Olga suddenly became excited and elated, and her speech became confused. She claimed that Christ had been talking to her and was coming for her. She *was* Christ and would save the world. At times the happy mood disappeared and she aggressively cursed and abused her parents. She refused food, saying that if she were to "live right" she must stop eating.

Olga was admitted to a mental hospital where other manifestations of her illness were observed. She complained that the women in the factory where she worked had said she was a bad girl because she touched herself. She did not wish to masturbate but the devil was making her do it. She could hear the critical voices of these women.

After her excitement abated Olga said that she was worried about her boyfriend (later her husband), who had gone to Africa to work for a year. She was afraid he would not want her when he came back because she had refused to have intercourse with him. The couple had engaged in mutual masturbation, which had made Olga feel guilty. Olga's parents said that she was a quiet, reserved girl, conscientious and well thought of at work. She had three siblings: an older brother and two younger sisters. Her mother said Olga had been "moody" for the month preceding the psychotic attack.

The acute symptoms gradually subsided, and Olga was discharged from hospital after four months. She was seen regularly as an outpatient for six months, during which time she returned to work and seemed well. But three years later she was readmitted to the hospital in an excited and overactive state. She said Jesus had been talking to her and had entrusted her with a mission. When the elated mood passed she claimed that the women at work had been calling her "a lesbian woman." "I am 'dirty'," she said; "I'll be all right if I keep my hands away from myself." Olga, who had been married for nine months, believed intercourse was a sin because it tortured God. She was not happy with her husband and did not like sex. She complained that her husband went out and left her by herself. He gambled and drank too much and was always asking her for money. She also thought that he wanted to make love to her sister.

Olga remained in the hospital for six months and was then seen as an outpatient. She seemed reasonably well though she complained of depression. A year later she relapsed and was readmitted. The women at work were again calling her a lesbian and a masturbator. She could hear their voices in the hospital. She feared that her actions, particularly masturbation, would get people into trouble. She did not want to masturbate but an evil force made her to so. As her symptoms receded she talked at length about her childhood conflict surrounding masturbation. At school she masturbated in the class and feared the teacher knew it. She was self-conscious with other children and avoided them because she thought they were aware of what she was doing. She remembered being punished by her father for touching her brother's penis. She recounted a memory of seeing her father's penis: he had pushed her to the floor when she had tried to touch it. Olga's mother had been very strict, always warning her not to touch herself. After the age of twelve she had lost interest in masturbation. During her engagement she had resisted her husband's attempts to touch her breasts. Later they had engaged in mutual masturbation. Olga was frightened by his wish to have intercourse.

Once more she remained in hospital for six months and was quite well on discharge. She needed no hospital treatment for three years, until she was pregnant with her first child. On this occasion anxiety and jealousy were the predominant affects. Olga accused her husband of having an affair with another woman. Her auditory hallucinations were the same as before. She was afraid she was to be punished for masturbating and for being a "queer." This acute phase lasted for three months. Olga's marriage remained unsatisfactory, and she stayed at her mother's house for weeks on end. She attended the outpatient clinic for six months. Then no more was heard from her for three years, by which time she had two children, aged one and three.

When Olga was seen on this occasion she was depressed in mood. She said her husband was having an affair, although she had no evidence. She said he did not love her or the children. She was not hallucinating or overactive, but her appearance showed that she was neglecting herself. Her husband reported that she had no interest in the children, in him, or in the house. Olga's mother was looking after the children. After some months Olga stopped attending the outpatient clinic without any material improvement in her mental state.

The fifth attack occurred four years later; Olga was again admitted to the hospital. In the intervening years she had been quite well for lengthy periods punctuated by bouts of depression, during which she neglected herself and the family. She had been particularly severely depressed for a month before her reappearance at the hospital. She was admitted in an overactive, elated, and excited state. "I'm tempted by the devil," she said; "he has made me interfere with young children. I'm going to jail for twenty years for wanking Trevor [her son] when my husband was out. I'm bad, I will be punished." At this point she burst into laughter. On another occasion she said, "They make me feel like a queer. It's not my fault. Aren't I a woman?" These ideas gradually disappeared, and her mental life returned to a relatively normal state. She was allowed home in her husband's care for a few days over the Christmas holiday. They had an argument, and her husband left her alone in the house. She ran to a nearby canal and jumped in. She was dead when taken out of the water.

Olga's utterances during her psychotic attacks indicate that prior to the psychosis she had struggled against the wish to masturbate. Lovemaking with her boyfriend had revived the masturbatory conflicts of her childhood. He had gone to work abroad and left her alone to deal with this newly awakened genital excitement. The content of the delusional ideas—that she was a "lesbian woman," that her husband wanted to seduce her sister, that her husband had another woman, that copulation tortured God, and that her masturbation injured others—suggests that the prepsychotic wish fantasies accompanying Olga's sexual excitement were of a homosexual and sadistic nature. She dreaded the consequences of giving way to her temptation to masturbate, hence her statement, "I will be sent to jail for twenty years for being a dirty, neglectful mother and for wanking myself."

Olga's sexuality, in the prepsychotic phase, was of a phallic-masculine character, evidenced by her claim that she was Christ. By becoming the asexual Christ she fulfilled her wish to be a man and simultaneously freed herself of her masturbatory conflict. Her refusal to eat during the first attack symbolized her wish to renounce bodily pleasure. At the same time the sight and memory of her boyfriend's penis had, prior to her first attack, revived her childhood castration wish. The delusion that intercourse tortured God meant that if she copulated she would castrate her husband and take the penis for herself. During Olga's last psychotic attack her wish to touch her son's penis was perceived as a fact, a repetition of touching her brother's and father's genitals. Was her wish to be a man reinforced or even provoked by the temporary loss of her boyfriend? Was object choice converted into identification in the psychotic attack under the influence of her wish to possess the penis?

The danger situation that led to the dissolution of Olga's psychic structure did not come from a threat to an existing incestuous object relationship, as with Penny. The danger arose from sexual wishes that had returned to their incestuous objects. Olga was able to establish an extrafamilial relationship, but sexual intimacy revived fantasies about the love objects of childhood. The excitement this generated led to acute anxiety. At first the ego reacted defensively, leading to the prepsychotic conflicts and the prodromal symptoms. But the continued instinctual pressure was too great. The defenses failed pari passu with a dissolution of the ego and superego.

The Developmental Antecedents of Schizophrenic and Schizophreniform Psychoses

The content of the mental conflicts occurring in schizophrenic psychoses differs hardly at all from that observable in the neuroses. It is the lack of harmony among the different elements of mental life that distinguishes the schizophrenic patient from the neurotic patient. Bleuler (1911) was the first to describe systematically this disjunction between volitional, cognitive, and affective functions. Mental functions that normally operate in unison are forced apart. Most striking and characteristic of the disease is the disharmony between material and psychic reality that Bleuler called *autism*. The fragmentation of the unity of the self (transitivism) that normally exists between intention and action, and the divorce of affect and thought, are only a few of the instances of disharmonious mental life existing at the onset or during the course of the schizophrenias.

When an individual believes that he or she is being observed and criticized by others, the normal function of self-scrutiny has been separated from the remainder of the self. This pathological phenomenon can best be explained on developmental grounds. The function of self-observation appears late in mental development, and its loss in psychosis suggests that it cannot resist psychic dissolution. A fault in development leaves the personality vulnerable to this kind of splitting. Might not other splits leading to the fragmentation of mental life in the schizophrenias be the result of developmental anomalies? Could it be, as Freud (1933) suggests, that the fragmentation of the personality in schizophrenic psychoses proceeds along pre-determined lines of weakness created during the individual's mental development.

The flaws in the personality structure postulated here as occurring in those susceptible to schizophrenic psychosis do not necessarily draw attention to themselves prior to the onset of the illness. Many such individuals claim important social, educational, vocational, and cultural achievements. If our hypothesis is correct, the faults arising during the course of personality development evoked a compensatory response that, in at least a third of the cases (Bleuler, 1978), allowed development to proceed without undue disturbance. In the rest of such cases the faults find expression in a neurosis-like deformation of the personality.

The symptoms of acute attacks both at the onset and in the chronic stage of schizophrenic psychoses hint at the faults believed to be present in the prepsychotic personality. The intense ambivalence that characterizes the patient's relations with others, for example, demonstrates that the libidinal and aggressive drive are no longer fused. Love and hate are alternately directed against the same person. At one moment the love object is *feared* to be dead; at the next the patient expresses a *wish* for his death. Sometimes he attempts to translate the wish into action. An inherent weakness in the synthesis between the two drive representations may account for such phenomena.

During acute attacks the combination of uncontrolled drive activity and disorganized cognitive processes can be attributed to the dissolution of psychic structure. Ego, superego, and id are no longer adequately differentiated from one another. The loss of object constancy is one consequence of this dissolution. Another is the failure of repression, which results in expression of pregenital drive derivatives. The injury to object constancy owes as much to detachment of cathexis as it does to disorganization of object representations. The latter merge with one another and with representations of the self. The zone of indetermination (Schilder, 1939) between self and objects is increased, leading to a confusion between external reality and its mental representations. Once again it is not unreasonable to postulate that structuralization during childhood has incorporated within it a series of defects rendering the personality vulnerable to dissolution.

If so, deficiencies in the mechanism of repression would be an inevitable consequence of the defective psychic structuralization. Repression can fully operate only when the ego retains the capacity to provide stable countercathexes against the drives. This change does not affect the object (displacement) or the aim (reversal) as it does in the case of mechanisms that developmentally precede repression (countercathexis). For repression to become established the drive cathexis must be partially transformed into the nucleus of the structure (Rapaport, 1951), which delays drive discharge. Repression can be conceived of, therefore, as a series of thresholds whose levels are set by the acceptability or unacceptability of the instinct seeking expression. It follows that in the absence of an effective mechanism of repression, the defense against unacceptable wishes will be undertaken by less stable defensive measures. Such a hypothesis is supported by the nature of the preillness personality in many schizophrenic patients, by observations of children suffering from "borderline" states,[1] and by the course of elderly patients who present with hallucinations and delusions in apparently clear consciousness.

Bleuler (1978) has noted that about half of the schizophrenic patients in his follow-up studies had what he calls schizoid preillness personality traits. These schizoid traits include lack of interest in others, disregard for others' feelings and sensitivities, emotional coldness, rigidity of outlook and behavior, ambivalent moods, and a ten-

---

1. Although these cases are referred to by Thomas et al. (1966) as borderline, many workers, including the authors, regard them as cases of childhood psychosis, at least in terms of outcome.

dency to distort meanings. These individuals also tend to act impulsively without consideration for others or for everyday reality. Some 28 percent of these personality traits were so pronounced as to be considered pathological (schizoid-aberrant), while in another 24 percent their presence was sufficiently limited that Bleuler categorized the preillness personality as nonaberrant. Other pathological personality traits, including the callously unstable and the infantile, were present in another 13 percent of the cases. An inquiry into the individual's sexual lives prior to the illness revealed only that those with schizoid personalities were less likely to have had loving sexual relationships.

The schizoid individual's need for vigilance in his dealings with others and reserve in his behavior must be contrasted with his or her episodic impulsive activity that disregards the feelings of others and reality. These extremes of behavior result from the instability of the mechanism of repression in the personality. Regulation of the affective and ideational derivatives of instinct depends on repression; without it, these derivatives are a constant source of danger, particularly in the course of contact with others. The individual must rely on the ephemeral defensive maneuvers of denial, displacement, withdrawal, reversal of instinctual aim (from active to passive), and externalization of physical and mental aspects of the self. Jacobson (1954) has drawn attention to the way preschizophrenic individuals use other as vehicles for the expression of unacceptable wishes and needs.

The defense mechanisms postulated to account for schizoid character traits compensate for deficiencies in the mechanism of repression. When mental development is partially or completely arrested, as in the borderline and psychotic states of childhood, the defense mechanisms called into play to offset the lack of repression appear to hinder rather than promote further development.

Latency-age children suffering from borderline and psychotic states are constantly oppressed by the demands of their pregenital and aggressive drives. Although these children attempt to control their instinctual drives (Thomas et al., 1966), the nature of this activity is patently different from that of repression. Under the influence of anxiety, which has a special quality in these childhood conditions (Rosenfeld and Sprince, 1963), these children attempt to disown the drive derivatives by means of displacement and externalization. Aggression is displaced to inanimate objects; and toys become the vehicles for the feared pregenital, sadistic sexuality. But unlike repression, these mechanisms can neither dispel anxiety nor provide a permanent respite from the drives.

Brain dysfunction in senile dementia, cerebral atherosclerosis, and toxic states can lead to a similar situation in which instinct derivatives become unstable because externalizations and projections substitute for repression. Anxiety in these cases, as well as in psychotic children and individuals with schizoid personalities, is unrelieved by these mechanisms, which merely change the source of the danger. In many elderly patients, a persecutory symptom complex appears at first sight to be functional in origin. But soon unequivocal evidence of intellectual deterioration is found. As these changes proceed toward dementia, the persecutory symptom complex recedes into the background. In such patients the organic basis of the repression mechanism is damaged and calls into play the defense mechanisms outlined.

These people experience anxiety and conflict surrounding instinctual wishes that were previously successfully contained. For example, an elderly man, a printer by trade, whose memory was failing became frightened and distressed because he believed that young men were secretly using his house to print obscene literature. Cerebral damage had so weakened repression that his sexual wishes revived memories of adolescence, when he and other apprentices had printed indecent verses and circulated them among their friends.

The release of instinctual derivatives from repression is even more dramatic in the acute brain syndromes precipitated by withdrawal from alcohol or drugs. The anxiety experienced is no less intense than in the long-standing organic mental states. Ruth, a woman of fifty, strained her back and was given a simple analgesic. As there was no improvement, four-hour pentozine was prescribed. About twenty-four hours later Ruth became delirious. She claimed that her husband and her best friend were dead and that she was now going to marry her friend's husband. The devil was trying to kill her because she had been unfaithful to her husband. She hallucinated and showed intense anxiety.

Unknown to her general practitioner, Ruth had been consuming up to a bottle (fifth) of alcohol a day; the delirium was a response to the combination of alcohol and pentozine. An explanation of the content of the delirium was soon forthcoming. Ruth's husband had been impotent for more than ten years, and she had turned to alcohol to

dull her sexual desire. In the delusion her unconscious or preconscious wishes for the deaths of her husband and her best friend were
fulfilled. In the absence of repression, Ruth attributed responsibility
for the wishes, via externalization, to the devil, but this mechanism
could not still her anxiety.

In the schizophrenias, in childhood psychosis, and in organic
mental states, object constancy is no less disturbed than repression.
The loss of object constancy is always accompanied by a failure to
differentiate clearly self- from object representation. The development of object constancy, like repression, requires contributions from
both the drives and the growing ego (Edgcumbe and Burgner, 1973).
It fails to mature if the instinctual drive energies on which the ego
draws to provide effective countercathexes cannot be adequately
modified.

Individuals who come to suffer from schizophrenic illness have
inadequate developmental foundations on which to base later healthy
mental life. The strength and resilience of the completed psychic
structure depend on the extent to which modifications are made to
compensate for the faulty foundations. In some cases the compensatory mechanism necessary to keep the individual in reasonable contact with reality, and at the same time to maintain control over the
instincts, are so unstable that they limit the growth of healthy mental
life. This is the case in people whose prepsychotic personality is of
the schizoid-aberrant type. In cases involving a healthy preillness
personality, there has been less need for these compensatory mechanisms. All manner of variations exist between these two extremes.

The question that presents itself is this: how can early development go astray without bringing about the generalized or selective
arrests in personality growth that occur in infantile autism or in the
borderline and psychotic states of childhood? It is now well known
that many transient and persistent symptoms and problems of behavior in young children are the result of faulty mental development
rather than internal conflict (A. Freud, 1974). The abnormal development is caused by asynchronous evolution of the ego and the drives.
Sometimes this disharmony results from an instinctual predisposition to fixations at pregenital stages, which interferes with drive fusion and leads to persistent infantile ambivalence. In other cases the
disharmony that disrupts progress along a given developmental line
(A. Freud, 1965) can be traced to adverse parental influences.
Whether the problem is innate or acquired, ego development is hin-

dered by drive pressures so that disorders of cognition, motility, and object relationships make their appearance.

The transience of many of the symptoms and behavioral problems (developmental disturbances) of childhood indicates that the disharmony between the ego and the id elements of a particular developmental line is often reconciled to some degree. Reconciliation uses whatever mechanisms are at hand, irrespective of their stability or pathological potential (Greenacre, 1960). As the discord is most active long before the psychic structure is complete, only such mechanisms as externalization, displacement, denial, and regression can play a part in the attempt to banish the more disturbing manifestations of the disharmony. When, for example, the bisexuality of early childhood is disturbed, it affects the harmonious evolution of sexual identity—the disturbing component (femininity in the boy, masculinity in the girl) is externalized. This is an expedient maneuver that bears subsequent pathological developments. Although the synthetic tendency often successfully creates unity out of discord within the developing personality, it cannot prevent the mental conflicts that subsequently arise from the mental disharmony.

The theory of developmental disharmony (chapter 2) is heuristic as well as explanatory. It explains how the conflicts of the schizophrenic come into being and why they are so intense. More significantly, it draws attention to the mental events of the patient's infancy and early childhood. Their study must be based on reconstruction despite the difficulties and limitations of this method. But there is always some access to the patient's childhood, and manifestations of the psychosis also provide a basis for the reconstruction. However, in established cases of schizophrenia, a treatment alliance within which transferences can arise to provide the details of early childhood relationships can rarely be attained. In the absence of such an alliance, and given the chaotic nature of the transference phenomena, the analyst can only speculate about the childhood experiences that promoted the disharmonious development.

A striking contrast is provided by cases of character neurosis and "disturbed" cases that undergo psychoanalytical treatment (chapters 5–6). In these instances treatment alliance and transference provide details that can only be guessed at in cases of schizophrenia. Invariably evidence is found of ill-advised parental interference, indifference, or overstimulation (Greenacre, 1960; A. Katan, 1973; Shengold, 1967, 1988) that led to disharmonious development of the drives and the ego. Even allowing for the tentative nature of reconstruction in schizophrenic psychoses, it should be possible, given the present state of analytic knowledge, to discover accurately some of the significant mental events of the schizophrenic patient's early childhood.

The schizophrenic patients described in this and the previous chapter gave abundant evidence in their acute attacks of psychic dangers that evoked anxiety. These dangers were present also in the prepsychotic phase, where they led to conflict and the prodromal symptoms. The predominant conflict of this phase was phallic-genital in type. Wish fantasies springing from the castration complex led to envy, jealousy, hatred, and anxiety. The intensity of this anxiety suggests that these prepsychotic wish fantasies are more virulently aggressive than those encountered in the symptom neuroses.

These pathogenic prepsychotic conflicts can be attributed to faulty libidinal-phase development (Greenacre, 1960). In the case of Penny, the anal phase was unduly prolonged, reflected in a history of bowel disturbances in early childhood. Did the intertwining of anal and phallic elements in Penny's acute psychotic attacks substantiate our belief that in childhood her awareness of her genitals began during an extended anal phase? The acute masturbatory conflict that followed Olga through her childhood must also have been caused by premature genital arousal following overstimulation and seduction.

The arousal of genital excitability during the anal phase is an important cause of acute anxiety attacks and phobias in young children (B. Bornstein, 1935; S. Bornstein, 1935; Furman, 1956). Premature excitation of the genitalia leading to masturbation can be caused by overstimulation (seduction, etc.) or by accidents of varying kinds (Greenacre, 1960). A persisting anal orientation of the libido imparts a sadistic element to the fantasies elaborated on the basis of the damaging (real) experiences (Shengold, 1967, 1988). The sadistic masturbatory fantasies that cause so much guilt in character neuroses and "disturbed cases" (see chapters 5–6) can be traced to infantile masturbation originating in the anal period. Similar events may have affected the preoedipal development of the patients described here and in chapter 8. The sadistic element may add to the intensity of the prepsychotic masturbatory conflict and its resulting anxiety.

Frosch (1983) has drawn attention to the importance of traumatic childhood events as predisposing to persecutory types of psychoses. In his opinion certain events assume the significance of psychical traumata because they are incompatible with the existing state of

drive and ego development. Arousal of genital excitability during the
anal phase is an example. These traumata introduce disharmony into
development. According to Frosch, male patients suffering from a
persecutory illness regard their passive-anal wishes as destructive
and dangerous because they have a sadomasochistic significance imparted by humiliating and degrading experiences at the hands of an
individual of emotional significance to the child. These experiences
occur prior to the phallic phase and prior to complete evolution of
sexual identity.

Reconstructions based on patients' recollections, dreams, and delusions illustrate how a disharmonious development comes into being, weakens the future personality, and leads to severe internalized
conflict. In the patients we have described, the ego was in its infancy
when the genital area became the leading erogenous zone and a focus
of interest and attention. No repression mechanism yet existed to act
against this trend. The distinction between the sexes was prematurely
recognized, and the pursuit of active and passive sexual aims was
overlaid by aims appropriate to masculinity and femininity. Phallic
arousal created an imbalance between these trends in favor of activ-
ity-masculinity. The ego, without the protection of repression, could
no longer remain in harmony with the sexual instincts. Parental pressure aimed at overcoming the effects of the disharmony aggravated it
still more.

As a further consequence of premature genital arousal, love objects continue to be regarded as need-satisfying objects. This can be
seen clearly in psychotic and borderline children (Thomas et al.,
1966). The persistence of this infantile mode of object relationship
interferes with the evolution of object constancy. The lack of stable
object representations creates deficiency in the structure of the ego,
whose optimal development depends on internalization of the representations of the love object. But this alone cannot account for the
vulnerability of object representations in those who succumb to psychosis. Other constitutional (innate) influences must play a part.

Continuing psychic differentiation even in the face of considerable disharmony between the instinctual needs of the child, his growing sense of self and others (ego aspects), and the wishes of the parents implies that in spite of the symptoms flowing from the disharmony, the areas of discord are patched up. The instability of this
solution is revealed by the splitting of mental life that occurs during
a schizophrenic attack. In several of the cases described above split-

ting led to manifest disharmonies between masculinity and femininity and between love and hate. These disharmonies are, in essence, no different from those believed to have been present in the child's earliest years.

It is postulated here that the ease with which object constancy and repression disintegrate during acute psychotic attacks can be regarded as the consequence of a disharmonious evolution of ego, id, and superego. The age at which a schizophrenic or schizophreniform illness occurs, the danger situations that initiate the psychosis, and the conflicts that can be reconstructed from the content of delusions and hallucinations all depend on the nature and extent of these childhood disharmonies, their effects on the developing psychic agencies, their integration, and their interrelationships. Until adolescence the natural tendency for synthesis in mental life limits the effects of earlier disharmonies through compromise and allows adequate functioning. But the new steps that must be taken in order to progress to adulthood, in individuals predisposed to schizophrenia, impose an intolerable strain on these syntheses. The individual lacks resilience as a consequence of danger situations and conflicts promoted by developmental disharmony and the measures employed to minimize its effects. Fixation to incestuous objects is one outcome of such disharmony: a threat to such a relationship or an attempt to leave it behind in favor of a new love object then creates the danger that initiates the psychotic attack.

Fragility in the psychic structure springing from a disharmonious development can also be postulated in individuals who fall ill some years after forming a permanent object choice. Many of these people made their choice on a narcissistic basis, the object representing the unconscious component of the patient's bisexuality. In other cases they choose a love object for reassurance (for example, of masculinity or femininity) or for protection against an unacceptable instinctual wish. Both these forms of object choice result from disharmonious development. Threats to these object relationships—loss, frustration, or disappointment, with attendant hatred—lead to a danger situation, to prepsychotic conflict, and to psychosis.

The great variation that exists among infants and young children with respect to their instinctual endowment, innate tendencies for psychic structuralization, and environmental circumstances means that developmental disharmonies, if severe, must be multifarious. Thus individual cases of psychosis vary, whether they belong to one clinical entity or several. Disharmonies make their impact in the preoedipal period. Apart from their effect on the stability of future psychic structures, they lead to pathological forms of the phallic-oedipal phase. Thus threats derived predominantly from the negative Oedipus complex foster the dissolution of ego and superego in individuals vulnerable to psychosis.

CHAPTER 10   On Mania and Hypomania

The characteristic and invariable feature of manic states is psychomotor overactivity. These phenomena contrast with the "inhibition" and retardation that signal severe depressive illnesses. As with depressions, there are various types and intermediate forms of mania. Intermediate forms were designated *mixed states* by Kraepelin (1899), who realized that not every patient suffering from mania exhibited elation of mood and that psychomotor overactivity did not uniformly affect thought and action in every case.

The psychoanalytic understanding of mania is based primarily on the various phenomena that constitute the typical psychomotor overactivity. The manic patient seems to have at his disposal an unlimited energy, which manifests itself in pressure of talk and continuous movement. This upsurge of energy is also reflected in the way the patient feels about himself. Mania brings with it an exaggerated sense of self-esteem and a heightened self-confidence and sense of well-being. He is quite uncritical of his thoughts and actions.

Both Abraham (1911) and Freud (1917) took as a starting point for their theoretical considerations those instances where mania succeeds depression. It appeared to Abraham that the energy no longer consumed in depression was set free in manic overactivity. Freud too laid stress on this economic factor in explaining the development of mania. In his opinion the expenditure of energy demanded by depression was no longer necessary once the patient had overcome the loss of the object (or his mourning over the loss, or perhaps the object itself). "And thereupon the whole quota of anticathexis which the painful suffering of melancholia had drawn to itself from the ego and 'bound' will have become available," Freud postulated (1917, p. 225).

The behavior, thinking, and feeling of the manic patient also seem to spring from a failure of repression (Abraham, 1911) and of reaction formations. Normal restraints on genital and pregenital activities are lacking. Wishes are freely expressed in both speech and action—conscience is held in abeyance. The patient believes he is omnipotent, ignoring considerations of reality. Mental functioning allows the primary process in this respect, and cognition is influenced by condensations and displacements. It is as if the distinctions between ego and id, on the one hand, and fantasy and reality, on the other, had ceased to exist.

Childhood Prototypes of Mania and Hypomania

If manic states result from a sudden dissolution of the ego and superego, a weakness must exist in these psychic agencies. Does this fragility of the ego and superego result from faulty (disharmonious) development? The difficulties that stand in the way of finding data in adult patients to test such a hypothesis have been referred to earlier. In the adult, direct manifestations of disharmony between the drives and the ego have long since passed from view, and so symptom and personality traits cannot automatically be attributed to conflict generated by an asynchronous development.

But such an anomalous development can be witnessed first hand in children whose hyperactivity is not the result of brain damage (Anthony and Scott, 1966). This hyperactivity may be accompanied by manifestations similar to those encountered in adults suffering from mania or hypomania. Many writers have described children whose hyperactivity occurs within a context of deprivation (Rochlin, 1953, 1959) or of trauma that provokes excitement as well as anxiety (Katan, 1979; Ritvo and Solnit, 1960). In all these instances drive development outstrips that of the ego and interferes with the growth of the secondary process (ego). Speech development is impaired, as is the ability to regulate motor activity. Hyperactivity is frequently accompanied, therefore, by a lack of bladder control. This uncoordinated development causes conflict not within the child himself but between the child and his environment. External conflicts appropriate to much earlier periods of childhood persist. The absence of internal discord acts as the greatest obstacle to psychotherapeutic work.

Hyperactive states also occur in children who are not excessively stimulated or emotionally deprived. In contrast with deprived overactive children, these nondeprived, nontraumatized children are not destructive. The aggression occurring under conditions of disappointment or frustration does not spill over into violence against animate or inanimate objects. They show concern for their bodies, although sometimes it is endangered by overactivity. In this respect they differ from deprived children, who fail to take care of their bodies and may even mutilate themselves.

Young children who are overactive and show mania-like phenomena as a rule lead traumatic, unsatisfying lives full of frustration and disappointment. Rochlin (1959), Wolfenstein (1955) and others have drawn attention to the fact that these hyperactive children are periodically withdrawn and apathetic—evidence of a depressed mood. Such a boy, aged nine, underwent periods of manifest unhappiness, in which he was inclined to be solitary. Later this state of mind was replaced by overactivity, boastfulness, and aggressive behavior. Is the hyperactivity of these emotionally deprived and overstimulated children defensive, as it may be for adult patients whose manic or hypomanic attacks are followed by depression?

It is possible to envisage the emergence, in these children, of a pathological ego state (Federn, 1953) with its own forms of defense and drive expression. This partial solution may enable the individual to create object relationships and make an adjustment to the environment. Ritvo (1974) cites the case of an overactive boy who achieved this kind of adjustment, though in this example the child was in psychoanalytic therapy and the mother in social casework treatment. Characteristic of this pathological ego state would be the readiness with which drive derivatives find direct expression through the motor system. The delaying function of thought is lost. The "permeability" of the ego organization to the primary process would result in a readiness for wishful thinking at the expense of reality judgment.

The presence of such a pathological state as the product of a disharmonious development between ego and id might have consequences in late adolescence or adulthood. If danger arose through fear of killing the object or from actual object loss, the outcome would not be, as in the neuroses, a compromise between id and ego. Instead dissolution would expose the disharmonious tendencies that had been unified by the synthetic function. Instinctual derivatives would find expression through a motor system no longer under control of the ego—leading to overactivity and wishful delusions.

Have adults who suffer from mania and hypomania passed through a similar condition in childhood? The fact that childhood prototypes exist does nothing to answer this question, nor does the accessible childhood history of adult manic patients. Nevertheless, we must take account of the fact that the psychic events that provoke childhood overactivity are similar to those that initiate manic and hypomanic states in adult life.

Manic States Following Object Loss

In manic states that follow depressions precipitated by bereavements or disappointments in love, the way the patient experiences himself and those about him is profoundly influenced by memories of the lost love object. These phenomena and the unconscious mental processes that give rise to them can best be illustrated by a clinical example.

Barry

Barry was an unmarried man of twenty-two. When he was first seen his depression was reflected in his appearance and manner. He offered no information about himself, and his speech was slow when he replied to questions. According to his father, Barry's health had gradually deteriorated since his mother's death two months before. (She had complained of severe headache for some time before her sudden collapse and death from cerebral hemorrhage.)

Barry said that he felt responsible for his mother's death because she had been concerned about his loss of interest in life following the loss of his job. He was retarded in speech and action. Before his depression began Barry had been regarded as a friendly and hard-working man. Since his depression quickly improved, the psychiatrist decided to let the illness follow its own course in the hope of spontaneous remission. This proposal was acceptable to Barry and to his family.

Four months later Barry was admitted to the mental hospital because of overactivity, talkativeness, and expression of ideas that worried his family. Apparently his depressed condition had continued since he was last seen but its intensity had gradually diminished. Suddenly his mood had changed. He became excessively cheerful and stayed up late at night, apparently needing very little sleep. He busied himself about the house in the small hours, to the annoyance of his family. He claimed that he was going to put the world to rights.

When Barry arrived at the hospital he was overactive and expressed grandiose delusions. He said that his village had been dead for a long time but he was now about to bring it life. He had already advertised its attractions on television and in the newspapers. He soon transferred these ideas to the hospital: "It's as dead as a graveyard, [but] I will bring it life." Barry insisted that evil forces were destroying the world and making everything seem dead. His task was to root out the evil and bring the world and everything in it back to life. He declared he was in contact with God, who had entrusted him with this undertaking. In this elated and omnipotent state Barry revealed that his mother had come to him in the night and that in fact she was not dead at all.

A few days later Barry's elation swung back toward depression, though the psychomotor overactivity persisted and the content of his speech was not uniformly depressive. He complained of a severe pain in his head, a bursting sensation as if he were bleeding inside his skull. He said he was in hell because he had killed his mother. She knew that he was wicked because she could see the devil in his eyes. This depressed mood did not last long, however, and Barry reverted to grandiosity: "I get cleverer every day," he said. He extended his good spirits and accomplishments to everyone else. He needed to have sexual intercourse with his "wife"—a girl from the village who had died some time before. He insisted that she was in the adjacent female ward and demanded that she be brought to him. "I'll fuck my wife in public if you want," he said; "her name is Maria, she was here the other morning."

Barry was easily stirred to anger if his wishes were not met immediately or if he were prevented from pursuing a particular interest, such as going to the female ward. He shouted, cursed, and threatened, yelling, "I have enough strength to wreck the place." Fortunately the aggressive outbursts were shortlived, although on one occasion he smashed a window and struck a nurse. Periods of depression disturbed his elated mood, and sometimes his speech resumed a normal flow. On one such occasion Barry told the psychiatrist that he had been in the habit of visiting his mother's grave, where he would weep profusely, crying out, "Why did I do this to you?" Then he turned to the psychiatrist and shouted, "She is not dead; I am going to dig her up."

Over the next few months Barry's behavior, affect, and thought content fluctuated in the way described. He frequently asserted, when he was elated and felt omnipotent, that there were evil people in the world whom he would punish. But when he was depressed he complained of pains and criticized himself for his wickedness. Sometimes Barry's depressed mood was accompanied by psychomotor overactivity, at other times by retardation. Usually the depressed phases lasted only for hours or a day at the most.

Slowly Barry gave up the misidentifications and delusions based on wish fulfillment. He no longer "saw" his mother or his "wife," although he thought the latter was now alive in the body of another girl. Gradually his overactivity subsided, his mood fluctuated less, and he eventually recovered. He appreciated that he had been mentally ill and looked back on his delusional ideas as foolish and over imaginative. After five years Barry remained well.

During his manic periods Barry identified with his dead mother, as he did also in his depression. He continued to suffer as he believed she did in the last moments of her life. The identification persisted in the manic attack whenever Barry's elation and grandiosity were absent, although his psychomotor overactivity continued. It is safe to assume that at such times much of Barry's libidinal cathexis was still bound in "the complex of melancholia" (Freud, 1917). When the identification weakened and its cathexis was freed, the drive derivatives turned again to external reality. The patient was then able to cathect the memory of a love object (the dead girl), first as a visual hallucination and then in the form of a misidentification of a real person.

As Freud (1917) pointed out, the transition to mania depends on changes in mental economics whereby libidinal cathexes are freed from an identification of self and object and turn to objects once again. He considered that the manic subject demonstrated his liberation from the object which had caused his suffering by seeking with a ravenous hunger for a new object (Freud, 1917). Barry displayed this tendency by externalizing one side of the conflict that had distressed him during his depression. At such times he blamed himself as wicked and believed he had caused his mother's death. In the manic state his aggression, previously self-directed, was aimed at evil men who should be punished. But this externalization was not always successful and Barry returned to self-blame. The fact that the primary process had gained ascendancy in the manic attack permitted Barry to fulfill wishes in the face of reality—in particular, his wish that his mother were still alive.

Other cases of mania provoked by object loss also show that the patient has made an identification with the object, and this influences the course of the attack. The only metapsychological difference between the manic and depressed states is that in the former the libidinal cathexes are not permanently locked in this total identification (Freud, 1917). Instead there is a repetitive recathexis of the representation of the lost love object which, for the moment, has become differentiated from the self. Real objects are condensed with the lost object and lead to misidentification.

Manic States Following Frustration and Disappointment

Cases of mania and hypomania frequently follow events other than object loss. The precipitants of these manias are highlighted during the acute attack—especially in cases of hypomania, in which the patient, usually married, complains bitterly about the behavior of the spouse, even going to the extent of claiming that he or she is the ill one (transitivism). Such attitudes were found in this case, in which the manic attack followed childbirth.

Marian

Marian, aged thirty-one, was admitted to the hospital because she had become restless and overactive and she refused to eat or sleep. This had started on her return from confinement ten days after the birth of her first child. When first seen, she was excessively talkative and overactive. She repeated the same thoughts over and over and showed distraction of thought. "I have three complaints: amnesia, a split personality, and a speech difficulty. Did you know I am a doctor? I studied psychology and medicine.... You should be admitted to this hospital, doctor, not me.... Can you confirm that I am right, as a doctor, because I am a doctor myself, being a doctor it is easy to diagnose myself. Is there a chance of getting a job in the hospital? ... I would like to help people rather than make their lives miserable." Marian did not acknowledge that she was ill: "My husband is the one who is ill; he should be in here, not me."

The patient had led a disturbed early life—war conditions had separated her from her mother at the age of three. She lived with relatives until she left school. She then held a number of clerical posts before her marriage at the age of twenty-nine to a divorced man. Three months after her marriage she became pregnant. She was extremely anxious and often depressed during her pregnancy, fearing that she might die during labor and that the child would be born defective. For weeks at a time she lost interest in her husband, the house, and herself. On occasion her spirits were so low that she thought of suicide. Later Marian said that her husband had become impotent within a few weeks after their marriage.

Marian persisted in her delusion that she was a doctor. She walked about the hospital ward in a white coat and acted as if she were examining the patients, much to their annoyance. She announced that she was Dr. Rogers, assuming the name of the male nurse who was in charge of the ward. She made no secret of her sexual interest in him, going so far as to call herself Mrs. Rogers. After some weeks these delusions subsided, only to reappear with great force when her husband refused to take her home for the weekend. "I am a famous doctor from London!" she shouted. If her orders were questioned she flew into a rage. In contrast to Barry, Marian showed no evidence of elation of mood throughout the manic attack: anger was the affect she most commonly expressed. Her overactivity was not accompanied by depressed affect or thought, again in contrast to Barry's symptoms.

Marian acted in a superior manner toward others and became angry if her wishes were not immediately met. During her first weeks in the hospital she believed that her husband was also a patient there. She said she knew exactly how he felt. When at times her overactivity subsided she was able to describe some of her recent experiences. She reported that just before entering the hospital, she had the feeling that "I was my husband as well as being me. . . . I could tell everything he was thinking or going to do. . . . It was a terrible ordeal. I was hypnotized by mistake, and that was why I had to come to the hospital." As some of the preceding material indicates, Marian's appreciation of reality was altered by the power of her wishes—"I can see you are married, your wife looks like me, that is why you liked me when you first set eyes on me," she told a doctor.

During her manic attack Marian indicated disappointment and anger with her husband. He was selfish and indifferent. She had to tolerate his inability to satisfy her sexually and she hated him for having deceived her into marriage. In the acute phase, she criticized the psychiatrist for thinking she was a lesbian and arranging for two nurses who were homosexual to look after her. She attacked another patient, claiming she was trying to seduce her. She blamed others for making her angry and causing her to behave so aggressively.

Two months after her admission Marian's psychomotor overactivity and delusional ideas subsided. She became depressed and apprehensive about the future. She was afraid that she would not be able to manage the baby. She feared that her husband would have a mental breakdown—and indeed, a few weeks later he had to stay home from work because of a "nervous upset." Though she expressed concern for her husband, she continued to criticize him for being childish and irresponsible. She was angry about the interference of her mother-in-law and wondered how she would manage should her husband fail to regain his potency. She felt lonely and unwanted. One night the thought of suicide entered her mind: "During the night I thought of killing myself. I went to the kitchen and took a knife. Then I found myself cutting the leaves off some plants."

Throughout this period Marian was apathetic. At no time did she express any kind of self-criticism. Several months passed before she could adjust herself to a future with her husband and leave the hospital.

In cases of mania that follow object loss, irrespective of a preceding attack of depression, the clinical phenomena show that the patient is in the process of reinvesting the lost love objects with libidinal cathexes. This is seen in the misidentifications and in the kind of wishes which, fulfilled, allow the individual to believe that the lost object has been restored. As the object representations become cathected, the patient gives up identification with the lost object. In contrast, individuals whose manic attacks occur after frustration and disappointment give no sign that they have replaced object cathexis by identification with the object. Wishes regarding the love object that find fulfillment are of a different order. Instead of a wish for restitution of the object there is a wish for vengeance. Marian's claims that her husband was the one who was ill and later that he was dead fulfilled her aggressive wishes. Similar wishes led her to believe that her husband was in the hospital. When she claimed that she and he were one, because she knew what he thought and felt, she was merely generalizing her own experiences to him. At no time did her behavior suggest the complete identification with the love object that occurs in mania that follows object loss.

Anger and aggressive behavior in manic attacks are most prominent when the illness has been provoked by frustration. Destructive wishes appear in the delusional content, which usually involves the conflict between good and evil. The destructive ideas also express elements of pregenital sadistic sexuality.

Marian's manic attack was preceded by a prolonged depression of mood, loss of interest in self and others, a sense of hopelessness, irritability, and sleep disturbance. Such symptoms precede both hypomanic and manic attacks, but they are not always sufficiently severe that the patient seeks help. This symptom complex is different from that of depressive states characterized by self-reproach and psychomotor retardation.

The Metapsychological Evaluation of Manic States

Patients' revelations in the manic phase and afterward indicate that typical psychomotor overactivity may have varying immediate causes and may result from varying unconscious mental events. In attempting a metapsychological analysis of a manic state we must first ask what kinds of conflict underlie the attack. Katan (1953) pointed to the commonly held view that, since mania often follows depression, the conflict in both phases may be similar. In depression, the conflict between the wish to retain the object and the wish to destroy it is momentarily resolved by turning the hatred against a self identified with the lost object. Katan proposed that in mania psychic structures are extensively dissolved and one side of the conflict is externalized. Destructive wishes are attributed to external objects, leading to the conflict between good and evil.

The cases described above suggest that conflict over aggression is applicable primarily to mania that follows a period of frustration and disappointment. During the prepsychotic "depressive" phase, which lasts for varying lengths of time, the patient tries to avoid a danger situation provoked by the frustrated libidinal wishes. The patient feels deprived of comfort and support. The frustrated libidinal wishes lead to an aggressive response—death wishes—that constitute a danger situation. The symptoms of this phase—fatigue, loss of drive, a sense of hopelessness—suggest that the death wishes are removed from consciousness and turned against the self. Although suicidal ideas occur to the patient, there are no self-criticisms.

The manic attack in these cases break out when the defensive measures are no longer effective. It is at this point that the economic aspects of the unconscious mental processes must be taken into account. Repression fails, either because of increased pressure from the instinctual drives or because the ego organization can no longer sustain the continuing stress. An eruption of the primary process coincides with the dissolution of psychic structures, particularly the superego. Both libidinal and aggressive wishes are freely expressed in both speech and action. The individual becomes openly aggressive to the spouse and looks elsewhere for genital satisfaction. Depending on the nature of the case this may take a homosexual or heterosexual direction. Hostile wishes against the spouse are fulfilled. The manic attack allows "discharge" of aggression, according to Jacobson (1954). This contradicts Katan's (1953) assertion that in mania aggression is limited to controlling the object and does not aim to destroy it. Katan's formulation is more appropriate to those manic states that follow severe depression and object loss.

Manic states precipitated by object loss are different in a number of ways, metapsychologically speaking, from manias surrounding frustrations and disappointments. The clinical phenomena indicate that even in the acute phase of the mania ambivalence characterizing the preceding state of depression can intrude (e.g., the case of Barry). The libidinal cathexes invest the self in its identifications alternately with the lost object and the object representations.

The fact that depressive states following object loss, characterized by psychomotor inhibition and self-reproach, precede the onset of mania suggests that the sequence of intrapsychic events leading to the acute attack differs from that envisaged for manias where frustration is the immediate cause. In the former cases the conflict revolves around the lost object, and object choice gives way to identification. In the latter, the object, still differentiated from self, is the focus of aggression.

In mania provoked by object loss, the dissolution of the psychic structure leads to the intrusion of the primary process. The anticathexis restricting the concentration of drive energy is no longer operative, perhaps because of superego collapse. At this point the ego functions under the comparatively unrestrained power of the instinctual drives. But the clinical phenomena indicate that the aggression thus set free is not aimed at the destruction of the object. Aggression arises only in response to opposition to the wish to regain contact with the lost object—psychically restored through wish fulfillment under the operation of the primary process. This type of manic state accords with Katan's (1953) view that the acute attack does not serve to discharge aggression previously bound in the depressive symptoms. This is true only for mania provoked by frustration: Katan failed to differentiate these two kinds of mania which, we believe, can be distinguished from each other both clinically and metapsychologically.

The manic state following object loss, with or without depression, expresses a primitive merging of self and love object—the psychotic identification described by Jacobson (1954).[1] This merger relieves the pain of loss. In this sense, the manic attack can be regarded as an attempt at recovery (Katan, 1953). As described elsewhere (chapter 8), a similar form of psychotic identification is to be found in cases of remitting schizophrenia, where, at the onset, delusions of this kind precede the persecutory phenomena. The manic individual, like the schizophrenic, becomes the real object. In mania, the patient identifies with the lost love object; in schizophrenia, with the object who is idealized and envied. In certain schizophrenias envy leads to the dread of retaliation—that is, persecution. The remission that occurs in both mania that follows object loss and remitting schizophrenia can be attributed to the return of the object, albeit in the form of primitive identification.

Since Freud (1917) put forward his theory of mania theorists have tended to emphasize the defensive nature of manic symptoms. This reached its culmination in Melanie Klein's concept of manic defense (1932). Pride of place is given to the role of denial in the individual's falsification of reality; wish fulfillment is relegated to a place of lesser importance. The material presented here shows, both clinically and theoretically, that only in the initial stages, before the

1. This psychotic form of identification, in which self- and object representations are merged, involves a structural regression. In this respect it is more primitive than the defensive identification also referred to in this study of mania. Intermediate forms also occur—as in the case of Marian, whose identification also includes a process of generalization. (There are of course other types of identification, not immediately relevant here, such as the *ego identification* of the adolescent who identifies with admired features of a favorite pop star.)

onset of the acute attack, are defenses brought into play to counter the effects of object loss or of frustration. These defenses eventually fail and there is a change in the clinical picture: the inhibition and self-criticism, the loss of energy, lack of will, and sense of hopelessness of the manic-depressive patient disappear. In both clinical categories the manic attack releases drive energy with the eruption of the primary process.

When the attack is precipitated by object loss the patient tends to recover, as libidinal wishes outweigh aggressive ones. Wishes based on the libidinal drives find fulfillment. When frustration causes the attack, aggressive and destructive wishes are directed against the disappointing object and sexuality seeks new outlets. Here it is predominantly the aggressive wishes that find fulfillment. In all cases of mania the patient's refusal to acknowledge that he or she is ill—denial—is secondary to the wishes that, as a result of the supremacy of the primary process, find psychic fulfillment.

Study of predisposition to manic and hypomanic states in adulthood is complicated by their inconsistent relationship to the depressive states usually associated with them. In clinical practice the most common cases are those in which depression follows the manic or hypomanic attack. These cases provide support for a concept of manic defense because the content of the attack reverses a disagreeable reality. But eventually the affect springing from this unsatisfying reality breaks through, leaving the patient depressed and self-reproachful. Where a depression precedes a manic attack a quite different psychic situation obtains: the attack signifies the resolution of an identification with an ambivalently regarded love object.

The vulnerability of those destined to suffer from manic attacks, in contrast to the schizophrenias, does not appear to lie in a difficulty in maintaining the object cathexis. Object cathexis is preserved during a manic attack, even though the investment changes in quality. Object relationships become need-satisfying. The loss of developmental achievements and their replacement by infantile modes of mental functioning suggest that the vulnerability to manic attacks lies in specific processes that maintain the differentiation of the ego from the id and from the superego.

CHAPTER 11 *Developmental Disharmonies and Manic-Depressive Depressions*

We hypothesize that a psychological predisposition to schizophrenia lies in a vulnerability within the personality created when the ego, id, and superego fail to evolve in harmony. In spite of attempts to integrate these disharmonies, the discordant development impairs the coordination of the ego and the drives. The ability to form object relationships and to establish self-representations, including those of the ego ideal, is insufficient to permit the modifications required from the time of puberty on. Instead object relationships become disorganized, and a break with reality follows.

Although this developmental hypothesis is equally applicable to manic-depressive depressions, the disharmony is of a different order from that postulated for predisposition to schizophrenia. In depressive individuals, signs of anomalous development must be sought in the symptoms and the mental contents that come to light during the course of the illness or that can be observed during psychoanalytic therapy.

Freud's Theory of Depression

The abnormal mental states called *manic-depressive depressions* or *endogenous depressions* are by no means homogenous. They differ according to age and mode of onset, immediate precipitant, clinical presentations, course of illness, and response to treatment. The theory

Freud advanced in "Mourning and Melancholia" (1917) was based on a single type of depressive illness—namely, psychotic depression precipitated by the loss, real or symbolic, of a loved person. Freud did not claim a general validity for his conclusions.

Those who work in psychiatric hospitals are familiar with this type of depression. For example, a fifty-five-year-old man may be admitted because his speech and action has become retarded and he is preoccupied with delusional self-reproaches. This attack has followed his son's suicide six months earlier. Such patients, whether retarded or agitated, tend to be inaccessible because their attention is entirely taken up with unrealistic self-criticisms and dread of imagined punishment.

Freud's interest in the psychopathology of depressive states was stimulated by Abraham, who had undertaken the treatment of a small number of depressive patients. The two exchanged a series of letters on the subject that were published in 1965.

In 1911, Abraham published the results of his work in a paper entitled "Notes on the Psychoanalytical Treatment of Manic-Depressive Insanity." The patients suffered from a relatively mild form of the illness and were therefore able to describe their life experiences, talk about themselves as persons, and show an interest in others. Although Abraham described these patients as "light cases of manic depression," each patient was possessed by a strong sense of guilt, which led to inappropriate self-criticism, some inhibition of thought and action, and serious loss of self-confidence. Abraham concluded on the basis of his work, that depressive symptoms arose from a violent anger that had been denied access to consciousness. Fear of injuring a loved person turned the hatred against the self, leading to self-criticism and sometimes suicide.

The phenomena Abraham described can be observed in the treatment of patients whose depressive illness is not sufficiently severe to obstruct psychoanalytic treatment. The deflection of hatred from a loved person to the self can easily be seen in the circular type of manic depression. In the manic or hypomanic phase the patient criticizes the apparently loved person in every possible way. When the depressive phase supervenes, this prominent rage disappears and is replaced by self-criticism, the content of which is identical to that of the reproaches made against the loved person during the hypomanic attack.

Freud was not convinced that the mental mechanism whereby

hatred is turned from the love object to the self was solely responsible for the symptomatology of severe depressions (Abraham and Freud, 1965). His reservations turned on the fact that aggressive death wishes are sometimes directed against the self in neuroses; in these conditions, however, the death wishes do not adhere so firmly to the self and can therefore more easily find their way to consciousness and to their real object.

As early as 1915, as the Freud-Abraham correspondence reveals, Freud had formed the opinion that people who develop depressive disorders do so because of psychic loss and an impaired capacity to replace the lost love object. Freud (1917) turned to a comparative study of mourning and depression in order to contrast the healthy psychic reaction of mourning with the pathological reaction to loss in a depressive illness.

Mourning differs from depression in a number of ways. The mourner's mind is taken up with memories of the deceased and the grief these memories evoke. The depressed patient whose disturbance follows loss does not have such memories. Instead he gives vent to his own failings, unworthiness and to his suffering. He knows that he has sustained an important loss but does not seem to be aware, as the mourner is, of what has been lost emotionally. Loss of self-esteem also distinguishes the depressed patient from the person who mourns. The mourner may feel deprived of love but he does not feel himself to be bad or unworthy of love. Although the depressed individual is unaware of the significance of the loss, he is unable to renounce his attachment to the lost love object, as the mourner is eventually able to do.

The depressed person's inability to free himself from the lost love object is reflected in the way he assumes mental and physical characteristics of that object, even to the point of presenting symptoms that belonged to the object in life. Freud's recognition that his depressed patients identified themselves completely with the lost object allowed him to see the self-criticism in an entirely new light—as criticisms of the lost love object.

When a middle-aged woman became deeply depressed after her husband's death, one sign of this identification was her assumption of his speech impediment. She accused herself of being a malingerer—the same criticism she had made of her husband when he had complained of not feeling well. Now that he was dead she continued her attacks against him by attacking herself. This total identification enables the patient to express the most violent hatred against the love object by way of self-reproaches and suicide.

Freud explains this special mode of reaction to loss on the basis of intense ambivalence. This patient's hatred for her husband was matched by her love. Her hatred was partially overt before his death, but in some cases it remains latent while the relationship continues. The depressed person's hatred thus finds its outlet in self-criticism while his or her love for the object ensures that the object is psychically retained through identification.

Although Freud emphasized that his theory was applicable to only one type of depressive illness, nevertheless it provides a conceptual framework within which the heterogeneous group of mental illnesses designated depressive disorders can be further distinguished from one another. The fact that patients whose symptoms are identical at the onset of the illness vary in their response to treatment emphasizes the need for such distinctions.

In typical cases the differentiation of depressive illnesses on descriptive grounds is quite straightforward. Patients of the kind Freud had in mind are easily distinguished from those who suffer from the type of depression that involves inappropriate self-criticism without delusional self-reproach and where the disorder of motility involves mild agitation rather than retardation. These depressions may seem to form spontaneously although they often occur after childbirth, after achieving a long-desired ambition, or after an attack of hypomania. Sometimes there is a lifelong history of recurrent depressive attacks. Those with long clinical experience know that the self-criticisms common to this type of depression are not of equal import when seen from the point of view of the course of the illness and the response to treatment.

Cases of depression can be differentiated on psychoanalytic grounds according to the extent to which adult mental life has been subject to regressive processes, measured by the nature of the patients' object relationships and the predominant intrapsychic conflict observed. In some cases the tie to another person is replaced by identification. When this identification is total, as illustrated by the case of Simon, below, the conflict surrounds wishes and fears springing from earliest childhood. In other cases the identification with the love object is only partial, and the conflicts originate in a somewhat later period of childhood dominated by anal sadism. These cases are similar to the obsessional neuroses. In other cases, the symptoms revolve around death wishes derived from jealousy and envy. In these cases object choice has not given way to identification. The conflicts belong to the oedipal-phallic phase and therefore offer the best possibility for treatment by psychoanalytical therapy.

Disharmony and Conflict in Severe Depression

Most severe depressions depend on a total or near-total identification with the love object: thus the conflicts observed play a secondary rather than a primary role in the genesis of symptoms. The primary role is played by a disharmonious mental evolution, beginning in infancy, which accentuates and aggravates the conflicts that surround successive phases of development.

In certain cases of depression, psychoanalytic treatment offers the opportunity to reconstruct the history of such a disharmonious development. Such reconstructions are more reliable than those proposed for established cases of schizophrenia, in which the patient's loss of contact with reality, the creation of a psychotic reality, and the effect of antipsychotic medications limit cooperation and interfere with recollection and the orderly repetition of memories and fantasies as transferences.

Simon

The following material emerged during a four-year-long psychoanalytic treatment of a severely depressed individual. Simon was a highly intelligent professional man, aged forty-five at the start of treatment. The depressive illness, which involved intense self-reproach, agitation, and suicidal thoughts, had lasted for over a year and had not responded to two separate courses of electroshock therapy. Simon had suffered from depression on two previous occasions—once at the age of twenty-one and once at twenty-seven, just before his marriage.

The current episode was precipitated by Simon's taking on a senior management position in a city about a hundred miles from his hometown. Simon had been born abroad and was the older of two boys. His father had been an official in the colonial office and had sent his sons back to England to be educated. At the age of five, Simon was sent to live with his paternal grandmother and a maiden aunt, to whom he became devoted. He continued to live with these relatives until his father retired and both parents returned to England. Simon was entering adolescence.

Simon had no apparent difficulty in following the basic rule of treatment. He talked freely, but primarily he talked about his suffering. He found it difficult to go to work each day because he was convinced that his assistant, who had held the job before Simon arrived, believed him incompetent and unfit to hold his position as head of the department. Simon was never satisfied by his own work performance—he always found something wrong that threw him into anxiety. He belittled all his achievements and felt hopeless and useless to his family.

During lengthy periods of the analysis the pattern of the transference was based on Simon's current relationship with his wife and that with his mother during adolescence. This alternated with a homosexual transference manifested through thoughts and feelings about his assistant. Simon believed that he was nothing but a burden to his wife and that she would be better off without him. He did not deserve such a good woman, nor was it right that he should benefit from the fact that she was wealthy. However, when his wife tried to reassure him about his work or make some suggestion to ease his situation, he criticized her to the therapist, claiming that she did not understand his state of mind and that her suggestions had the quality of demands. These data allowed some exposure of preconscious transference thoughts. Reluctantly Simon admitted that while he feared he would prove an impossible burden to the analyst, he also found the analysis very demanding. Every day he feared that he would have nothing to say and that the treatment would fail as a result, because of a deficiency within himself.

At the beginning of the analysis Simon described his mother as kindly and considerate, but later he recalled her as expecting a great deal from him. He remembered going for a walk with his mother at about eight years of age. They came to a steep hill, and he complained of being tired and asked to go back home. His mother refused his request and forced him to on. He shouted at her, calling her "a cruel mother." This led to a recollection of his adolescence, during which his mother perpetually pressed him to work hard at school and at university. He then recalled that he had blamed his mother for his first breakdown. It was she who had suggested that he ought to proceed to a graduate degree.

About the middle of the second year of treatment Simon's elderly mother fell dangerously ill. The improvement he had made vanished immediately. He blamed himself for not having devoted more time to her, calling himself selfish and thoughtless. He believed with an almost delusional intensity that her death would bring his life to an end. His extreme distress was accompanied by a renewal not only of self-criticism but of criticism of others. His wife and family and his colleagues at work made endless demands on him. During this time Simon made no further mention of his mother.

When Simon's mother died his symptoms became even more disturbing. He said he could no longer work. He called himself a parasite, criticizing himself for his wish to retire and live on his wife's income. As long as he had to work he could never be free of a crushing sense of inadequacy. Work sucked him dry. His wife did the same. The analyst, Simon complained, did not seem to appreciate his inability to continue with life, work, and treatment. When he tried to relax he could not free himself from the nagging feeling that he should be planning a new project at work or keeping up with current literature.

Simon responded constructively when connections were made between these utterances and his attitudes toward his mother in the past and toward the analyst in the present. His hatred of work, on the one hand, and the demands he made of himself, on the other, represented a childhood struggle between his mother and himself. This struggle was being repeated in treatment. Simon bitterly complained that his mother had sucked him dry; she had never been satisfied with his achievements; she had pushed him to greater and greater efforts. Like a vampire, she had exhausted him of his resources and then abandoned him. When Simon was able to express these criticisms of his mother he felt no anger against the analyst or against his wife.

This analytic work led to the revival of new memories and the repetition of others only briefly mentioned earlier in the treatment. Among these was Simon's recollection of arriving in England at the age of five with his teddy bear. His aunt made a number of outfits for the teddy bear, replicas of Simon's own clothes. He spent hours playing with the bear and always had to have it with him. He relinquished it only when he reached the age of seven or eight. Simon knew that he had taken separation from his mother very badly. He recalled a fantasy of wanting to stick a hatpin through his head. In later years he suffered badly from headaches, as his mother had when he was a child. His earliest memories of his mother were of her expectations that he be neat, tidy, and obedient. She would not tolerate outbursts of temper. In early childhood Simon had been cared for by a nurse-maid; he had been told that for the first six months of his life he was suckled by a wet-nurse. According to his mother he was extremely distressed when this feeding ended suddenly. Simon's father was a distant figure who failed to act as a counterweight to the mother with whom Simon became so closely identified.

Simon's mental development was interfered with by external circumstances. He was suddenly weaned, subjected to excessive expectations in toilet training, and his expression of aggression in the second and third years of his life was opposed by threats of loss of love. His father played no part in his early upbringing, and there was never any closeness between them. At the age of five Simon effectively lost his mother. The discord between his ego and superego, which found expression in his illness, was characterized by a sadism directed against a self wholly identified with the mother. The superego drew on an oral sadism characterized by greed, cruelty, and insatiability. These traits were projected in the transference and expressed in fantasies about his mother, his wife, and his work, which was also personified. Simon's unrealistic ideals and grandiose ambitions reflected an overvaluation of the self, concealed by modest, self-effacing behavior.

It is not unreasonable to suppose, on the basis of the clinical phenomena, that Simon's early experiences interfered with the fusion of libido and aggression, which imparted an excessive sadism to his oral, anal, and phallic instincts. This discordant development, which promoted and perpetuated an intense ambivalence in object relationships, was further aggravated by his rapid internalization of the commands and anger of his mother and nurse. His precociously advanced ego development was soon out of sympathy with the drive derivatives. Simon experienced panic attacks in childhood and was afraid of being left alone. These consequences of death wishes were powerful determinants of his need to acquiesce to his mother's demands.

The disharmony between ego and id exacerbated the usual developmental conflicts that characterize the first years of life. Reaction formations against hatred, greed, and cruelty soon became a part of Simon's personality. The loss of his mother disturbed the integration of the discordant elements of his evolving personality and enabled the sadistic tendencies to return. But by this time they turned upon the self, exemplified by Simon's fantasy of sticking a hatpin into his head. His play with a teddy bear, with whom he identified, must have given expression both to his loss and to his aggressive reactions against it.

Simon's later childhood development gave no cause for concern. On the surface, adolescence presented no particular problems, although Simon experienced an intense masturbation conflict that caused him shame because of the strong anal influence on his genital development. The sadistic quality of his genital sexuality was apparent in masturbation fantasies in which soldiers ravished innocent young women. Material from the analysis not quoted here revealed that Simon's excessive identification with women (to be distinguished from the pathological identification that provided the basis for the self-criticism and self-hatred) impaired his masculinity. He felt a sense of inferiority and a passive attitude toward other men, which reached pathological proportions in his dealings with his assistant.

From time to time during his adolescence and adult life Simon showed signs of the greed and impatience that had been curtailed in his early years. Material possessions were very important to him, and he expected to be well provided for. He remembered that as a student he had insisted that his mother buy a new carpet for his room because a friend was coming to visit. He was indifferent to the fact that his mother, then a widow, was short of money. Simon's oral, acquisitive needs found short-lived satisfaction when he married a woman who came from a wealthy family.

Environmental interference hindered the development of object cathexis that requires for its optimal development a harmonious combination of instinctual drives on the one hand and their aim-inhibited derivatives on the other. Simon's object cathexis was excessively instinctualized and so his object relationships were characterized by oral traits and ambivalence. Much of the libidinal cathexis that should have invested the object representation had fallen back onto the self. The outcome was a narcissism that found expression in adolescent fantasies of omnipotence and, in adult life, in unattainable ideals and ambitions. This ego-ideal component of the superego based on excessive self-love paralleled those aspects of this agency derived from his oral-sadism. Whatever Simon did failed to satisfy the standards he set for himself, hence his continual disappointment and self-criticism.

The latent disharmony between Simon's ego and the superego showed itself when, at twenty-one years of age, he was on holiday and due to begin at the university in the autumn. He feared he would not succeed and began to brood about this. Anxiety turned into agitation and Simon had to be hospitalized, but after a few months he recovered completely without the need for active treatment. His second attack began just before his marriage. He feared he might be impotent and again became agitated and self-critical. This time Simon did not need to go into the hospital, but some months elapsed before he felt well enough to go ahead with the wedding. Both these attacks and the one that led to psychoanalytic treatment occurred when Simon was confronted with a situation that would have been exciting and challenging to a mentally sound individual.

A danger was created by the superego in these situations. The anticipation of a new experience from which Simon might derive pleasure was denied him. It became instead a potential source of disappointment and frustration, with the consequent arousal of aggression followed by guilt. This sequence of responses led, just before Simon's marriage, to the fear of impotence. The regression that followed superego anxiety in his third attack laid bare the latent disharmony between ego and id. The ego remained firm except in a temporal sense: Simon became overdependent, feared separation from his wife, and constantly sought reassurance. The instincts regained their infantile quality with further defusion of libido and aggression, and the oral-sadistic elements of the superego came to the fore. The superego was vulnerable to regressive alterations because at the time of its formation, also at the time when the love objects were internalized, the instincts had not been sufficiently modified in their quality. Instinctual rather than aim-inhibited drive derivatives cathected the identifications that come to constitute the superego, accounting for the severity of Simon's superego even when he was apparently well.

Florence

Florence, a married woman of twenty-five, became mentally ill two days after the birth of her first child, a girl. The baby was born by caesarian section after a pregnancy that was uneventful except in the last days. During her pregnancy Florence had worried considerably that the baby might be born defective. Her first sign of mental disorder was a confusion of mind—she was afraid she would not know how to manage the baby. There followed a series of fears. Florence told the nurse that the baby was deformed and was going to die. She feared

she had given the baby too much milk and that she would fall ill.
Florence's agitation and restlessness became so great that she was
transferred to the psychiatric ward of the hospital. She refused to stay
and returned home, but her mental state was so bad that she had to
be readmitted forty-eight hours later.

On her return to the psychiatric ward Florence was withdrawn
and agitated. Her speech was slow, but she did answer questions. She
said that she was afraid to take care of the baby lest she failed to carry
out the various procedures correctly and harm the infant. She could
not decide what line of action to follow. She was also angry with her
husband for sending her to the hospital.

The nursing staff reported that Florence said other patients in the
ward did not like her and were talking about her in a critical way.
Some were saying that she was a thief. The staff and patients were
doing everything they could to annoy her. They did not think she
should be in the hospital, as there was nothing wrong with her: she
was just a bad person. Even the most trivial acts seemed to have the
purpose of conveying this message to her. Florence hated everyone
in the ward and wanted to annoy them. She did so by refusing to sleep
and being noisy.

Florence regretted having had the baby and claimed she had no
interest in her. She said, "I can neither laugh nor cry." Everyone
wanted to punish her, but for her part she wanted to punish them.
The baby was taking up everyone's attention, and soon no one would
bother with her. Her mother would take over the baby's care, and
Florence would have to sit and watch and do as she was told. She
slept poorly and frequently tried to leave the ward.

Gradually these acute symptoms subsided and Florence's interest
in her baby returned. She was allowed home for a weekend and enjoyed caring for the child. During this period of improvement
Florence spoke of her relations with her parents, particularly her
mother. She was an only child but had never gotten along with her
parents. Her mother was critical and domineering and insisted that
Florence do things the way she herself would have done them. In
adolescence Florence had struggled constantly to gain independence
from her mother. Although there were no overt quarrels, they sometimes did not speak to each other for long periods.

Florence's mother told her what to do and when to do it. Florence
resented this because her mother had not looked after her needs properly. When she was four months old her mother had gone back to

work, leaving Florence with her grandmother, who lived across the street. Her mother looked after her only in the evenings and on weekends. Her mother and grandmother often quarreled, causing Florence to feel a conflict of loyalties. Her father played a passive role in domestic affairs and avoided the arguments over Florence's care.

Florence's improvement, which lasted through the third week after her admission to the hospital, came to a sudden end. As later events confirmed, this relapse was precipitated by her parents' departure on holiday. They had been spending several hours each day with her, almost excluding her husband. This behavior was entirely consistent with her mother's lifelong overconcern, which Florence remembered ever since childhood. Not only did her mother worry excessively about her daughter's health but she queried her every intention and action. It was this that had led to disagreements in Florence's adolescence.

During the relapse Florence refused to eat or drink. Although retarded in speech and action she burst out periodically with self-reproach. Everyone said she was wicked. This was true because she wished everyone dead, including the baby, her mother, and her husband. She wished she were dead too. She asked if the town had changed: were the buildings still all right? When told they were she accused the analyst of lying to her. The town had been destroyed, she insisted, as a punishment for harboring such an evil person as herself. Everyone had changed. When her husband had visited the day before it was some time before she recognized him. He did not seem to be the correct size: he looked like a small boy. Asked who he was, she replied that he was a boy called Ian Jackson whom she had known at school.

The acute attack continued—Florence claimed that her mother would never come back because she was dead. She was glad because she was a rotten mother. Then Florence reproached herself with the thought that she had ruined her family because she was evil. She switched repeatedly between free verbal expression of hatred for the baby, husband, mother, doctors, and nurses, followed by the belief that they were all dead, and statements to the effect that she had damaged everyone and so deserved to die as a punishment.

This episode passed within a day or so of Florence's mother's return home. That the attack had been initiated by the mother's departure on holiday was confirmed by the husband's report that, about two years earlier when Florence was apparently quite well, she became agitated and anxious when her parents went away on holiday. She and her husband had agreed to take them to the airport. At the last minute Florence refused to go. She said she had the idea that there would be a plane crash and her parents would be killed. She could not face the thought of saying goodbye to them.

For two weeks after her parents' return there was a considerable improvement in Florence's mental state. Again she talked about her childhood and adolescence, recalling fears similar to those just described. She remembered being anxious around about the time her mother was due home from work. She feared that her mother might be struck by a car and killed. Because her grandmother was always nearby she was never lonely, but she recalled being afraid of the dark and reluctant to go to bed. She talked about her need to keep her mother at a distance when she got home from the hospital. Although she did not recall real difficulties at school, she had a faint memory of not wanting to leave the house during the first few months after school had begun.

Florence said that throughout adolescence and early adulthood she was given to bouts of depression during which she was oppressed by a sense of her inferiority to her friends and colleagues. On such occasions she found it difficult to speak or to derive help from other people's reassurance. Both mother and husband confirmed these statements and added that at such times it was impossible to break through Florence's withdrawal. The tendency to silence was most evident if she was unhappy with her mother in the past, or her husband in the present. In becoming silent she was acting as her mother had done when she was angry with her husband. Florence's condition improved and she was allowed to go home for a long weekend. Although she looked forward to the visit, it did not go well—she did not feel at ease caring for the baby by herself. Within a day or so of her return to the hospital her depressive mood reappeared. She refused to eat or drink and became extremely negativistic. During one meeting with the analyst she sat immobile for over half an hour. This catatonic-like behavior was also observed by the nursing staff. The few words Florence did utter revealed that she was taken up again with her delusional ideas. Her attachment to the ward sister enabled her to disclose that she did not drink or eat because she thought the water was urine—even if it were water it came from the sewer, as did the food. After a number of days she gradually relaxed when in the company of the ward sister and finally improved again.

During the acute phases of Florence's illness the dissolution of her personality caused the instinctual drives and the superego to act independently of one another, while the ego passively "looked on." This discord meant that either the superego or the id was at any one time in control and giving rise to the symptoms. At one moment the ascendancy of the id allowed Florence to believe that everyone was dead, in accordance with her conscious wishes. The next moment the superego would take over, and she would hold herself responsible for the destructive acts she believed had occurred. The omnipotence of her death wishes led to self-condemnation: she was an evil witch, and everyone knew of her destructiveness. When her aggressive tendencies had free rein, she attributed wickedness to her mother. During these acute phases, ego regression resulted in loss of reality testing. The sense of volition was lost, and Florence experienced reality in terms of her wishes, memories, and fantasies. She misidentified her husband as a small boy, for example, and misperceived water and food as urine or as contaminated by feces.

This asynchrony between ego, id, and superego can only be explained on the basis of the hypothesis that there existed in Florence's personality a defective integration of the three psychic systems—ego, id, and superego. The birth of her child disturbed the precarious adjustment that existed between them.

There is considerable evidence that such a lack of integration had its origin in a disharmonious development. Florence's relations with her mother were never satisfactory. In her early childhood she had been handled by two different people, who disagreed about her management. Object constancy was established, but drive development did not progress normally. The intense ambivalence so evident clinically suggests that drive fusion was only partially successful. Florence had to cope with aggressive drives forbidden by her mother, which later became unacceptable to her. Anal interests were similarly opposed at an inappropriate time. A forced and premature ego development led to an excessive repudiation of instinctual wishes (cf. George, chap. 4). This explains Florence's delusion about being given contaminated food and water. Maternal pressure to repudiate anal-erotic tendencies during early feeding must have contributed to such a reaction, with its combination of oral and excretory elements.

Developmental conflicts were exacerbated by the disharmony between the drives and the ego. Fear of loss of love led to instinct repression and to the establishment of reaction formations. In spite of these, Florence's repressed hatred found representation in fears for her mother's health and safety. Hate for her mother found a limited outlet in adolescence, but only as a means of establishing some distance between herself and the love object of childhood. For the most part her ambivalence remained hidden from view until the onset of the psychosis. Her need for independence from her mother became a compulsion, hiding from view a dependency based on anxiety and death wishes that were expressed, in adulthood, in the morbid fear that her parents would be killed in a plane crash.

In this case, as in the case of Simon, the development of the superego suffered because of a defective evolution of the drives. Florence's aggression was never sufficiently modified by libido. Not only were aspects of her mother's personality, including her criticism of Florence, internalized, but the girl's part in the aggressive exchange was reinternalized. Her ego prematurely became an instrument for the execution of her mother's instructions and commands, which took a particularly punitive form. The discord between ego and id was further compounded by the establishment of the maternal introject as the "moral" core of the superego. This agency was now endowed with the aggressiveness that the mother's behavior provoked as well as with the mother's own aggressiveness. This self-directed aggression from the superego caused the periodic bouts of depression of mood from which Florence suffered in adolescence and adulthood.

Ambivalence rather than love was evoked by the birth of Florence's child. She feared she would harm the child. Once the dissolution of the ego took place, the wish to kill the child became manifest. This aggression provoked by the arrival of the baby was not attenuated by fusion with libido, nor could it be rendered harmless through the formation of neurotic symptoms. The disharmonious development had left its mark on the ego, depriving it of the power to mediate between the drives and the superego. The compulsive fear of harming the child can be compared with Grace's compulsive need to wash (described later in this chapter). In neither case did the symptoms arise from a compromise between a sexual (phallic-genital) wish altered by regression (anal-sadistic) and the requirements of the superego. Instead, the compulsive phenomena were the direct outcome of instinctual pressures, aggressive here, anal-erotic in the case of Grace. The psychic structures gave way at the point of weakness created by the underlying discord between the drives, the ego, and the superego. As a result, Florence experienced overt death wishes.

At the onset of this illness, and in accordance with current practice, Florence was given antidepressant and phenothiazine drugs. Her initial improvement was attributed to these medications. After her relapse, however, all drug therapy was stopped, and her final recovery from the illness was entirely spontaneous. Only rarely has the question been asked how patients suffering from severe mental disorders achieve a spontaneous remission of their illnesses. Freud (1917) suggested that recovery was due to a redistribution of libidinal cathexes. The mania that follows a depressive state in circular manic-depressive psychosis in Freud's view was caused by the libido's attempt to make a new object choice, now that it had been detached from the introjected object. Clearly, a redistribution of libido has occurred at the time of remission in patients whose psychotic depression is neither preceded nor followed by a manic or hypomanic attack. However, other factors must operate in cases where a complete remission occurs. Recovery is also contemporaneous with a reduction in drive pressure, as the clinical changes reveal. This may be due to a relative convergence of libido and aggression with a concomitant lessening of ambivalence—which in turn reduces the pressure exerted by the superego.

The Developmental Fault in Depressive States

The onset and course of severe (psychotic) depressive states tell us that the libidinal cathexis is not withdrawn from the object. When depression is precipitated by loss, object choice is replaced by identification. This type of depressive identification is comparable to the psychotic identifications observed at the onset of the schizophrenias (Jacobson, 1954; See chapter 7). In these cases the identification follows from a loss of the boundaries of the physical and mental self. The self and object merge in the manner described in chapter 10. But the boundaries of the self- and object representations remain intact in non-psychotic depressive states since there is no dissolution of psychic structures.

A striking feature of depressive states is the tenacity with which the patient clings to the lost object. It is "a love which cannot be given up" (Freud, 1917), even when the opportunity for an alternative love object becomes available. The new conscious choice of a love object does not succeed in attracting to itself the cathexis invested in the lost object. The patient remains depressed and self-critical in spite of his new love relationship. This and other observations suggest most strongly that the developmental fault in depressive states cannot be traced to a failure in the creation of a stable object representation (ego) or to lack of ability to cathect such a representation firmly. The converse seems to be the case in those who are destined to suffer from a schizophrenic psychosis.

The ambivalence that characterizes depressive states, irrespective of their immediate causes, hints at the nature of the developmental fault predisposing individuals to depression. Such a degree of ambivalence is possible only if the fusion of libido and aggression, of love and hate, has never been satisfactorily achieved.

One of the ways the young adolescent frees himself from his incestuous love for his parents and siblings is by replacing love by hate (A. Freud, 1958). In the mentally healthy adolescent, manifestation of this hatred is confined to criticism of the parents and expressions of disillusionment. The restriction of the expression of hatred results from an adequate fusion of aggression and libido. This contention is borne out by contrast to cases of severe manic-depressive depression that arise in early or middle adolescence.

Tony

Tony, aged fourteen and a half, was admitted to the hospital because over a period of several weeks he had expressed depressive ideas and his speech and action had become increasingly retarded. The retardation was pronounced at the time of his admission. With encouragement he was able to say that he had deceived his parents into believing that he was a good person, whereas in fact he was wicked and bad, lazy, and hypocritical. He added that he had the impression television announcers were calling him a thief and a liar. "What have I done?" he repeatedly asked.

Tony's condition gradually improved over the next few weeks. As he moved toward recovery he avoided talking about himself or his relationships with his parents and two older sisters. According to his father, Tony was ordinarily a bright, outgoing young man with friends and many interests. No immediate cause for his illness presented itself. The only event that may have upset Tony, according to his mother, was a trip by sea to a football match. The extent of the drunken behavior on the ship had upset him.

Tony's depression recurred three years later. In the intervening period he had been perfectly well, had returned to school and resumed his work, friendships, and athletic interests; had studied without difficulty and passed his exams. A month or so before the second attack Tony's mother noticed that he was dejected and in low spirits. She wondered if this was the result of his having joined an evangelical group. He appeared to be preoccupied with moral and ethical problems.

The symptoms of the second attack were identical to those of the first. On the second occasion, however, Tony made a serious attempt to injure himself, seizing a knife and cutting his forehead badly. On admission to the hospital he said that he had destroyed his family and wanted to die. During his first days in the hospital he had to be restrained from injuring himself. The psychomotor retardation that was otherwise present gradually lessened as the weeks passed. The quantity of Tony's speech varied from day to day. Once recovery was under way he again showed reluctance to talk about himself and asked to discontinue his daily interviews with the analyst.

Tony did, however, indicate how he experienced himself and others. Thoughts were repetitively expressed during the sessions. For example, he believed that he was evil because he hated people and judged them. In turn they hated him. "I wanted to kill people," he said. Tony reproached himself for hating his parents but did not say that he wanted to kill them. He admitted hating his doctor and feared that she must also hate him. He criticized himself for not caring about anyone, particularly his parents. "Everything reminds me of hurting my parents—every move I make."

Tony criticized himself for his jealousy. His father paid too much attention to his mother and sisters, and that made him angry. Another theme that appeared and led to self-criticism consisted of "grandiose" daydreams in which Tony imagined he was famous and special.

Tony's mother said that he was very close to her and from time to time confided in her. She reported that he had told her how wicked he felt because he had been sexually aroused by the sight of his sisters. The mother implied that he had hinted that thoughts of his sisters entered into his masturbation fantasies, which caused him shame. During his daily interviews with the analyst Tony made no reference to his sexual life, and when an appropriate moment arose to introduce the subject of masturbation he made no response.

These data suggest that before the attack Tony was oppressed by incestuous wishes. Hinting to his mother about masturbation was a plea for help in controlling himself. He had not been able to displace his libido to extrafamilial substitutes. He was momentarily conscious of hating his family, but this changed to hatred of himself. Through hating his parents and sisters Tony hid his incestuous wishes from himself. The intensity of the hatred was a measure of the intensity of the incestuous wishes.

The hatred, the means by which incestuous ties were weakened, created a danger situation in which the superego played a part. Instead of giving rise to repression, the dangerous aggressiveness Tony periodically experienced was turned against himself, leading to verbal and physical self-attacks. The necessary conditions for a smooth transition to adolescence were lacking. The punitive quality of the superego was uppermost.

Tony shows the same developmental disharmony evidenced by the illnesses of George and Florence and the reconstructions of their childhood development. Not only did the aggressive and libidinal drives develop unevenly, prolonging the intense ambivalence of infancy, but in addition the ego and superego evolved precociously. Every object relationship, its maintenance guaranteed by the capacity for continuing object cathexis, became the focus of hate as well as love. The libidinal tie to the mother ensured internalization and introjections so that hatred molded central elements of both ego and superego. The development of these structures was progressively affected by the freedom afforded to the aggressive instincts. The internalized conflicts that followed structuralization were intensified. This hypothesis, initially advanced by Hartmann (1953) to explain schizophrenia, seems more applicable to depressive states

The effects of an asynchronous evolution of the drives may make themselves felt at any period of childhood. When ego development is too rapid, the potential for acute conflict is heightened and may result in symptoms similar to those in the adult.

Grace

Grace, an intelligent girl of eleven years, had symptoms that caused both herself and her parents some distress. She had become afraid of catching a fatal disease. This fear had led to an abhorrence of dirt and to compulsive cleanliness. At bedtime Grace was frightened because she feared she would die in her sleep.

Grace's parents did not get along well together. The mother had been working outside the home for a number of years, and Grace and her sister, who were usually on good terms, spent a great deal of time with their maternal grandmother. Grace was very fond of both grandparents, and the shock of her grandfather's death was thought to have precipitated her illness.

Grace especially loved her father. On weekends she accompanied him to the golf course or watched him work on his car. She later complained that he treated her more like a boy than a girl, since he had wanted his second child to be a boy. But Grace had always looked on herself as a tomboy, whereas her sister was interested in all things feminine.

Meeting with the psychiatrist appeared to reduce her anxiety and her compulsive need to keep clean. Grace washed her hands less often and seemed less afraid of contracting a fatal disease. During her sessions she talked about the grandfather of whom she had been so fond. Since his death she often had the idea that he wanted her to join him.

Just as she was about to be discharged from the hospital Grace complained of new symptoms. She said that the world around her often seemed unreal. This symptom was attributed to the fact that Grace's mother had detected a lump on her own breast and feared she might have cancer. A biopsy revealed only a benign cyst. The reassurance this finding gave to Grace's mother and family may have caused Grace's symptoms to disappear. She was finally discharged.

No more was heard from Grace until she turned thirteen, when she was referred once again. Her earlier fears had returned, although they were less severe. She had also become low-spirited and tearful, expressing a sense of hopelessness about the future, and talking of suicide. Grace felt she must be mad because of the thoughts that came into her head. Unless her attention were occupied, she could not rid herself of the idea that the devil had entered her mind and possessed it. If she could think of God the devil was driven out, but she was not always successful in this.

Whenever Grace was sitting by herself, thoughts, ideas, and feelings came into her mind that she believed could only be the work of the devil. She might look the same, but she felt like a different person inside. She was envious of her sister's physical appearance and wanted to possess it herself. Her sister's femininity made her feel inferior and childish. She envied her sister her boyfriend. When in the company of her sister or mother she sometimes had a frightening urge to stick a knife into them. This made her think of herself as evil. She wept bitterly as she related these experiences and said that she must be mad. She wished she were dead. Several weeks earlier Grace had swallowed some of her mother's tranquilizers in the belief that she was wicked while her mother was good. She was convinced that her evil nature was injuring both her mother and her sister.

The analyst decided to approach Grace's illness psychotherapeutically and in a more systematic way than had been done before. Grace responded well to regular appointments and quickly gained relief from talking about her symptoms. Fortunately, her symptoms did not interfere with her good school performance, and her difficulty sleeping did not recur. These observations supported the view that a psychotic outcome was unlikely. It was not long before Grace was able to recognize that her evil feelings and thoughts were not caused by the devil or by monsters but had originated spontaneously inside herself. The development of this insight into the origin of her symptoms may have followed her recollection that, in the previous two years, she had read many horror stories in which people were possessed by the devil. These stories had come to mind when she was searching for an explanation of her strange experiences, and she now looked on the treatment as a way of getting rid of them.

Grace explained that some months before the poor relationship between her parents had culminated in her father's leaving home to live with another woman. This had been a great blow to Grace: she had been very close to her father and now felt lost, as her mother and sister were closer to each other than to her. Her low spirits were reflected in a loss of interest in activities she had previously enjoyed. She spoke little in the house and was very irritable toward her sister. On several occasions Grace visited her father. The woman with whom he was living had a son, and Grace's father took a great interest in him. Grace felt jealous of the boy, and her attitude toward her father began to change. She was critical of him, felt disillusioned, and sympathized with her mother. Nevertheless, whenever she thought of her father she found it hard to restrain her tears.

Against this background of events Grace had gradually become aware of feeling different from others. At times she imagined herself to be a superior person with powers to attain whatever she wanted. She thought of killing people one by one, but then said to herself that she had no wish to kill anyone. Sometimes she wondered who her mother really was, in spite of knowing that she was her mother. These destructive ideas gradually gained momentum, and Grace began to feel that she must be someone else. Her loss of control over her thoughts heightened her anxiety. One day she suddenly pictured in her mind "a green wizard with a long nose." He was laughing at her. She at once feared that she would turn into this wizard. She knew it was impossible but could not rid herself of the idea. She thought she was mad and wanted to die. At such times she wished to be "brain-washed" so that all her unpleasant experiences could be swept away. This wish had made it much easier for her to see the psychiatrist.

Grace was thought to have been mentally healthy before her grandfather's death. After the bereavement she first became conscious of thoughts that she would be carried off by the devil. But it was with her father's departure that she became plagued by "evil" thoughts, though they had been present to a minor degree after her grandfather died.

Grace's grandfather's death had left her vulnerable to aggressive wishes which had hitherto been quiescent. Her grandfather, for whatever reason, had been the object of her death wishes, and with his demise she feared retribution. Projection of the death wishes resulted in the fear that the devil, a substitute for the grandfather, would come in the night and carry her off. This explanation of her initial symptoms is supported by her thought that her grandfather wanted her to join him in death. When it looked as if her mother might have breast cancer, Grace's death wishes were briefly reactivated, but it was not until the father's departure that they made their full impact.

The clinical phenomena observed in this case, so similar to those of Florence, who suffered from puerperal depression, reflect the intensity of the conflict between the aggressive drive derivatives and the remainder of the personality. But this conflict does not explain why death and object loss should provoke intense ambivalence and fear of aggression. Grace's instinctual development may have been more heavily weighted on the side of aggression than libido. This readiness for aggression at every stage of instinctual development would introduce a disharmony into the interactions between the love objects, the drives, and the ego. According to Grace's early history, her ego had evolved rapidly in both its cognitive and its defensive aspects. In turn the superego became the vehicle for aggression bound to the love objects.

This formulation does not exclude other considerations relating to Grace's sexuality, which was rapidly becoming a source of conflict. When Grace fell ill at age eleven she was approaching puberty, but at thirteen, when the relapse occurred, she still had not begun menstruating. Psychotherapeutic work indicated that her sexuality to this point had had a phallic orientation, but that this was now in conflict with her developing femininity. It seems to us that the sexual conflicts may well have been intensified by the effects of disharmonious development, in particular by aggression, which reinforced the sadistic aspects of the anal and phallic drives that were being reactivated in the prepubertal period. They made their own contribution to symptom formation.

It is often said that predisposition to a particular mental illness is based on a defect within the personality. The defect cannot be identified by direct observation alone because the personality is already disordered by the impact of the morbid process. A circuitous approach must be followed, studying the clinical phenomena, and gathering whatever additional information the patient can offer, through behavior as well as speech, during the course of psychotherapeutic or psychoanalytic treatment. In the cases presented here, including that of Grace, conflicts of great severity were the first psychopathological manifestations to come into view. The content of these internalized conflicts was unexceptional; it was their *intensity* that distinguished them from those found in the mentally healthy and in those who suffer from neurosis.

Excessive aggressiveness and sadism is common in individuals predisposed to manic-depressive depression. The part played by a disharmony between anality and its repudiation in premature ego development, together with the premature development of superego precursors, is strikingly similar to the developmental disharmony described by Anna Freud in her discussion of predisposition to obsessional personality (1966).

In the cases described here, destructive orality also plays in important part. Whereas in the obsessional individual later development locates the pathology in the thought processes and emphasizes the defense mechanisms of isolation of affect and intellectualization, in the depressive person the disturbance manifests itself in the drives and affects. These depressive disorders are accompanied by undue hostility, insatiability, and a disturbance of self-cathexis.

These characteristics originate in the later part of the oral stage. The extreme ambivalence of this phase is carried forward into succeeding instinctual phases. The destructive oral-incorporative trends remain inadequately modified and color all subsequent development. The cases of Simon and Florence illustrate how the negative narcissism[1] of the oral phase is reinforced by the mother's failure to respond to the child's insatiable wish for love. According to Abraham, in these patients positive and negative narcissism are closely juxtaposed.

When oral ambivalence of this intensity is carried forward into the anal phase, death wishes become singularly threatening. The persistence and intensification of the child's belief in the omnipotence of thought threaten him or her at every turn with the loss of the object of his or her love.

In consequence, the child encounters the disappointments of the Oedipus complex at a time when oral sadism has not sufficiently receded. Abraham maintains that this "traumatic" disturbance makes the later loss of love such an important precipitant of depressive episodes. In considering these later developments, Abraham (1924) had in mind Freud's comment that the melancholic individual was unable to shift the objects of his love, remaining tied to the "lost" object in spite of his strong hostility.

The intensity of the depressive conflicts should not be viewed apart from the disposition to aggressiveness discerned throughout the course of these patients' mental development. To attribute this potential for aggression, whatever its expression in childhood, to constitutional factors alone fails to do justice to the developmental pathology recounted in the histories. We suggest that aggressiveness arises as a byproduct of discordant development between the drives themselves and the consequences that follow from the first interactions with external objects. Abraham's view of the special nature of the oedipal disappointment in these cases suggests a further disharmony arises and contributes to predisposing factors in manic-depressive depression. When this is combined with rapid and premature evolution of the ego, conditions are created that facilitate psychic discord. This discord can remain latent for long periods, but under certain conditions, it becomes manifest and the ego is deprived of its power to influence either drive expression or the superego. A depressive illness results.

---

1. Abraham (1924) used the terms *positive* and *negative narcissism* to refer to self-love and self-hatred, which he thought were rooted in the later part of the oral phase—that is, after the acquisition of teeth.

CHAPTER 12 *Psychiatry and Psychoanalytic Nosology*

We close this book with a brief discussion and review of the psycho-analytic nosology on which it is based, beginning by putting the thinking behind it into the broader historical context of general psychiatry.

In psychiatry, the era of taxonomy, with its meticulous observations and detailed descriptions of insanity, reached fruitful and systematic organization in the classical formulations of Kraepelin. The work of many years was distilled in the sixth edition of his textbook (1899); the basic structure of Kraepelin's system has proved remarkably resilient, despite repeated criticisms and attempts at substantial revision, and is easily recognizable in diagnostic classifications used all over the world, even though contemporary nosographies cover a much wider field than that clinically encountered in the mental hospitals of the late nineteenth century. The usefulness of Kraepelin's system is most readily apparent in his classification of the psychoses, and his descriptive clarification of the manic-depressive disorders is still of clinical value today. In spite of all the circumscriptions of its application, weaknesses of Kraepelin's general classification must be assigned to the limitations of any descriptive system, rather than taxonomic inaccuracy.

Although in the days when Kraepelin was putting together his system many mental afflictions were ascribed to "hereditary taint," "degeneracy," and the like, many believed that, over and above the disturbances stemming from organic brain disease, all forms of insanity must have a physiopathological bases. Kraepelin himself thought dementia praecox was a disease due to an "endogenous intoxication," and he instructed his assistant, Alzheimer, to track down the underlying brain lesions. This Alzheimer failed to do, but within a few years he discovered instead the characteristic pathological changes of the form of organic dementia to which his name is given (Alzheimer, 1907). Such searches continued, some of them rewarding; and it seems likely that the demonstration of 1905 of a bacteriological basis for "general paralysis of the insane" (which until the advent of penicillin accounted for about 10 percent of all admissions to mental hospitals), and the comparable disclosures of an identifiable physical basis for other psychiatric syndromes, supported the hope, still unrealized, that sooner or later firm links between physical pathology and clinical presentation would be widely, even universally, established.

Meanwhile, taxonomy had begun to reveal its inadequacies. Neurosis in particular had failed to lend itself to classification as readily as psychosis. It is a curious paradox in the history of diagnostic endeavor that the alienist (the mental hospital doctor) was most concerned with the psychoses and attempts to link them with organic pathology, while it fell to the neurologist to study and treat the neuroses. This development came about from the need to distinguish hysterical from organic paralyses. It was through neurology, therefore—particularly in France with men like Charcot and his pupil Janet, and also with Bernheim—that psychopathology entered the scene: allying itself with etiology on the one hand and taxonomy, on the other, providing an indispensable bridge between the two, and introducing fresh thinking into a field that had remained for many years outside psychiatric practice.

Further progress necessitated a more scientific psychopathology. A move was made in this direction once the limitations of the French school became clear to Freud and hypnotic suggestion gave way to the "talking cure." Freud, with Breuer (1895), delineated a causal chain between etiology (seduction in childhood), psychopathology (strangulated affect), and surface symptomatology (hysterical phenomena). The weakness of this attempt did not survive the rigors of the new investigatory method, and the early discoveries of psychoanalysis proper soon began to lay the basis for a truly scientific psychopathology.

A distinguishing feature of this pathology was, and remains, the developmental principle. This too has important origins in neurology—and of course Freud was a neurologist and neuropathologist before he became a psychoanalyst. In On Aphasia (1891), he readily acknowledged his indebtedness to the English neurologist Hughlings Jackson, whose views were far in advance of their time and failed to attract the support of most of his fellow neurologists (Jelliffe, 1937; Jones, 1953; Stengel, 1953). Jackson (1884) was strongly influenced by both Darwin and Herbert Spencer in his theory of evolution and the dissolution of the nervous system. On the basis of clinical observations he rejected the contemporary "precise" cerebral localization hypothesis, which fitted so very well with the Associationist psychology of the day. Instead, Jackson understood nervous functioning in terms of a complex hierarchical or "vertical" model, in which the process of dissolution gave rise to two kinds of symptom. The negative, pathological symptoms were brought into being once higher levels of organization were lost. The positive symptoms, on the other hand, were not intrinsically pathological. They represented the operations of much older structures whose activities were revealed once the checks and inhibitions of developmentally more recent nervous organizations had been lost. Negative symptoms stemmed from the loss of function consequent on dissolution; positive symptoms from the operations of the intact structures to which dissolution had reverted.

Although Jackson (1894) also applied his thinking to what he called "the insanities," he insisted on the absolute distinction between mind and brain and warned against a confusion of the physical and the psychic, a view that Freud wholeheartedly endorsed. Freud was particularly impressed by Jackson's formulation of the processes of evolution and dissolution, on which were founded his own concepts of fixation and regression, which played a profound part in his thinking on normality (dreams) and psychopathology (hysteria).

Freud observed these processes in operation in his clinical analytic work and saw, through dreams and transference phenomena, the regressive reactivation of childhood experience. Arriving at a clearer understanding of infantile neurosis as the forerunner of adult pathology, he also added immeasurably to our knowledge of child development. These advances in turn inspired analytically trained professionals to observe children directly for confirmation of what they had learned from adults about them. Such observation provided first-hand awareness of normal as well as pathological child development. Anna

Freud repeatedly pointed out that adult patients bring to analysis the conflicts that continue to disturb them rather than those they have resolved—these conflicts are the residues of childhood failures and defects rather than the roots of early successes and satisfactory development. The direct observer has the chance to redress the balance, to see positive areas of mental growth in children and not simply those that may indicate present disturbances or lay the ground for future pathology. But something more was still needed: something that could be provided only by the analysis of children themselves. Child analysis proper began with Siegfried Bernfeld, who worked with adolescents, and grew via the contributions of Berta Bornstein, Melanie Klein, Steff Bornstein, Alice Balint, and Anna Freud, followed by Dorothy Burlingham, Margaret Mahler, D. W. Winnicott, and a rapidly expanding body of distinguished contributors too numerous to mention here.

Early psychoanalytic success in linking clinical presentation of symptoms with underlying psychopathology based on internal conflict and unconscious processes meant that many psychoanalysts not only lost interest in taxonomy but dismissed the importance of symptoms altogether. Anna Freud, however, never supported this view. She recognized that similar symptoms would indicate different psychopathologies and that similar psychopathologies gave rise to differing symptoms. She was aware of the need to ask, "Why this symptom or that pathology rather than another?" although the question often defied an easy answer. Nor did she despise phenomenology: she knew well that one was sometimes unable to go beyond it.

But in seeking to go beyond phenomenology, Anna Freud was aware of the need to consider the complexities of the whole personality—the interactions of competing mental agencies both with each other, within each agency, and with the outside world. Her approach to nosology insisted that due weight be given to possible genetic, constitutional, and physical factors as well as psychological ones. Environmental influences, both past and present, played a role, as did beneficial and injurious events, successes and failures, the development of defensive organization, symptoms, and all those manifold elements that together make up the personality as seen at a particular time. This approach is formalized in Anna Freud's diagnostic schema (1962), while the developmental factors outlined by the child analyst underlie the concept of developmental lines (chapter 2).

Developmental arrests, delays, deviations, and disharmonies, as well as healthy and adaptive progress, contribute to the personality as seen in horizontal cross-section and in vertical, historical dimension. To the genetic reconstruction made possible by the analytic process in adults must be added observation of actual development. While the latter is not always possible in any individual case, the cumulative material of child observation within and without analysis, so-called objective developmental histories, and innumerable specialized child studies has built up a body of knowledge that informs the attempt to reconstruct development, however imperfect the reconstruction may be in any given instance.

Phenomenology, psychopathology, and nosology are essential for the proper psychoanalytic understanding of normative and pathological states in both adult and child. Informed assessments of children whose development is still continuing and whose structures are incomplete differ from assessments of those in whom psychic organization is more or less settled, as Anna Freud recognized in her contribution to the understanding of the symptomatology of children (1970). This is the standpoint from which we have approached the subject of nosology.

The historical background we have just outlined would be regarded by many of our colleagues as inadequate for reasons that have nothing to do with brevity. Although the classical approach to psychoanalytic theory and practice has continually advanced, along with its contributions to psychoanalytic nosology based on accumulating data derived from therapeutic and observational work with children and adults, we have given little, if any, attention to many coterminous developments. Over the years, the need for new discoveries and the wish to extend the range of therapeutic method have led to a proliferation of theories and technical recommendations, some of them far removed from the theory of mind (and the treatment method) that Freud called psychoanalysis. Today *psychoanalysis* refers to a number of psychological theories of mind (Sullivan's, Klein's, Fromm's and many others'), each with its own distinctive treatment technique; or it can refer, as it does in this book, to the body of knowledge built upon Freud's metapsychological principles. Before turning to a summary of the psychoanalytic nosology used in this book, we should say a little more about metapsychology itself.

Freud's metapsychological principles have recently become the target of criticism by many clinicians for whom the content of the psychoanalytic session is unique and irreducible. To evaluate clinical observations in terms of metapsychology, they believe, is to depreciate their value and to perpetuate an outmoded explanation of mental life based on nineteenth-century physics and chemistry. According to these critics, metapsychological evaluation reduces highly organized and differentiated mental activity to the language of forces, energies, and structures. The economic concepts of metapsychology have taken much of the brunt of this criticism.

This by no means ends the list of charges made against metapsychology: for others see Holt, 1981; Peterfreund, 1975. Some of the accusations have weight because undisciplined use of metapsychological concepts has encouraged analysts to regard explanatory concepts as facts. However, the basic objection to metapsychology, common to every critical publication (Gill, 1976; Lidz, 1972), is that this approach to clinical phenomena is rendered redundant by advances in contemporary psychobiology (Hill, 1971).

This criticism, attractive at first sight, fails to come to grips with the fundamental question of the purpose of metapsychological concepts. The critics of metapsychology, in spite of their devotion to the scientific spirit, forget that explanatory concepts can only be means, never ends. The concepts of displacement and condensation of drive cathexis, for example, originated in a theoretical model constructed to describe dreams as resulting from interaction between an elementary mode of mental functioning characteristic of the state of sleep (primary process) and a more advanced form (secondary process), which completes the manifest dream content.

The meaning of a dream for the dreamer's present life cannot be known until the concepts devised to describe the action of the elementary level (displacement, condensation) and those constructed to describe the action of the more advanced level (as in secondary revision) are used by the dream interpreter. These metapsychological concepts act as a tool whose use brings to light wishes, fears, memories and fantasies which would have disturbed REM sleep had they not been transformed by the dreamwork. The latent dream content is the primary concern of the psychoanalyst who makes use of metapsychological concepts. The concepts were never designed to substitute for the analysis of a dream or a neurotic symptom.

The abstract nature of metapsychological concepts and the role they play in demonstrating the presence and significance of clinical phenomena render the charge of reductionism inappropriate. As Noy

(1977) has pointed out, metapsychological concepts provide the framework for a series of models illustrating aspects of mental phenomena. These models can be likened to topographic, geologic, and climatic maps of one geographical area. Each is relevant for its own particular sphere. The models, like the maps, can be changed in the light of new knowledge.

Critics insist that a new approach in psychoanalysis must be based on what is consciously experienced and what can become the object of experience. But their refusal to acknowledge the relevance of metapsychology for clinical work excludes the possibility of explaining how behavior patterns and symptoms arise in the healthy and in the mentally ill.

As controversy is rarely based on the facts of clinical observation, we have based these studies on a review of commonly encountered symptom complexes, setting them against the background of normal and abnormal mental development as informed by classic psychoanalytic observations and their later elaboration. This developmental orientation is the motif of the book, and we hope with this short discussion to reassure those who fear that the use of metapsychological concepts must result in the transformation of clinical experiences into arid abstraction without heuristic or therapeutic potential.

Turning to a summary of the psychoanalytic nosology illustrated in our studies, we find no need to jettison basic metapsychological principles.

Some abnormal psychological states show deterioration in the psychic structures. These are the psychoses and the dementias. In other states a disordered drive organization and the ego's reactions against it are centered on conspicuous fixation points, while the psychic structures themselves remain more or less intact. These disturbances are the neuroses, whether of symptom or of character. Lastly, there remains a large group of disparate conditions that cannot be ascribed to either of the major groups of disorders. These conditions involve serious developmental deficiencies, including delays, arrests, deviations, and disharmonies. They do not form a recognizable clinical group, even descriptively; their diversities are more impressive than their similarities. We now consider each of these groups in turn.

The Psychoses

The structural dissolution involved in the psychoses of adolescence and adult life bears on the clinical forms and presentations of these illnesses. For example, partial loss of the "binding" functions of the ego means that secondary process functioning yields to a degree of incursion of the primary process with resulting disturbance in ideation or form of thinking. The concomitant loss or impairment of neutralization means that the drive derivatives, which were hitherto well sublimated, recover something of their original character. Certain activities that were formerly socially adaptive are now excessively instinctualized. The ability to distinguish between past and present, to order events in sequence and in time is impaired as a consequence of ego dissolution; and this impairment of the repression barrier permits drives and their associated mental content to intrude more readily into consciousness. Distinctions between reality and fantasy, which were not formerly dynamically repressed, become blurred. Incestuous wishes, for example, may be freely expressed and even acted upon in some way. The defusion of drives into comparatively unmodified love and hate compounds this process. Excessive use of such primitive defense mechanisms as externalization and projection (at the expense of the more sophisticated ones), together with impaired reality testing, sets the scene for the formation of delusions, commonly of a paranoid or erotic kind.

To all this must be added the consequences of superego dissolution. This structure no longer remains an autonomous introject within the ego but reverts to a more primitive developmental level where it may be experienced as an external influence, critical or benign. The superego recruits the readily available, deneutralized, and defused drive energies, reinforcing the patient's experience of delusional and/or hallucinatory love and hate from seemingly external sources. Delusional objects from these different sources readily merge with or become identified with real objects, mostly through primary condensation.

The process of dissolution affects all three psychic agencies and their dynamic interactions. The foregoing description does not apply equally to all the psychoses, which show considerable individual variation, but it is suitable for the purposes of summary. However, a few additional points may be made. While the psychoses may involve various regressions, the dissolutions described sometimes reveal phenomena unseen, even in prototype, in the course of normal development. This is due partly to the fact that dissolution is only partial, as Hughlings Jackson (1884) recognized, and a "regressed" adult is not at all the same as a child. But this observation does not of course dispense with the important question of childhood antecedents of later psychotic phenomena—a point that has been repeatedly emphasized in our text. A task—as interesting as it is essential—that remains to be tackled more thoroughly than it has been hitherto is to discern the relationship between infantile psychosis on the one hand and the psychotic states of adolescence and adulthood on the other. The developmental history of the psychoses is just as important as that of the other psychiatric groupings.

An influential group of psychoanalysts has taken the view (discussed in chapter 7) that the psychoses can be understood on the same lines as the neuroses and take a unitary view of their psychopathologies. The apparent contradiction between their view and the one summarized here is substantially resolved if we take due account of the prepsychotic phase of psychotic illness—which indeed has a neurotic character. When psychosis supervenes, we can assume that a psychological attempt to resolve the conflicts by neurotic compromise has failed. Perhaps in this light one might consider psychosis as a failure of restitution.

The Neuroses

Although in the neuroses ego functioning and superego functioning may be somewhat impaired and interfered with by unconscious conflict (rather than damaged), the personality retains sufficient strength to ensure, in the symptom neuroses, a coordinated drive regression to a particular fixation point. Even at the height of the economic disorder the ego is sufficiently powerful to integrate into a structured symptom all the disparate and contending forces involved. The same cannot be said for a delusional symptom in a psychosis, which does not have the character, as in neurosis, of a foreign body within an otherwise reasonably integrated personality.

The question of how the character neuroses are formed is not an easy one. As in the symptom neuroses, fixation points are prominent in the presentation. But neither regression nor dissolution plays an essential part in the clinical picture. Developmental studies suggest that individuals who develop character neurosis negotiated the oedipal phase differently from the kind of oedipal resolution occurring in people predisposed to symptom neurosis. In summary, character neuroses involve a mutual accommodation of id and ego of a different order from that of the symptom neuroses, so that compromise formations are more readily acceptable to their possessor.

Neurotic , normal, and many adult psychotic individuals have all reached a level of development that leaves open to them certain kinds of pathology. This level of development must have been reached on the object-relations developmental line before such pathological "solutions" are possible. The point may be summarized in turning to the third broad grouping of adult pathologies.

The Developmental Disorders

All the neurotic and psychotic conditions have significant developmental components and contributants. What distinguishes this group from other disorders is their failure to reach, in important respects, certain levels of development in childhood. Without the attainment of these levels, subsequent resolution of later economic disturbance becomes impossible through neurotic or even psychotic recourse.

The difficulty in delineating this grouping arises first from its heterogeneity and second from serious defects, arrests, and deviations not easy to infer from the presenting picture alone. These problems often take pseudo-neurotic or pseudo-psychotic forms; but the significant pathology is not built around instinctual fixation points, with or without regression, as in the neuroses; nor does it rest on dissolution, as in the psychoses. The developmental arrest or deviation has remained salient through all subsequent evolution of the personality, so that the psychopathology linked with the initial disturbance forms a continuum and shows its effects at any given age.

These clinical conditions are protean in their manifestations. The absence of a developmental history may add to the difficulties in differentiating them from the other disorders. Anxiety is poorly controlled in many and can sometimes be assuaged, if at all, only by adventitious means. Insofar as this phenomenon involves a failure to develop the forms of ego control necessary to restrict anxiety to signal levels, this group of patients overlaps with those loosely referred to as "inadequate" or "immature." Patients with personality disorders of this type may, however, have married, achieved parenthood, or advanced themselves professionally; and their apparent capacity, with or without these attainments, to sustain nonintimate relationships may deceive the observer into thinking that they have achieved a high level on the object-relations line of development. Nonetheless, careful scrutiny reveals that object relationships are arrested at an early level where consideration of the object as a person in his own right has never taken place: the balance of libidinal investment is heavily tilted in favor of narcissism and away from objects. Quite often, the capacity for confusing the interests of the self with those of the object far exceeds the normal or neurotic capacity for self-deception. These developmental abnormalities are often compounded by a primitive level of defense activity including a striking use of projective and externalizing mechanisms, reversals, and denials. In many instances the personality approximates the "as if" type described by Winnicott (1955).

In some developmentally disturbed patients fantasy and reality are only tenuously separated, and the poor control of fantasy may superficially resemble delusions. The majority of these cases do not, however, show these borderline psychotic features. Although closer consideration may suggest neurosis, a conspicuous element of external blame may suggest a more ominous prognosis. In treatment these individuals cannot form a working alliance; they form destructive transferences in which an angry and complaining attachment is especially common. In the course of treatment their behavior may deteriorate, often developing anomalies such as self-destructiveness or externally directed aggression. It is all too easy to mistake these clinical phenomena for regressive reactivation of preoedipal relationships; however, they are not true transference neuroses but, rather, spontaneous transferences consequent on the arrest or defect.

Borderline psychosis is closely related to monosymptomatic hypochondriases; and in their severest forms these patients have little cathexis to spare for any sort of transference relationship. Certain forms of chronic depersonalization may differ in their surface manifestations but are similar in terms of their treatment relationships. But they may deceive the observer and prompt a misdiagnosis if they had showed a superficial capacity for ostensibly satisfactory social relationships. A fuller account or even an extended list would have to include, among others, the condition of mental subnormality and such disorders as the paranoid personality.

The serious developmental defects, deviations, or arrests that these cases have in common, whether these are brought about internally or through failures of environmental influences, the result is fateful for subsequent development. If ordered instinctual phase development comes to a halt (instead of establishing fixation points), or if its serial progress is conspicuously disordered, interactions with the developing ego and superego will result in substantial arrests or serious disturbances on the developmental lines—above all the object relations line. Similarly, conspicuous failures, defects, or deviations in the structuralization of the ego or superego interfere with these agencies' interactions with the id, and serious interference with the developmental lines mars all subsequent evolution of the personality.

Some cases may involve structural defects in the repression barrier (a term that has dropped out of general use but needs to be revived; see Kennedy et al., 1985; Shengold, 1980). Some of these developmental anomalies result in what Anna Freud (1980) has called disharmonies: the agencies are maturationally out of step, and their disparities are synthesized in abnormal interactions. In some instances such disharmonies predispose to neurosis: for instance in the obsessional, where the ego and superego are prematurely advanced in comparison to the dawdling id. In other instances, disorders may supervene. To understand more fully the processes that wreak permanent damage on personalities, it is necessary to turn to childhood disorders in which we may observe them in *statu nascendi*, as we have done herein.

References

Abend, S. M. (1983). Theory of character (Panel report). *J. Amer. Psychoanal. Assn.*, 31:211–224.

Abraham, K. (1908). Psychosexual differences between hysteria and dementia praecox. In *Selected Papers on Psycho-analysis*. London: Hogarth Press, 1927.

———(1911). Notes on the psychoanalytical investigation and treatment of manic-depressive insantiy and allied conditions. In *Selected Papers on Psycho-analysis*. London: Hogarth Press, 1927.

———(1920). Manifestatins of the female castration complex. In *Selected Papers on Psycho-analysis*. London: Hogarth, 1927.

———(1921). Contributions to the theory of the anal character. In *Selected Papers on Psycho-analysis*. London: Hogarth Press, 1927.

———(1924). The influence of oral eroticism on character-formation. In *Selected Papers on Psycho-analysis*. London: Hogarth Press, 1927.

———(1925). Character-formation on the genital level of the libido. In *Selected Papers on Psycho-analysis*. London: Hogarth Press, 1927.

Abraham, K. & Freud, S. (1965). *A Psychoanalytic Dialogue: The Letters of Sigmund Freud and Karl Abraham, 1907–1926.* London: Hogarth Press.

Alzheimer, A. (1907). Über eine eigenartige Erkrankung der Hirnrinde. *Allgemeine Zeitschrift für Psychiatrie*, 64:146.

Anthony, J. & Scott, P. (1966). Manic-depressive psychosis in childhood. *J. Child Psychol. Psychiat.*, 1:53–72.

Arlow, J. A. & Brenner, C. (1969). The psychopathology of the psychoses. *Int. J. Psychoanal.*, 50:5–14.

Bak, R. (1943). Dissolution of ego, mannerism and delusion of grandeur. *J. Nerv. Ment. Dis.*, 98:457–468.

────── (1971). Object relations in schizophrenia and perversion. *Int. J. Psychoanal.*, 52:235–242.

Batchelor, I. R. C. (1964). The diagnosis of schizophrenia. *Proc. Roy. Soc. Med.*, 57:417–420.

Baudrey, F. (1983). The evolution of the concept of character in Freud's writings. *J. Amer. Psychoanal. Assn.*, 31:3–31.

────── (1984). Character: a concept in search of an identity. *J. Amer. Psychoanal. Assn.*, 32:455–477.

Bion, R. (1967). Notes on the theory of schizophrenia. In *Second Thoughts*. London: Heinemann.

Bleuler, E. (1911). *Dementia Praecox, or the Group of Schizophrenias*. New York: International Universities Press, 1955.

────── (1924). *Textbook of Psychiatry*. London: Macmillan.

Bleuler, M. (1978). *The Schizophrenic Disorders*. New Haven: Yale University Press.

Blum, H. (1978). Reconstruction in a case of post-partum depression. *Psychoanal. Study Child*, 33:335–362.

────── (1980). Paranoia and beating phantasy. *J. Amer. Psychoanal. Assn.*, 28:331–362.

────── (1981). Object Inconstancy and Paranoid Conspiracy. *J. Amer. Psychoanal. Assn.*, 29:789–813.

Bornstein, B. (1935). Phobia in a 2½ year old child. *Psychoanal. Quart.*, 4:93–113.

Bornstein, S. (1935). A child analysis. *Psychoanal. Quart.*, 4:190–225.

Boyer, L. B. & Giovacchini, P. L. (1967). *Psychoanalytic treatment of characterological and schizophrenic disorders*. New York: Science House.

Burgner, M. & Edgcumbe, R. (1972). Some problems in the conceptualization of early object relationships. *Psychoanal. Study Child*, 27:315–333.

Burlingham, D. (1973). The preoedipal infant-father relationship. *Psychoanal. Study Child*, 28:23–47.

Bychowski, G. (1952). *Psychotherapy of psychosis*. New York: Grune and Stratton.

———— (1956). The concept, delineation and structure of latent psychosis. Contribution to scientific proceedings, reported by L. L. Robbins. *J. Amer. Psychoanal. Assn.*, 4:553.

Edgcumbe, R. (1975). The border between therapy and education. In *Studies in Child Psychoanalysis: Pure and Applied*. New Haven: Yale University Press.

Edgcumbe, R. & Burgner, M. (1973). Some problems in the conceptualisation of early object relations. *Psychoanal. Study Child*, 27:283–333.

———— (1975). The phallic-narcissistic phase. *Psychoanal. Study Child*, 30:161–180.

Fairbairn, W. R. (1956). Considerations arising out of the Schreber case. *Brit. J. Med. Psychol.*, 29:113–127.

Federn, P. (1953). *Ego Psychology and the Psychoses*. London: Imago.

Fenichel, O. (1946). *The Psychoanalytic Theory of Neurosis*. London: Routledge.

Fisher, C.; Byrne, J.; Edwards, A. & Kahn, E. (1970). The psychophysiological study of nightmares. *J. Amer. Psychoanal. Assn.*, 18:747–782.

Fleischmann, O. (1956). Contribution to scientific proceedings, reported by L. L. Robbins. *J. Amer. Psychoanal. Assn.*, 4:557–560.

Fleiss, R. (1961). *Ego and Body Ego*. New York: Schultz.

Forrest, A. (1973). Paranoid states and paranoid psychoses. In *New Perspectives in Schizophrenia*. Ed. J. Affleck and A. Forrest. Edinburgh: Livingstone.

Fraiberg, S. (1952). A critical neurosis in a 2½ year old girl. *Psychoanal. Study Child*, 7:173–215.

Frank, J. (1956). Contribution to scientific proceedings, reported by L. L. Robbins. *J. Amer. Psycchoanal. Assn.*, 4:561–562.

Freeman, T. (1955). Clinical and theoretical observations on male homosexuality. *Int. J. Psychoanal.*, 36:1–13.

———— (1963). The concept of narcissism in schizophrenic states. *Int. J. Psychoanal.*, 44:293–303.

———— (1965). *Studies in Psychoses*. London: Tavistock.

———— (1968). On the psychopathology of repetitive phenomena. *Brit. J. Psychiat.*, 114:1107–1114.

———— (1969). *Psychopathology of the Psychoses*. London: Tavistock.

———— (1976a). On the psychopathology of transitivism and appersonation. *Brit. J. Psychiat.*, 129:414–447.

———— (1976b). *Childhood Pathology and Adult Psychoses*. New York: International Universities Press.

—— (1977). On Freud's theory of schizophrenia. *Int. J. Psychoanal.*, 58:383–388.

—— (1978). Developmental aspects of psychosis. *Int. Rev. Psychoanal.*, 5:449–455.

—— (1981). The prepsychotic phase and its reconstruction in schizophrenic and paranoiac psychoses. *Int. J. Psychoanal.*, 62:447–453.

—— (1982). Schizophrenic delusions and their pre-psychotic antecedents. *Int. J. Psychoanal.*, 63:445–448.

Freeman, T.; Cameron, J. L. & McGhie, A. (1958). *Chronic Schizophrenia*. London: Tavistock.

Freeman, T. & Davie, J. M. (1961). Disturbances of perception and consciousness in schizophrenic states. *Brit. J. Med. Psychol.*, 34:33–42.

Freeman, T.; Wiseberg, S. & Yorke, C. (1984). Psychoanalytic psychiatry: some past and present studies at the Hampstead Clinic. *Bull. Hampstead Clinic*, 7:247–269.

Freud, A. (1936). *The Ego and the Mechanism of Defense*. London: Hogarth, 1961.

—— (1951). Observations on child development. In *Writings*, 4:143–162. New York: International Universities Press.

—— (1952). Studies in passivity. In *Writings*, 4:245–259. New York: International Universities Press.

—— (1958). Adolescence. *Psychoanal. Study Child*, 13:225–278.

—— (1962). The emotional and social development of young children. In *Writings*, 5:336–351. New York: International Universities Press.

—— (1963a). Assessment of childhood disturbances. *Psychoanal. Study Child*, 17:149–158.

—— (1963b). The concept of developmental lines. *Psychoanal. Study Child*, 18:245–265.

—— (1965). Normality and pathology in childhood. In *Writings*, 6. New York: International Universities Press.

—— (1966). Obsessional neurosis: a summary of psycho-analytic views. In *Writings*, 5:242–261. New York: International Universities Press.

—— (1967). Comments on psychic trauma. In *Writings*, 5:221–241. New York: International Universities Press.

—— (1970). The symptomatology of childhood: a preliminary attempt at classification. In *Writings*, 7:157–188. New York: International Universities Press.

——— (1972). The widening scope of psychoanalytic child psychology, normal and abnormal. In *Writings*, 8:8–33. New York: International Universities Press.

——— (1974). A psychoanalytic view of developmental psychopathology. In *Writings*, 8:57–74. New York: International Universities Press.

——— (1979). Child analysis as the study of mental growth, normal and abnormal. In *Writings*, 8:119–136. New York: International Universities Press.

——— (1981). The concept of developmental lines: their diagnostic significance. *Psychoanal. Study Child*, 36:129–136.

——— (1983). Problems of pathogenesis. *Psychoanal. Study Child*, 38:383–388.

Freud, S. (1891). *On Aphasia*. Trans. E. Stengel. London: Imago, 1953.

——— (1900). The interpretation of dreams. In *Standard Edition of the Complete Psychological Works*. Trans. James Strachey, 4–5. London: Hogarth Press, 1953. (Hereafter referred to as *SE*.)

——— (1907). *A Psychoanalytic Dialogue: Letters of Sigmund Freud and Karl Abraham, 1907–1926*. London: Hogarth Press.

——— (1908). Character and anal erotism. *SE* 9:169–175. London: Hogarth Press, 1959.

——— (1909). Analysis of a phobia in a five-year-old boy. *SE* 10:3–149. London: Hogarth Press, 1955.

——— (1911a). Formulations on the two principles of mental functioning. *SE* 12:215–230. London: Hogarth Press, 1958.

——— (1911b). Psychoanalytical notes on autobiographical account of a case of paranoia. *SE* 12. London: Hogarth Press, 1958.

——— (1912). Types of onset of neurosis. *SE* 12:229–238.. London: Hogarth Press, 1958.

——— (1914). On narcissism: an introduction. *SE* 14:69–104. London: Hogarth Press, 1957.

——— (1915a). The unconscious. *SE* 14. London: Hogarth Press, 1957.

——— (1915b). A case of paranoia running counter to the psychoanalytic theory of the disease. *SE* 14. London: Hogarth Press, 1957.

——— (1917). Mourning and melancholia. *SE* 15. London: Hogarth Press.

——— (1920). Beyond the pleasure principle. *SE* 18:7–64. London: Hogarth Press, 1955.

────(1921). Group psychology and analysis of the ego. SE 18:67–143.

────(1923). Ego and the id. SE 19. London: Hogarth Press.

────(1924). Neurosis and psychosis. SE 19. London: Hogarth Press.

────(1926). Inhibitions, symptoms and anxiety. SE 20:77–172. London: Hogarth Press, 1959.

────(1933). New introductory lectures on psychoanalysis. SE 22:3–158. London: Hogarth Press, 1964.

Freud, S. & Breuer, J. (1895). Studies in Hysteria. SE 2. London: Hogarth Press, 1955.

Frosch, J. (1983). The Psychotic Process. New York: International Universities Press.

Furman, E. (1956). An ego disturbance in a young child. Psychoanal. Study Child, 11:312–335.

Gill, M. M. (1976). Metapsychology is not psychology. In M. M. Gill and P. S. Holzman: Psychology vs. Metapsychology. New York: International Universities Press.

Gitelson, M. (1955). Contribution to scientific proceedings, reported by L. Rangell. J. Amer. Psychoanal. Assn., 3:294–295.

Glover, E. (1948). Psycho-analysis. London and New York: Staples.

────(1950). Functional aspects of the mental apparatus. Int. J. Psychoanal., 31:125–131.

────(1955). The Technique of Psychoanalysis. New York: International Universities Press.

────(1958). The use of Freudian theory in psychiatry. Brit. J. Med. Psychol., 31:143–152.

Greenacre, P. (1960). Regression and fixation. J. Amer. Psychoanal. Assn., 8:703–723.

Greenson, R. R. (1955). Contribution to scientific proceedings, reported by L. Rangell. J. Amer. Psychoanal. Assn., 3:288–289, 295–296.

Grotstein, J. (1977). The psychoanalytic concept of schizophrenia, pts. 1–2. Int. J. Psychoanal., 58:403–426, 427–452.

Guntrip, H. (1956). Recent developments in psychoanalytic theory. Brit. J. Med. Psychol., 29:82–99.

Hartmann, H. (1939). Ego Psychology and the Problem of Adaptation. New York: International Universities Press, 1958.

────(1950). Psychoanalysis and developmental psychology. In Collected Papers. London: Hogarth Press, 1964.

——— (1953). Contribution to the metapsychology of schizophrenia. *Psychoanal. Study Child*, 8:177–198.

Hill, D. (1971). On the contribution of psychoanalysis to psychiatry: mechanism and meaning. *Int. J. Psychoanal.*, 52:1–10.

Holt, R. R. (1981). The death and transfiguration of metapsychology. *Int. Rev. Psychoanal.*, 8:129–143.

Jackson, J. H. (1884). Evolution and dissolution of the nervous system. In *Selected Writings of John Hughlings Jackson*, Ed. J. Taylor, vol. 2. New York: Basic Books, 1931.

——— (1894). The factors of insanities. In *Selected Writings of John Hughlings Jackson*, ed. J. Taylor, vol. 2. New York: Basic Books, 1931.

Jacobson, E. (1954). On psychotic identifications. *Int. J. Psychoanal.*, 35:102–108.

——— (1967). *Psychotic Conflict and Reality*. London: Hogarth.

Jelliffe, E. S. (1937). Sigmund Freud as neurologist. *J. Nerv. Ment. Dis.*, 85:696–711.

Jones, E. (1953). *Sigmund Freud: Life and Work*. Vol. 1. London: Hogarth Press.

Katan, A. (1973). Children who were raped. *Psychoanal. Study Child*, 28:208–224.

Katan, M. (1950). Structural aspects of a case of schizophrenia. *Psychoanal. Study Child*, 5:145–159.

——— (1953). Mania and the pleasure principle in affective disorders. Ed. P. Greenacre. New York: International Universities Press.

——— (1954). The non-psychotic part of the personality in schizophrenia. *Int. J. Psychoanal.*, 35:119–127.

——— (1959). Schreber's hereafter: its building up and its downfall. *Psychoanal. Study Child*, 14:314–362.

——— (1960). Dream and psychosis. *Int. J. Psychoanal.*, 41:341–351.

——— (1969). A psychoanalytic approach to the diagnosis of paranoia. *Psychoanal. Study Child*, 24:151–180.

——— (1974). The development of the influencing apparatus. *Psychoanal. Study Child*, 29:473–510.

——— (1975). Childhood memories as contents of schizophrenic hallucinations and delusions. *Psychoanal. Study Child*, 30:357–375.

——— (1979). Further explorations of the schizophrenic regression to the undifferentiated state. *Int. J. Psychoanal.*, 60:145–176.

Kennedy, H. (1971). Problems in reconstruction in child psychoanalysis. *Psychoanal. Study Child*, 26:386–402.

—— (1986). Trauma in childhood: signs and sequelae as seen in the analysis of an adolescent. *Psychoanal. Study Child*, 41:209–219.

Kennedy, H.; Moran, G.; Wiseberg, S. & Yorke, C. (1985). Both sides of the barrier: some reflections on childhood fantasy. *Psychoanal. Study Child*, 40:275–283.

Kennedy, H. & Yorke, C. (1980). Childhood neurosis v. developmental deviations: two clinical case histories. *Dialogue: A Journal of Psychoanalytic Perspectives*, 4:20–33.

Kernberg, O. (1967). Borderline personality organization. *J. Amer. Psychoanal. Assn.*, 15:641–685.

—— (1974). Further contributions to the treatment of narcissistic personalities. *Int. J. Psychoanal.*, 55:215–240.

Klein, M. (1932). *The Psychoanalysis of Children*. London: Hogarth Press.

—— (1946). Notes on some schizoid mechanisms. In *Development in Psycho-Analysis*, ed. J. Riviere, 292–320. London, Hogarth Press, 1952.

Knight, R. P. (1956). Contribution to scientific proceedings, reported by L. L.Robbins. *J. Amer. Psychoanal. Assn.*, 4:553–554.

Kohut, H. (1971). *The Analysis of the Self*. New York: International Universities Press.

Kraepelin, E. (1899). *Psychiatrie*. 6th ed. Leipzig.

Kris, E. (1956). The recovery of childhood memories in psychoanalysis. *Psychoanal. Study Child*, 11:54–88.

Langfeldt, G. (1960). Diagnosis and prognosis of schizophrenia. *Proc. Roy. Soc. Med.*, 53:1047–1055.

Lidz, T. (1972). Schizophrenic disorders: the influence of conceptualization on therapy. In *Schizophrenia*, ed. D. Rubinstein and Y. O. Alanen. Amsterdam: Exerpta Medica Press.

London, N. (1973). An essay on psychoanalytic theory: two theories of schizophrenia. *Int. J. Psychoanal.*, 54:169–194.

Low, B. (1920). *Psycho-Analysis*. London: Allan and Unwin.

Mahler, M. (1952). On childhood psychosis and schizophrenia. *Psychoanal. Study Child*, 7:286–305.

—— (1968). *On Human Symbiosis and the Vicissitudes of Individuation*. New York: International Universities Press.

Meissner, W. H. (1978). *The Paranoid Process*. New York: Aronson.

Niederland, W. G. (1959). The miracled world of Schreber's childhood. *Psychoanal. Study Child*, 14:383–413.

Noy, P. (1977). Metapsychology as a multimodel system. *Int. Rev. Psychoanal.*, 4:1–12.

Nunberg, H. (1921). The course of the libidinal conflict in schizophrenia in practical theory of psychoanalysis. In *Mental and Nervous Disease Monographs*. New York.

Ogden, T. H. (1980). On the nature of schizophrenic conflict. *Int. J. Psychoanal.*, 61:513–534.

Pao, P. N. (1979). *Schizophrenic Disorders*. New York: International Universities Press.

Peterfreund, P. (1975). The need for a new general theoretical frame of reference in psychoanalysis. *Psychoanal. Quart.*, 44:534–549.

Radford, P.; Wiseberg, S. & Yorke, C. (1972). A study of "mainline" heroin addiction: a preliminary report. *Psychoanal. Study Child*, 27:156–180.

Rangell, L. (1955). The borderline case. Panel report of scientific proceedings. *J. Amer. Psychoanal. Assn.*, 3:285–298.

——— (1982). The self in psychoanalytic theory. *J. Amer. Psychoanal. Assn.*, 30:863–891.

Rank, O. (1952). *The Trauma of Birth*. New York: Brunner Mazel.

Rapaport, D. (1950). On the psychoanalytic theory of thinking. *Int. J. Psychoanal.*, 31:161–170.

——— (1951). *The Conceptual Model of Psychoanalysis in Psychoanalytic Psychiatry and Psychology*. New York: International Universities Press.

Reich, A. (1960). Pathologic forms of self-esteem. *Psychoanal. Study Child*, 15:215–232.

Reich, W. (1928). On character analysis. In *The Psychoanalytic Reader*, ed. R. Fleiss. London: Hogarth Press, 1950.

Retterstol, N. (1966). *Paranoid and Pranoiac Psychoses*. Springfield: Thomas.

Ritvo, S. (1974). Current status of the conflict of the infantile neurosis, implications for diagnosis and technique. *Psychoanal. Study Child*, 29:159–182.

Ritvo, S. & Solnit, A. J. (1960). The relationship of early identifications to superego structures. *Int. J. Psychoanal.*, 41:295–300.

Rochlin, G. (1953). Loss and restitution. *Psychoanal. Study Child*, 8:288–309.

——— (1959). The loss complex: a contribution to the aetiology of depression. *J. Amer. Psychoanal. Assn.*, 7:299–316.

Rosenfeld, H. (1954). Considerations regarding the psychoanalytic approach to acute and chronic schizophrenia. *Int. J. Psychoanal.*, 35:135–140.

——— (1968). *Psychotic States: A Psychoanalytic Approach.* London: Hogarth Press.

Rosenfeld, S. K. & Sprince, M. (1963). An attempt to formulate the meaning of the concept "borderline." *Psychoanal. Study Child,* 18:603–663.

Schilder, P. (1935). *The Image and Appearance of the Human Body.* New York: International Universities Press.

——— (1939). The psychology of schizophrenia. In *On Psychoses.* New York: International Universities Press.

Searles, H. (1963). Transference psychosis in the psychotherapy of chronic schizophrenia. *Int. J. Psychoanal.,* 44:249–281.

Shengold, L. (1967). The effects of overstimulation: rat people. *Int. J. Psychoanal.,* 48:403–415.

——— (1988). *Halo in the Sky.* New York: Guilford.

Spitz, R. A. (1947). *Birth and the First Fifteen Minutes of Life.* 16 mm. film.

——— (1965). *The First Year of Life.* New York: International Universities Press.

Stengel, E. (1953). Introduction. In S. Freud, *On Aphasia,* trans. E. Stengel. London: Imago.

Tausk, V. (1919). On the origin of the influencing machine in schizophrenia. In *The Psychoanalytic Reader,* ed. R. Fleiss. London: Hogarth Press.

Thomas, R.; Edgcumbe, R.; Kennedy, H.; Kawenoka, M. & Weitzner, L. (1966). Comments on some aspects of self and object representations in a group of psychotic children. *Psychoanal. Study Child,* 21:527–580.

Vaillant, G. B. (1964). An historical review of the remitting schizophrenias. *J. Nerv. Ment. Dis.,* 135:48–56.

Waelder, R. (1960). *Basic Theory of Psychoanalysis.* New York: International Universities Press.

Wexler, M. (1971). Schizophrenia, conflict and deficiency. *Psychoanal. Quart.,* 40:83–100.

Willick, M. S. (1983). Clinical aspects of character (panel review). *J. Amer. Psychoanal. Assn.,* 31:225–245.

Winnicott, D. W. (1955). Metapsychological and clinical aspects of regression within the psycho-analytic set-up. *Int. J. Psychoanal.*, 36:16–26.

——— (1960). The theory of the parent-infant relationship. In *The Maturational Processes and the Facilitating Environment*. London: Hogarth Press, 1965.

——— (1965). Clinical regression compared with defense organisation. *Int. Psychiat. Clinics*, 5:3–11.

Wiseberg, S. & Yorke, C. (1986). "Physicality" and conversion hysteria: developmental considerations. *Bull. Hampstead Clinic*, 9:3–18.

Wiseberg, S.; Yorke, C. & Radford, P. (1975). Aspects of self-cathexis in "mainline" heroin addiction. In *Studies in Child Psychoanalysis: Pure and Applied*. New Haven: Yale University Press.

Wolfenstein, M. (1955). Mad laughter in a 6-year-old boy. *Psychoanal. Study Child*, 10:381–394.

Yorke, C. (1980). The contributions of the diagnostic profile and the assessment of developmental lines to child psychiatry. *Psychiat. Clinics N. America*, 3:593–603.

——— (1983a). Clinical notes on developmental pathology. *Psychoanal. Study Child*, 38:389–402.

——— (1983b). Anna Freud and the psychoanalytic study and treatment of adults. *Int. J. Psychoanal.*, 64:391–400.

——— (1985). Fantasy and the body-mind problem. *Psychoanal. Study Child*, 40:319–328.

——— (1986). Reflections on the problem of psychic trauma. *Psychoanal. Study Child*, 41:221–236.

——— (1988). A defect in training. *Brit. J. Psychiat.*, 152:159–163.

Yorke, C. & Burgner, M. (1980). Obsessional phenomena in children. *Dialogue: A Journal of Psychoanalytic Perspectives*, 4:35–47.

Yorke, C.; Kennedy, H. & Wiseberg, S. (1981). Some clinical and theoretical aspects of two developmental lines. In *The Course of Life*, 1:619–637. Adelphi, Md.: U.S. Dept. of Health.

Yorke, C.; Putzel, R. & Schacht, L. (1975). Some problems of diagnosis in children presenting with obsessional symptomatology. In *Studies in Child Psychoanalysis: Pure and Applied*. New Haven: Yale University Press.

Yorke, C. & Wiseberg, S. (1976). A developmental view of anxiety: some clinical and theoretical considerations. *Psychoanal. Study Child*, 31:107–135.

Index

Abraham, Karl: on character types, 70; and female castration complex, 88; on relationship between mania and depression, 171–72; on manic-depressive states, 185–86; on narcissism, positive and negative, 207n

Acute brain syndrome: alcohol or drug induced, 164

Adolescence: symptom neurosis in, illustrated (Dennis), 38–40; oedipal conflict in, 51; character traits in, 74; psychosis in, illustrated (Mark), 143; psychosis in, 148–49; schizophrenia in, exemplified (Penny), 149–56; psychosis in, exemplified (Olga), 157–60; disorders of, compared with adult mania/ hypomania, 172–74; depression in, exemplified, 196; freeing of incestuous ties in, 200; manic-depressive depression in, illustrated (Tony), 200–202; manic-depressive depression in, illustrated (Grace), 202–07

Affect: sampling of, 7; trial, 7; fear of, 65; isolation of, 65; divorced from thought, 161; strangulated, 209. See also Anxiety; Depression; Guilt; Shame

Aggression: in obsessional neurosis, 56–59, passim; phallic, in character neurosis, 77; attacks of, in psychotic states, 153; outbursts of, in manic patient, 175; in depressed patient, 197; and sadism, in manic-depressive

depression, 206. See also Ambivalence; Death instinct; Death wishes; Drives; Obsessional neurosis; Sadism, anal

Agitation: in depressive state following childbirth, illustrated (Florence), 194, 196

Alienist, 209

Altruism, as reactive trait, 85, 87

Alzheimer's disease, 209

Ambivalence: and failure of drive fusion, 59, 161, 191; increased by childbirth, 198; oral, 206–07. See also Obsessional neurosis

Anal phase: and pregnancy theories, 39; and obsessional neurosis, 56–69, passim; genital excitability in, 167; in passive wishes, schizophrenic, 168

Anal sadism. See Sadism, anal

Antidepressant drugs, 199

Anxiety: described, 1; and pleasure principle, 1; and basic danger situations, 2–5; as trial affect, 7; and vegetative excitation, 10; in borderline children, illustrated (Brian), 11; attack, 16; and trauma, 17; persecutory, 123; leading to psychotic states, 136; acute, in schizophreniform states, 160; in chronic organic states, 164; in psychotic children, 164

—pervasive: 3–4, 8–9; distinguished from automatic, 4; post-traumatic, 10

—signal: 5, 7, 8; concept of, 4; initiating

233

Anxiety (continued)
 pathology, illustrated (Harvey), 12–14;
 in childhood neurosis, 12–14; and
 defense mechanisms, 33
—automatic: 9–10; distinguished from
 pervasive, 4; illustrated (Brian), 11;
 reversion to, illustrated (James), 16–17
Anxiety hysteria. See Hysteria, anxiety
Anxiety state: chronic, illustrated (James),
 16–17
Appersonation: 138; illustrated (Michael),
 129–30; in schizophrenia, 138; and
 identification, 138; in regression from
 object choice, 139
Autism: as feature of schizophrenia, 160–
 61; infantile, 165

Bak, Robert C.: on prepsychotic symptoms,
 128–29; theory of conflict in psychosis,
 128–29
Balint, Alice: and start of child analysis,
 211
Baudrey, Francis: on concepts of character,
 71–72
Belle indifférence, 47
Bernfeld, Siegfried: and start of child
 analysis, 211
Bernheim, Hyppolite: and psychopathology, 209
Bion, Wilfred: view of psychosis, 131; and
 bizarre objects, 132
Bleuler, Eugene: and psychic disjunction
 in schizophrenia, 160
Bleuler, Manfred: on schizophrenia,
 criteria for diagnosis of, 137; study of,
 147; severe endstates in, 149; follow-up
 studies, 162–63
Blindisms, 57
Blum, Harold: on persecutory delusions,
 genesis of, 132; homosexual theory of,
 133
Body: neglected in case of character
 neurosis (Isabel), 86; loved and hated in
 adolescent schizophrenia, 148; loved in
 schizophrenic (Penny), 152
Body/mind equation: illustrated (Billy),
 96–97
Borderline psychotic states: in children,
 illustrated (Brian), 11, 162–64. See also
 Developmental disturbances
Bornstein, Steff: and start of child analysis,
 211
Brain dysfunction: in cerebral
 atherosclerosis, 164
Breuer, Josef: and linking of etiology,
 psychopathology, and symptom, 209

Burlingham, Dorothy: and early child
 analysts, 211

Cancerophobia: in depressive state,
 illustrated (Grace), 202–03
Cannibalistic impulses: in normal and
 deviant development, 23
Cannon, Walter B.: and fight or flight,
 principle of, 1
Castration complex, female: revenge type,
 81, 88; wishful type, 88
Castration wishes: in psychosis, illustrated
 (Erica), 121–23; in schizophreniform
 psychosis, 160
Cerebral atherosclerosis: in psychotic
 state, 152; brain dysfunction in, 164
Character and character types, 70–72
Character disorders: and developmental
 disharmonies, 27; illustrated (Keith),
 28–29
Charcot, Jean M.: and psychopathology,
 209
Child analysis: historical note on, 211
Child observation, 210
Childhood disturbances: borderline,
 illustrated (Brian), 11; neurotic,
 illustrated (Harvey), 12–14, (Clare), 26–
 27; and disharmony, illustrated (Keith),
 28–29, (Alice), 29–30; symptom
 neurosis, illustrated (Dennis), 38–40; as
 prototypes of mania and depression in,
 172; as prototypes of mania and
 hypomania in, 172–74. See also
 Adolescence; Fears
Childhood history: in later psychoses, 148;
 in manic-depressive states, 174
Childhood neuroses, 47–48. See also
 Childhood disturbances
Children: and "experiential disturbances,"
 134
Cleanliness: compulsive, in a prepsychotic
 phase, 154
Coitus, childhood interpretations of, 44
Compromise formation, in dreams, 37–38;
 in neurosis, 41–42; in conversion
 hysteria, illustrated (Jean), 45–46;
 absence in borderline disturbance, 98
Compulsion to repeat, 7
Condensation, in dreams and symptom
 formation, 47
Conflicts, internalized: 32; as opposing
 organismic trends, 32; and repression
 barrier, 32; and defense, 32–33;
 avoidance of, 33; and ego weakness, 33;
 and superego, 33; and inhibition, 33–35;
 simpler solutions of, 33–36; without

Schizophrenic attack: acute, illustrated (Ivy), 149

Schizophrenic process (nuclear), 134

Schizophrenic psychosis, 115; case illustration (Olga), 157–60

Schreber case, 142; his psychosis, description of, 115; Flesching as male persecutor, 115–16

Screen memories, 95, 96

Secondary process: admixture with primary process in dreams and symptom neurosis, 36; and manifest dream content, 213

Secondary process functioning: and anxiety line, 8

Secondary process thinking: developmental interference with, illustrated (Keith), 29

Seduction in childhood: twelve year old, 52; overstimulated, 52; in relation to etiology, 209

Self, physical loss of boundaries from mental self, 199

Self-blame: in manic-depressive patient in depressive phase, 177

Self-interest: versus those of objects, 218

Self-object boundary: loss in nonremitting schizophrenia, 144

Self-object differentiation: loss of, 127–29; schizophrenias, 144; loss in psychosis, 144; reconstruction in psychosis, 144; loss of distinction in psychotic states, 165

Self-object fusion: following wish-fulfilling identification, 139

Self-observation, 161

Self-scrutiny: function of, lost in schizophrenias, 161

Separation-individuation phase: in normal and deviant development, 23, 133

Shame: in character neuroses, 75–77; in case of character neurosis, 81, 88; and urethral erotic wishes, 81; of parents, 154

Shengold, Leonard: and defects in repression barrier, 219

Sleep, REM: 38; and dreams, 213

Smearing: fecal and urinary (in psychotic state), 152; fecal, 153

Smiling response (R. Spitz), 6

Somatic compliance, 44–45; 47

Specific theories of schizophrenia, 135–36

Speech development: impairment of, in childhood prototypes of mania and hypomania, 172

Spencer, Herbert: influence on J. H. Jackson, 210

Spitz, Rene: view of birth trauma, 2; stranger anxiety, 3; smiling response, 6

Spontaneous remission, 199

Sprince, Marjorie: on borderline states in latency, faulty development in, 163

Sublimations: relationship to inhibition, 34–35

Suicide: successful, in schizophreniform psychosis, 157

Superego: fear of loss of love, 3; and conflicts, 33; dissolution of, in schizophreniform psychosis, 160; sadistic relation to ego, in case of manic-depressive depression, 191; in patient with manic-depressive depression, 192–93

Symptom-formation: neurotic steps in, 41–42; transient in childhood, illustrated, 48–50

Symptom neurosis: comparison with dreams, 36; compromise formation in, 36; illustrated in child (Dennis), 38–40; steps in formation of, illustrated in adult (Jean), 40–42; conversion hysteria, 43–48

Symptoms, positive: in schizophrenia, as repetition of infantile wish fantasies, 136

Superego collapse: in mania following object loss, 181

Taxonomy, psychiatric: Kraepelin's contributions to, 208; inadequacies of, 209

Therapeutic method: need to extend range to understanding, 212

"Thing presentations," 60; treated as "word presentations," 63

Thinking: primary process, 22; secondary process, 22

Thomas, Ruth: 11; and borderline states in children, 162; on borderline states in infancy, faulty development in, 163

Thought: as trial action, 7; divorced from affect in schizophrenias, 161; delaying function of, blocked, 173; distraction of exemplified (Marian), 177

Thought disturbance: in obsessional neurosis, 63–64

Time, sequential order in: impairments of, in psychoses, 215

Topographical regression: leading to tactile hallucinations, illustrated (Joan), 124; leading to auditory hallucinations, illustrated (Maura), 124–26

Toxic states: brain dysfunction in, 164

Transference: in dreams, 37; death wishes in, in borderline-type disturbance, 95; in